SAVING THE CONSTITUTION FROM LAWYERS

This book is a sweeping indictment of the legal profession when it enters the realm of constitutional interpretation. The adversarial, advocacy-based American legal system is well-suited to American justice, where one-sided arguments collide to produce a just outcome. But when applied to constitutional theorizing, the result is selective analysis, overheated rhetoric, distorted facts, and overstated conclusions. Such wayward theorizing finds its way into print in the nation's more than six hundred law journals – professional publications run by law students, not faculty or other professionals, and in which peer review is almost never used to evaluate worthiness. The consequences of this system are examined through three timely cases: the presidential veto, the "unitary theory" of the president's commander-in-chief power, and the Second Amendment's "right to bear arms." In each case, law reviews were the breeding ground for defective theories that won false legitimacy and political currency. This book concludes with recommendations for reform.

Robert J. Spitzer is Distinguished Service Professor of Political Science at the State University of New York, College at Cortland. His books include *The Presidency and Public Policy, The Right to Life Movement and Third Party Politics, The Presidential Veto, The Bicentennial of the U.S. Constitution, President and Congress, Media and Public Policy, The Politics of Gun Control, Politics and Constitutionalism, The Right to Bear Arms, Essentials of American Politics,* and *The Presidency and the Constitution.*

Saving the Constitution from Lawyers

.... HOW LEGAL TRAINING AND
LAW REVIEWS DISTORT
CONSTITUTIONAL
MEANING

Robert J. Spitzer

State University of New York, College at Cortland

CAMBRIDGE
UNIVERSITY PRESS

CAMBRIDGE
UNIVERSITY PRESS

University Printing House, Cambridge CB2 8BS, United Kingdom

One Liberty Plaza, 20th Floor, New York, NY 10006, USA

477 Williamstown Road, Port Melbourne, VIC 3207, Australia

314-321, 3rd Floor, Plot 3, Splendor Forum, Jasola District Centre, New Delhi - 110025, India

103 Penang Road, #05-06/07, Visioncrest Commercial, Singapore 238467

Cambridge University Press is part of the University of Cambridge.

It furthers the University's mission by disseminating knowledge in the pursuit of education, learning and research at the highest international levels of excellence.

www.cambridge.org
Information on this title: www.cambridge.org/9780521896962

© Robert J. Spitzer 2008

First published 2008

A catalogue record for this publication is available from the British Library

Library of Congress Cataloging in Publication data
Spitzer, Robert J., 1953–
Saving the Constitution from lawyers : how legal training and law reviews distort constitutional meaning / Robert J. Spitzer.
   p.   cm.
Includes bibliographical references and index.
ISBN 978-0-521-89696-2 (hardback) – ISBN 978-0-521-72172-1 (pbk.)
1. Constitutional law – United States – Interpretation and construction.   2. Lawyers – Training of – United States.   3. United States. Constitution.   I. Title.
KF4552.S65   2008
342.73–dc22   2007045109

ISBN 978-0-521-89696-2 Hardback
ISBN 978-0-521-72172-1 Paperback

To
Jinny Spitzer and Tess Spitzer,
the two most brilliant and beautiful women I know

Contents

Acknowledgments

As with any endeavor such as this, I owe a debt of gratitude to many people. In particular, I thank Seth Asumah, Erik Bitterbaum, Deb Dintino, Michael Genovese, Nancy Kassop, Mary McGuire, and Mark Prus. David Latimer, John Siliciano, and David Wippman read key portions of the manuscript and provided genuinely incisive and immensely helpful suggestions. It has been a pleasure to work with Cambridge University Press editor John Berger, as well as with Marcus Hinds and Maggie Meitzler. I also thank the many unnamed people with whom I have discussed the ideas that comprise this book over the space of many years, as well as the anonymous readers who offered very important and beneficial recommendations and suggestions. In addition, I gratefully and happily acknowledge Mellissa and Aaron; Shannon, Scott, Alexis, and Luke; Gary, Gail, Skye, and Jinny; and Joe and Dorothy Duncan, who understand and practice not only citizenship but also partisanship in the best sense. Most of all, I acknowledge my deepest love for and gratitude to my wife, Teresa, for the nearly inexpressible joy she brings to my life every single day. Take it from me, I'm one lucky guy.

Although unrelated to the subject matter of this book, I also acknowledge my good friends in the Cortland musical theater community, including Kevin and Cindy Halpin, Tom and Cathy Hischak, and David Neal. I completed this project during a sabbatical that allowed me to do this work during the day, and sing and dance at night. Although there's no chance whatsoever that I'll be giving up my day job, it's hard to put into words the special kind of joy that comes only from musical theater. So I won't try.

.... Introduction

A few years ago, I read a lengthy article in a prominent law journal about the constitutional power to declare war. The article ably presented opposing views regarding the enduring debate between those who argue for congressional preeminence over war-related decisions and those who believe that the president possesses great war-making discretion. But, the author offered a startling categorical finding that he said "all scholars have missed": namely, that "the Founders denied the President a veto over congressional decisions to wage war. . . ."[1] This finding was, in turn, offered by the author as decisive support for greater congressional power over war-related decisions. "Wow," I thought. Had the author uncovered a previously unknown letter by the likes of James Madison, for example, stating in unambiguous terms that declarations of war could not be vetoed by the president? Such a finding would be of major historical and constitutional significance. And, was it true that *all* scholars had missed this finding?

On its face, such a claim would seem to contradict a straight reading of the Constitution. According to Article I, sec. 7, "Every bill which shall have passed the House of Representatives and the Senate, shall, before it becomes a law, be presented to the President of the United States" for signature or veto. The succeeding paragraph in sec. 7 further explains that "Every Order, Resolution, or Vote to which the Concurrence of the Senate and House of Representatives may be necessary . . . shall

---

[1] William Michael Treanor, "Fame, the Founding, and the Power to Declare War," *Cornell Law Review* 82(May 1997): 700.

be presented to the President of the United States. . . ." Passage of bills
requires a simple majority vote in both houses. If the president chooses
to veto, Congress may override the veto by a two-thirds vote.[2] The only
exceptions are measures that require a two-thirds vote on initial passage:
proposed constitutional amendments and treaties (which only require
approval from the Senate). It has long been understood that presidents
may not obstruct these measures passed by super-majorities. Yet, a declaration of war requires only a simple majority vote of both houses, suggesting that presidents could, indeed, veto a declaration of war (although
it has never occurred in the five times war has been declared in American
history).[3]

As I read the balance of the article, I discovered that the author had
not, in fact, uncovered any new historical evidence. His emphatic and
categorical assertion that the Constitution's founders expressly denied
the president a veto over declarations of war was not based on any newly
discovered evidence but rather on familiar quotations and other related
sources from the country's early history in which early presidents, constitutional founders, and others referenced the sentiment that Congress
alone possessed the power to start war.[4]

It turns out that the author's flat assertion that the founders denied
the president a veto over war declarations was simply not supported by
the evidence presented and in all likelihood is false (or at least a highly
debatable proposition), and his other emphatic assertion – that "all scholars" had missed or overlooked this matter – was demonstrably false. In
1951, for example, the noted presidential scholar, Clinton Rossiter, wrote
this in his classic book on the commander-in-chief (CIC) power: "But
of course the President could veto a declaration of war, something that
[President Grover] Cleveland for one was probably quite ready to do –
in the case of war with Spain."[5] In a 1918 article, constitutional scholar,

---

[2] If the president does nothing, the bill automatically becomes law after ten days, unless
Congress by its adjournment prevents return of the bill, in which case it is pocket-vetoed.

[3] The number of separate declarations of war is actually greater than five because Congress
in some instances passed multiple declarations for single conflicts, such as World War II.
The five instances of formal war declaration are the War of 1812, the Mexican-American
War, the Spanish-American War, World War I, and World War II. These declarations
were enacted as joint resolutions, which do cross the president's desk for signature or
veto.

[4] Treanor, "Fame, the Founding, and the Power to Declare War," 700.

[5] Clinton Rossiter, *The Supreme Court and the Commander in Chief* (Ithaca, NY: Cornell
University Press, 1976; first published 1951), 66.

Simeon E. Baldwin, wrote, "As a declaration of war takes thus the shape
of a special Act of Congress, it requires, like any other bill, order, vote,
or resolution, the approval of the President." Later in his article, Baldwin
says that "Two things are certain, when the functions of the President
are considered with respect to their relation to a declaration of war. He
has the right . . . to communicate to Congress, before such a declaration
is made, the facts and circumstances that in his opinion may call for it.
It is also of no force, unless he approve it. . . . He must, as in the case of
any other measures of legislation, approve the whole or disapprove [i.e.,
veto] the whole."[6] Whereas the matter of a presidential veto of a war
declaration receives little attention in modern writings on the war power,
extant writing and evidence pretty clearly support the proposition that
presidents may, indeed, exercise such a veto.[7] And, it is obvious that the
matter had not been "missed" by "all scholars."

I mention this article not so much because of its subject matter but
rather because of its inappropriate (and, as it turns out, inaccurate) overstatement and its mischaracterization of the literature on the subject. Both
traits are startling because they are rarely, if ever, seen in such bald form
in the scholarly literature of other disciplines. In fact, it is customary to
dampen, if not excise, inflated rhetoric of this sort and for the obvious
reason that it is unnecessary, unwarranted, unprofessional, and risky: no
matter how carefully one conducts research, unbounded assertions about
trends in research usually run afoul over claims like "all" and "none." More
to the point, the facts should speak well enough for themselves, and the
conclusions should not outrun the evidence.

Yet, in the many hundreds of law journal articles I have read in the last
two decades while studying the two primary subjects of my research –
the American presidency and gun control – I have often found overstated
claims, rhetorical excesses, gaps in basic research, and conclusions that
simply did not follow from the evidence presented. I subsequently discovered that I was not the first to puzzle over this. An article published in a
prominent law journal a few years ago that was based on an analysis of more

---

[6] Simeon E. Baldwin, "The Share of the President of the United States in a Declaration
of War," *The American Journal of International Law* 12(January 1918): 1, 10. See also
Clarence A. Berdahl, *War Powers of the Executive in the United States* (Urbana, IL:
University of Illinois Press, 1921).

[7] Constitutional Convention delegate James Madison, as president, signed the declaration of war that commenced the War of 1812 on June 18, 1812, an action that supports the prima facie case for the ability of the president to also veto such an act.
http://britannica.com/eb/article-9032132/war-of-1812, accessed on September 12, 2006.

than two hundred law journal articles noted the same phenomenon in legal publications: "stridently stated, but overly confident, conclusions. . . ."[8] A book about six prominent legal writers observed a similar phenomenon in noting that the six have promoted "simple, elegant, and utterly wrong conclusions almost at every turn."[9]

I should quickly add that I have read many outstanding and illuminating law review articles. Undoubtedly, there is much superb writing to be found in these pages.[10] Yet, the central problem is not that there is no limit to superb writing and analysis but rather that there is no floor to dreadful writing and analysis. To understand the principles of legal training and the workings of law reviews is to understand why there are so few restraints on so much of its writing. The presence of no little wayward writing on constitutional subjects in the professional writings of the legal discipline – at least, as I observed it in the two otherwise divergent subjects of the American presidency and gun control that have comprised my primary areas of research for more than twenty years – was one observation that eventually spawned the argument of this book:[11] that law reviews are a breeding ground for wayward constitutional theorizing. Such defective theories, in turn, may not only distort academic debate and popular understanding of important constitutional principles but also generate wayward public policy.

This argument finds immediate support from several distinctive features of the legal publishing realm. Nearly all of the hundreds of law reviews published by America's law schools are run by law students, meaning that students choose what to publish and what form those publications will take. The articles published are not, with the rarest exceptions, subject to any kind of peer review, meaning that the decision to publish is not based on any expertise-based assessment of articles' logic, accuracy, significance, or relationship to the larger literature to which it purports to

[8] Lee Epstein and Gary King, "The Rules of Inference," *The University of Chicago Law Review* 69(Winter 2000): 7. See also their discussion of the penchant for the overstatement of claims in law review articles (49–50).

[9] Daniel A. Farber and Suzanna Sherry, *Seeking Certainty: The Misguided Quest for Constitutional Foundationalism* (Chicago: University of Chicago Press, 2002), ix. Farber and Sherry examine the views and writings of Robert Bork, Antonin Scalia, Richard Epstein, Akhil Amar, Bruce Ackerman, and Ronald Dworkin.

[10] For the sake of full disclosure, I have published five articles in law reviews. This experience helped provide me with a fuller understanding of how the law review process works.

[11] I first advanced this argument in Robert J. Spitzer, "The Constitutionality of the Presidential Line-Item Veto," *Political Science Quarterly*, 112(Summer 1997): 261–84.

contribute. To return to the example cited at the beginning of this Introduction, how could a law student be expected to know that "all scholars"
had not, in fact, missed the truth of what the president can and cannot
veto?

Further, the law review publishing realm is incomparably vast: in 2006,
there were more than 1,100 law publications, meaning that a persistent
author could find a publishing outlet for nearly any kind or quality of writing. And, the principles and norms of the legal profession, as taught in law
schools, are markedly different from – indeed, at odds with – those of every
other academic discipline: legal training (understandably and properly)
emphasizes and elevates the principles that are the hallmark of American
law in practice, including the adversary principle and the preeminence of
client loyalty as advanced by advocacy for the client's interests, even if it
results in the presentation of something less than the truth. No wonder
some academic legal writing sounds more like Perry Mason's melodra-
matic summation to a jury than like a carefully (if tediously) phrased and
parsimoniously constructed academic argument couched in qualifiers that
are less dramatic but more accurate.

In the light of these traits, it is not difficult to explain the all-too-typical
strident tone and basic factual lapses as a logical, even natural consequence
of legal training and legal publications. If one thinks of the author of the
law journal article described previously as a lawyer making a case to a
jury, the sureness of tone and emphatic assertion of fact are suddenly
explicable. And, the ability for an error-laced article on an important
matter of constitutional law to find its way into print in a prestigious law
review is also explicable given that the article was never subject to peer
review by, in this case, experts on the constitutional basis of the war power.
I do not mean to suggest that the system of peer review, gold standard
though it is in every other academic discipline, is a perfect or foolproof
system – far from it. But, it possesses the saving virtue of providing the
best system yet devised to separate good, publishable research from that
which is defective. That is why it continues to be used in every other
academic discipline. Peer review is neither vanity nor snobbery but rather
an acknowledgment that the best judges of competent work are those who
already have detailed knowledge of the subject matter. The simple but
incontrovertible fact is that no such expertise-based barrier exists in law
publishing.

The problems I have described are by no means new, or news, to the
legal community because it has engaged in much laudable examination

of and soul-searching about the values that underlie legal education and the system of student-run law reviews that attach to virtually every law school. Yet, virtually no attention has been turned to the pivotal question of what, if anything, this means for our understanding of the Constitution and constitutional law. For law is not just a profession, like plumbing or teaching; rather, it is also an academic enterprise, with an academic literature like every other academic discipline – except that law scholarship is not like that of every other discipline. It is those differences, and their consequences for our understanding of constitutional meaning in politics and policy, that are the focal point of this book.

To be sure, the argument of this book offers a serious criticism of the constitutional writings of the legal community. But, although critical, this book is emphatically not about lawyer-bashing. The legal community and the American judicial system sustain far too many cheap shots, from scurrilous political attacks to the endless stream of lawyer jokes. Although I am not a lawyer, I revere the law and those who study and practice it. I have encouraged many of my students to attend law school to pursue this noble and necessary profession. Further, as a political scientist, I have spent much of my professional career studying aspects of the law, and I share an abiding love and respect for constitutional law, a connection underscored by the long and intimate relationship between the fields of law and political science. It is no coincidence that the foremost constitutional scholar of the first half of the twentieth century, Edward S. Corwin, was, in fact, a political scientist.[12]

The phenomenon I describe here is not the product of scheming or unscrupulous lawyers nor of any nefarious individual behavior. This is not a tale of academic fraud. Rather, it is a by-product of institutional forces shaped through the growth and maturation of American legal education spanning more than a century. The ability of institutions to shape behavior is well understood in political science, and it is a phenomenon that applies not just to the nation's governing institutions but to academic disciplines

---

[12] Corwin actually received his doctoral degree in history from the University of Pennsylvania in 1905, but this came at a time when political science was not yet a fully formed discipline. As a faculty member at Princeton, Corwin was a founding member of the Politics Department, of which he was the first chair and where he was later named the McCormick Professor of Jurisprudence. Political science can thus rightly claim Corwin for itself. See Glenn H. Utter and Charles Lockhart, eds., *American Political Scientists* (Westport, CT: Greenwood Press, 1993), 52.

and professional occupations as well.[13] To state the matter differently, this is not a case of "rotten apples spoiling the barrel"; there is, instead, a problem with the barrel.

Outline of the Book

Chapter 1 describes the basic principles and tenets that compose law school education. These principles, including the adversary system, preeminent loyalty to a lawyer's client, and zealous advocacy, are well suited to the American system of justice. But, they are poorly suited to the endeavor of academic inquiry and stand in stark contrast to the principles and norms of academic inquiry as they are found in every other academic discipline. Chapter 2 examines the professional publishing realm of legal scholarship: law reviews. I first examine their history, their relationship to law as an evolving and maturing profession, and the origins and consequences of student control over these publications. When legal writing in such publications expanded beyond its traditional areas of case analysis (i.e., explication of specific court cases) and doctrinal writing (i.e., analysis of a body or doctrine of law) to encompass an ever-expanding realm of subjects and disciplines in the last several decades, it opened the door wide to the problems described in this book. Scholarship is defined not by who writes it, or whether that writing includes values or other normative concerns, but rather by the process by which it finds its way into print. In the case of law, that process is deeply flawed.

Chapters 3 through 5 examine in considerable detail three specific cases of wayward constitutional theorizing cultivated in the pages of law reviews – that is, constitutional theories that, by virtue of their law journal provenance, acquired a degree of legitimacy and respect as "scholarly" constitutional doctrine that is, I argue, unwarranted. Chapter 3 describes a constitutional theory arguing that the president possesses a constitutionally based item veto power – that is, a preexisting power to veto portions or items of legislation. This theory gained such currency that, at one point, a sitting president publicly pledged to exercise such a power, notwithstanding any ensuing litigation. Chapter 4 examines a new interpretation of the

---

[13] For example, former American Political Science Association president, Theodore J. Lowi, argued that "U.S. political science is itself a political phenomenon and, as such, is a product of the state." "The State in Political Science: How We Become What We Study," *American Political Science Review* 86(March 1992): 1.

president's power as CIC as it has been expounded during the George W. Bush presidency. The provenance of this theory proves to be more complex because it arose as part of a wide-ranging and grandiose theory of executive power called the "unitary theory," which also has roots in law reviews. Chapter 5 examines a different subject, the Second Amendment's right to bear arms. In this instance, an interpretation of this right emerged in law reviews dubbed the "individualist view" in opposition to the prevailing militia-based or "collective" view that has understood the amendment's reference in the second half of the wording (i.e., the right to bear arms) in concert with the first half of the amendment's sentence referencing arms-bearing as pertaining to service in a government-organized and -regulated militia. Chapter 6 offers a brief conclusion, including a discussion of possible reforms that might ameliorate the problems described herein.

1 . . . . . The Logic, and Illogic, of Law

"It is not what a lawyer tells me I *may* do; but what humanity, reason, and justice tell me I ought to do."
Edmund Burke, "Speech On Conciliation With America"
March 22, 1775

1. In an interview with reporters on July 25, 1989, President George H. W. Bush disclosed an eyebrow-raising decision: it was his intention, he said, to exercise a selective or item veto over some piece of legislation if the appropriate circumstance arose where he believed that some provision of an otherwise acceptable bill merited such an action.[1] This pronouncement by the first President Bush was startling for two reasons: first, no other president in American history had ever claimed to possess, much less attempted to exercise, an item veto under the terms of the veto power's description in the Constitution (although many presidents have asked that the power be given to the president); and second, no legal or constitutional change in the president's power had been made to accommodate an item veto.

2. Two weeks after the devastating attacks by terrorists against American targets, launched on September 11, 2001, the Deputy Assistant Attorney General in the Office of Legal Counsel, John Yoo, authored a lengthy memorandum in which he staked out an unprecedentedly sweeping, even grandiose definition of President George W. Bush's powers pertaining to

---

[1] Michael B. Rappaport, "The President's Veto and the Constitution," *Northwestern University Law Review* 87(Spring 1993): 736, note 2.

military actions against other nations and terrorist groups. According to this analysis, the president's constitutional CIC powers were essentially unbounded; they could not, the memorandum asserted, be limited or constrained by Congress or the courts.[2] In subsequent memoranda, Yoo and others reiterated these vast power claims as the country girded for a protracted conflict with Islamist fundamentalist terrorists, and President Bush took every opportunity to embrace and extol this view of the powers of his office.

3. In March 2007, the U.S. Court of Appeals for the District of Columbia Circuit ruled, for the first time in American history, that a gun law was unconstitutional based on the Second Amendment's right to bear arms. In the case of *Parker v. District of Columbia*,[3] two members of a three-judge panel struck down a District of Columbia law barring DC residents from keeping handguns in their homes. The ruling was stunning because it contradicted four Supreme Court cases and nearly fifty lower federal court decisions spanning more than a century, all of which have concluded (or accepted the view) that the Second Amendment protects citizen gun ownership only when those citizens are serving in a government-organized and regulated militia, as the Second Amendment says. According to the *Parker* majority, the Second Amendment protects an individual's right to own guns, even for purposes that include hunting and personal self-protection.

These three seemingly disparate disputes over constitutional meaning have several traits in common. First, they all articulate what are claimed to be constitutionally based powers or rights, based on what purports to be careful scholarly research. Second, they all contradict received wisdom. Third, all of these constitutional theories were born, cultivated, and legitimated in the pages of law reviews, a venue deigned to be "scholarly" rather than political or polemical. Fourth, in each instance, the constitutional theories described reverberated beyond the academic world's narrow confines, influencing national public debate, and even public policy, on these profoundly important constitutional matters. And fifth, they are all based on constitutional and historical analysis that is – or so I argue

---

[2] John C. Yoo, "The President's Constitutional Authority to Conduct Military Operations Against Terrorists and Nations Supporting Them," Memorandum Opinion for the Deputy Counsel to the President, September 25, 2001, accessed at http://www.usdoj.olc/warpowers925.htm on September 12, 2006.

[3] 478 F.3d 370 (D.C.Cir. 2007).

in this book – stunningly, and fatally, defective. In chapters to come, I examine each of these cases in great detail.

No academic discipline, from the humanities and social sciences to the natural sciences, is immune from error or wayward analysis. But, among the vast realm of academic writing, law stands alone in its training, principles, and publishing practices. These distinctive traits, I argue, make legal writing uniquely vulnerable to the cultivation of wayward constitutional theorizing.

Lawyers as Liars?

In an article written in 1998, at the height of the Bill Clinton–Monica Lewinsky scandal, Bronx public defender David Feige posed this question: "Is a lawyer free to tell, with as much passion as he cares to muster, something he believes to be a lie?"[4] Drawing on the behavior of President Clinton's lawyer, Bob Bennett, and Lewinsky's lawyer, William Ginsburg, Feige first cited the American Bar Association's Model Code of Professional Responsibility, which bars a lawyer from "knowingly mak[ing] a false statement of law or fact." Sure, said Feige, a lawyer is not supposed to knowingly lie; on the other hand, a lawyer is not obligated "to know the truth or to draw logical inferences from what he or she does know." And because lawyers are almost never eyewitnesses to the events or actions precipitating legal action involving the client, lawyers are essentially free to make whatever argument best suits the client. In fact, the lawyer's professional obligation to advocate zealously on behalf of the client means that the professional obligation to the truth could be eclipsed by the greater obligation to defend the interests of the client. Moreover, the long-established principle of lawyer–client privilege means that lawyers are obliged (with some narrow exceptions) not to divulge information about the client, even if highly incriminating, because to do so would undercut the adversary process itself (however, the standards that apply to prosecutors are higher; see subsequent discussion). Does this mean that lawyers think it is allowable to lie on behalf of a client? Certainly not. But it does mean that the values and norms of the profession may have the effect of placing truth farther down the list of lawyer priorities.

---

[4] David Feige, "Lying Lawyers," *Slate Magazine*, March 22, 1998, accessed at http://www.slate.com/id/1088/, viewed on January 21, 2006.

Journalist and lawyer Michael Kinsley addressed similar issues in an article analyzing the politics of the nomination hearings of Supreme Court Justices John Roberts and Samuel Alito in 2005 and 2006. Like Feige, Kinsley noted the "tension between advocacy and honesty" and concluded that the tenets of the legal profession often "encourages or even requires outright lying."[5] During his confirmation hearing, Roberts was asked about briefs he had written in the 1980s when he worked for President Ronald Reagan's Justice Department, in which he argued that the 1973 abortion rights case, *Roe v. Wade*, was "wrongly decided and should be overruled." Roberts and his defenders sought to avoid pegging him as overtly hostile to abortion rights by explaining that this statement did not necessarily represent Roberts's actual views because he was "simply arguing the position of the United States, his client." Alito penned even more hostile views toward *Roe* in Reagan's administration when he wrote in 1985, "the Constitution does not protect a right to an abortion." Alito also wrote that overturning *Roe* was something "in which I personally believe very strongly." Such "smoking-gun" statements seemed to leave no doubt about Alito's disapproval of abortion and *Roe*. Yet, Alito's defense during his confirmation hearings was that he was simply functioning as a "line attorney" expressing views that were consistent with the president's (i.e., his client's) policy agenda, and that Alito expressed these opinions because he was "seeking a job" in the administration.[6]

In other words, two of the most highly regarded legal figures in the country were seeking a seat on the highest court in the land by arguing, successfully (both were confirmed to the Supreme Court), to the Senate and the country that their apparently unequivocal personal expressions of antipathy toward the controversial *Roe* case were not necessarily that at all; instead, Roberts and Alito were simply functioning as good lawyers. In that capacity, it was allowable for them to lie to their client regarding what they really thought about *Roe* because they knew that their client, Ronald Reagan, opposed *Roe*. Did they, in fact, lie to their client about their actual views or to the Senate Judiciary Committee about the truth of

[5] Michael Kinsley, "Why Lawyers Are Liars," *Slate Magazine*, January 20, 2006, accessed at http://www.slate.com/id/2134510/, viewed on January 21, 2006.

[6] Kinsley, "Why Lawyers Are Liars." One representative of the conservative legal team that prepared Alito said that "He worked for the Reagan administration, he was a lawyer representing a client...." David D. Kirkpatrick, "Group Fueled Effort to Shift Court to Right," *New York Times*, January 30, 2006, A1.

their prior statements? Were their anti-*Roe* writings insincere expressions about whether *Roe* was, in fact, good law? Not very likely; after all, President George W. Bush almost certainly nominated them to the nation's highest court precisely because they were known for antipathy to *Roe* and abortion rights. Yet, what is most instructive is that Roberts and Alito could plausibly (if not very believably) distance themselves from their unequivocal expressions of antipathy to abortion rights by arguing that those views were not necessarily theirs because their job as good lawyers was to put the preferences and interests of their client first – even if that meant lying to their client or to the country.

If this sounds like a slam against the legal profession or against Roberts and Alito, it is not so intended. Instead, these examples are offered to illustrate some important traits of legal training and of the legal profession. The traits discussed here – the adversarial system, lawyer–client privilege, the elevation of client needs even above those of truth-telling – are integral to the American judicial system and are eminently defensible when functioning within that system (although lawyers and legal ethicists have debated these questions for centuries). Yet, when these traits are transplanted into what is deemed to be the world of scholarly inquiry and subsequently into the broader political or policy realm, their probity seems far less certain. That, in a nutshell, returns us to the argument of this book: American legal values and principles function effectively and properly when lawyers practice law – when they apply their training and trade within the bounds of the civil and criminal justice systems or in similar, traditional legal activities. But when individuals with those principles and training engage in academic scholarly analysis regarding the Constitution, the results may well be inimical to an accurate understanding of constitutional meaning.

This chapter examines the pedagogical underpinnings and core principles that compose legal training and then compares them with professional training in other academic fields. These characteristics and traits of legal training are well known to lawyers and even to many in the general public, thanks – in part, at least – to the blizzard of movies, television programs, and other elements of popular culture that depict what lawyers do. My purpose is *not* to question the propriety or adequacy of legal training as preparation for a conventional career in law but rather to clearly identify these traits in order to explain how they contribute, even if unwittingly, to the distortion of constitutional knowledge, especially among the small number of lawyers who later engage in academic and scholarly pursuits. Legal training is fine for lawyering but inadequate for – even antithetical to – the conduct of academic and scholarly inquiry.

Thinking Like a Lawyer

The discipline of law, as it is taught in American law schools, emanates from the nature of the legal profession. According to a widely used law text, the teaching of "legal reasoning" lies at the heart of a law school education. It is "a kind of reasoning which is adapted to the reaching of decisions for action. . . . It is like the kind of reasoning characteristic of . . . any other applied, or practical, art or science. It is a quite different kind of reasoning from that which is adapted solely to the establishment of general principles. . . . The pure scientist seeks – primarily – truth; the applied scientist seeks – primarily – right action."[7] Stated more bluntly, "the objective of law school education is to indoctrinate students into the legal profession."[8] Another law professor puts it this way: "In teaching law we also teach lawyering. . . . ,"[9] and yet another: "Law schools exist to prepare students to be attorneys."[10] Thus, by its nature, law school education is designed to train future lawyers to qualify for a specific vocation. This training process is summarized by law-text author, John Bonsignore, as one of transforming law students from laypeople into novice lawyers. Law school provides them with some competence in legal rules and problem solving. It develops in them a nascent concept of themselves as professionals, a commitment to the values of the calling, and a claim to that elusive and esoteric style of reasoning called "thinking like a lawyer."[11]

This training or "indoctrination" encompasses both a standard curriculum and a disciplinary-based set of values. Thus, the typical first-year law

---

[7] Harold J. Berman, William R. Greiner, and Samir N. Saliba, *The Nature and Functions of Law*, 6th ed. (New York: Foundation Press, 2004), 13. See also chap. 6 on legal reasoning.

[8] Steven Vago, *Law and Society*, 5th ed. (Englewood Cliffs, NJ: Prentice-Hall, 1991), 279. See also Ruggero J. Aldisert, *Logic for Lawyers* (New York: Clark Boardman Co., 1989).

[9] Howard Lesnick, "Infinity in a Grain of Sand: The World of Law and Lawyering as Portrayed in the Clinical Teaching Implicit in the Law School Curriculum," *UCLA Law Review* 37(August 1990): 1158.

[10] D. Don Welch, "'What's Going On?' in the Law School Curriculum," *Houston Law Review* 41(Spring 2005): 1607.

[11] John Bonsignore et al., *Before the Law: An Introduction to the Legal Process*, 8th ed. (Boston: Houghton Mifflin, 2006), 344. See also Kenneth J. Vandevelde, *Thinking Like a Lawyer: An Introduction to Legal Reasoning* (Boulder, CO: Westview Press, 1996).

student takes a fairly standard coursework covering basic areas of the law, including criminal law, property law, torts, contracts, civil procedure, and perhaps constitutional law. Upper-level coursework is more loosely constructed, focusing on aspects of legal reasoning, doctrine, and social-policy analysis. The still-common if no longer universal method of instruction includes the reading of cases and the application of the legendary Socratic method, whereby the instructor questions students about the facts and principles of the cases read by the students, in the fashion of a Socratic dialogue of question-and-answer.[12]

America's two hundred–plus law schools[13] have not been static because they today reflect greater diversity in curriculum, pedagogy, and faculty training than was true in earlier decades, including a growing number of faculty with degrees other than or in addition to law. At the same time, however, it would be a mistake to overstate the degree of personnel and curricular change in law schools. A study of the faculties of forty-one top law schools in 2003–04 found that, on average, 9 percent of the tenure-track faculty had doctorates in the social sciences. About 22 percent of these schools had no social scientists holding a tenured appointment. (One might reasonably infer that lower-ranked law schools would have even fewer non-lawyers by comparison.) Thus, law schools continue to be populated overwhelmingly by faculty with law degrees.[14]

---

[12] Karl E. Klare, "The Law-School Curriculum in the 1980s: What's Left?," *Journal of Legal Education* 32(September 1982): 337–38; Vago, *Law and Society*, 354–55; Steven J. Burton, *An Introduction to Law and Legal Reasoning* (Boston: Little, Brown, 1985), xiii. A recent article notes that the assignment of casebooks and use of the Socratic method are still central features of the education found in most law schools. Welch, "'What's Going On?' in the Law School Curriculum," 1607–23. The reading of cases and use of Socratic method was introduced by the Dean of the Harvard Law School, Christopher Columbus Langdell, in 1870. Prior to this time, legal education focused mostly on the study of legal treatises. By the early twentieth century, the revolutionary Harvard case method had swept through an ever-growing number of university-associated American law schools. This transformation in teaching method coincided with another: the decline of apprenticeship as the standard process for joining the legal profession. In 1870, only a quarter of those admitted to the bar attended law school, with the rest receiving their legal training through apprenticing themselves to lawyers. By 1910, two-thirds of bar-admitted lawyers had graduated from law schools. See Lawrence M. Friedman, *American Law in the 20th Century* (New Haven, CT: Yale University Press, 2002), 33–35.

[13] The legal Web site FindLaw reports 218 American law schools. See http://stu.findlaw.com/schools/fulllist.html, visited May 16, 2007.

[14] Tracey E. George, "An Empirical Study of Empirical Legal Scholarship: The Top Law Schools," *Indiana Law Journal* 81(Winter 2006): 152–53.

Regarding law school curriculum, Lawrence Friedman's contemporary verdict on law school education is no less true: "There is an almost numbing sameness about the law schools."[15] Even with more recent changes in the law curriculum of leading institutions, historian of legal education Laura Kalman noted in 2006 that "The curriculum in most first-year law schools is one with which Langdell [Harvard Law School dean in the 1870s] would be largely familiar."[16]

As a component of law school curriculum, the learning of legal reasoning is rarely the express subject of coursework[17] because law professors infrequently "deal explicitly or systematically with how lawyers think."[18] An exception is survey coursework in subjects like Introduction to Law, Legal Methods, and Legal Reasoning. By and large, law students are expected to learn legal reasoning – "thinking like a lawyer" – through the cumulative experience of a law school education, incorporating the case method, use of analogy and analytical reasoning, deductive legal reasoning, doctrine, and acquisition of discrete bodies of knowledge pertinent to the different areas of law.[19] Stated another way, traditional legal education revolves around "learning law, organizing it, and applying it."[20]

---

[15] Friedman, *American Law in the 20th Century*, 486.

[16] Jonathan D. Glater, "Harvard Law Decides to Steep Students in 21st-Century Issues," *New York Times*, October 7, 2006, A10. Harvard Law School Dean Elena Kagan announced that it was revising the curriculum so that first-year students would be required to take courses in legislation and regulation, international law, and legal problem solving. Yet, the traditional core curriculum would remain.

[17] In the introduction to his book on legal reasoning, Ruggero J. Aldisert noted that he was prompted to write his book in large measure because "there was no, repeat no, book strictly devoted to legal reasoning for law students, lawyers, or judges." *Logic for Lawyers: A Guide to Clear Legal Thinking* (New York: Clark Boardman Co., 1989), ix–x. A recent contribution to this slim literature by Sarah E. Redfield, *Thinking Like a Lawyer: An Educator's Guide to Legal Analysis and Research* (Durham, NC: Carolina Academic Press, 2002), focuses narrowly on the sources or types of law, the process of reading case law, and legal research. Edward H. Levi's classic, *An Introduction to Legal Reasoning* (Chicago: University of Chicago Press, 1949), is an extended essay on the case-law method as it bears on statutory and constitutional interpretation. Lief H. Carter's wonderful *Reason in Law* (New York: Longman, 1998) illustrates the virtue of bringing a political science sensibility to traditional legal-case analysis.

[18] Burton, *An Introduction to Law and Legal Reasoning*, xiii.

[19] Burton, *An Introduction to Law and Legal Reasoning*, passim; Ransford C. Pyle, *Foundations of Law: Cases, Commentary, and Ethics* (Albany, NY: West Publishing, 1996), 27–28.

[20] Steve Sheppard, "Casebooks, Commentaries, and Curmudgeons: An Introductory History of Law in the Lecture Hall," *Iowa Law Review* 82(January 1997): 643. Sheppard's careful history of legal education concludes that the case method and use of traditional

The Adversary System, Advocacy, and Truth

The purpose of legal education is, of course, to produce lawyers – that is, "to prepare and to socialize students for entry into a very narrow range of career lines."[21] The job of the lawyer is to function successfully within the framework of the American legal system. And that system – indeed, the "central tenet"[22] of American justice – rests on the adversary system. A practicing lawyer is an advocate, whether in private practice (accounting for the employment of about 75 percent of all practicing lawyers); government service (12 percent); private industry or the business world (12 percent); or in the employ of special interest, advocacy, legal aid, or similar groups.[23]

The hallmark of Anglo-American law, adversarial adjudication, dates to the Middle Ages, evolving in Britain along with the jury system and the pivotal role played by lawyers.[24] The adversarial role of lawyers was firmly established in Britain by the seventeenth century and in America by the eighteenth century. Indeed, even in the eighteenth century, the distinguishing characteristic of the successful American lawyer was finely honed debating and persuasion skills. Witness Andrew Hamilton's legendary (and successful) defense of John Peter Zenger in the famed early American free-press case from 1735, or John Adams's sagacious defense

---

case books are still pre-eminent in law school teaching. A rising chorus of critics has argued that legal education, especially at top law schools, is shunting aside traditional, doctrinal-oriented legal education "by emphasizing abstract theory at the expense of practical scholarship and pedagogy," including such subjects as critical legal studies, feminist legal studies, and various "'law and' movements" such as law and economics, law and literature, and law and sociology. Harry T. Edwards, "The Growing Disjunction Between Legal Education and the Legal Profession," *Michigan Law Review* 91(October 1992): 34.

[21] Klare, "The Law-School Curriculum in the 1980s," 336.

[22] Bonsignore et al., *Before the Law*, 368.

[23] Vago, *Law and Society*, 330.

[24] For more on the history of the American legal system and the adversary principle, see Marion Neef and Stuart Nagel, "The Adversary Nature of the American Legal System," in *Lawyers' Ethics: Contemporary Dilemmas*, ed. Allan Gerson (New Brunswick, NJ: Transaction Books, 1980), 73–97. The Anglo-American adversary system contrasts with that used in many European countries, the inquisitorial process, in which judges play a much more active role, juries and lawyers play a lesser role, and greater emphasis is placed on the discovery of material truth. Each system has its advantages, but any comparison of the relative merits of each is beyond the scope of this inquiry. See Landsman, *Readings on Adversarial Justice: The American Approach to Adjudication* (St. Paul, MN: West Publishing, 1988), 38–39.

of British soldiers prosecuted in the aftermath of the Boston Massacre of 1770. What Stephan Landsman calls "flamboyant courtroom advocacy"[25] of the sort identified with today's well-known celebrity defense attorneys is as applicable to Johnnie Cochran or Gerry Spence as it was to the brilliant backwoods lawyer Abraham Lincoln.

The adversary system is predicated on the belief that the best way to determine the truth (or to at least arrive at a relatively just outcome) in a legal dispute is for opposing sides to present their strongest possible arguments to an impartial and passive arbiter, whether a judge or jury. Truth to tell, the adversary system in operation tends to serve "the objective of resolving disputes rather than searching for material truth."[26] As a standard law school text notes, "Taking sides is the root notion of the Adversary System (the clash of mad dogs) as opposed to the Inquisitorial System (one very nice dog, sniffing). The idea is that truth is more likely to emerge from conflicting positions than from the most well-meaning of neutral investigations."[27] The adversary system is thus composed of three key elements: a neutral and passive decision maker (i.e., judge or jury), partisan advocates representing the opposing sides (i.e., lawyers), and a highly structured set of rules that govern the activities of the advocates (i.e., rules of procedure or conduct, evidence, and ethics). These guidelines are essential because long experience with the adversary system has demonstrated "the natural tendency of advocates to win by any means available. . . ."[28]

The nature of the adversary system means that a lawyer's foremost obligation is to the lawyer's particular position or client.[29] Even though lawyers function as officers of the court, they "have no obligation to parties or interests other than their own clients. . . . Consequently, justice, or the right result, is not the responsibility of either lawyer."[30] In fact, although lawyers are ethically barred from lying or knowingly allowing their clients

[25] Landsman, *Readings on Adversarial Justice*, 17.

[26] Landsman, *Readings on Adversarial Justice*, 3.

[27] Kenney Hegland, *Introduction to the Study and Practice of Law*, 3rd ed. (St. Paul, MN: West Publishing, 2000), 16.

[28] Landsman, *Readings on Adversarial Justice*, 4–5.

[29] For example, federal district court judge, Marvin F. Frankel, wrote that the "advocate's prime loyalty is to his client, not to the truth as such." "The Search for Truth: An Umpireal View," *University of Pennsylvania Law Review* 123(May 1975): 1035.

[30] Stephen Gillers, "The American Legal Profession," in *Fundamentals of American Law* (New York: Oxford University Press, 1996), 166–67. The adversary system has its limits; lawyers are not supposed to lie to clients or encourage clients to lie, for example.

to lie, lawyers may encourage a fact-finder to reach a wrong conclusion by, for example, knowingly presenting perjured testimony or cross-examining truthful witnesses in a manner that undercuts their credibility, if such an end promotes the goal of effectively defending the client.[31] These tenets of the adversary process are not limited to the criminal and civil realms but also emerge, for example, during contract negotiations.[32]

There is an important exception to the preeminence of advocacy. Prosecutors are held to a higher standard, one that specifically recognizes the importance of seeking justice. This responsibility arises from the fact that prosecutors wield the awesome power of the state. As the American Bar Association notes in its Model Rules of Professional Conduct, "A prosecutor has the responsibility of a minister of justice and not simply that of an advocate. This responsibility carries with it specific obligations to see that the defendant is accorded procedural justice and that guilt is decided based upon the basis of sufficient evidence." Similar sentiments are expressed by the National District Attorneys Association.[33] Bearing these special rules for prosecutors in mind, legal education precedes prosecutorial service, and it is a profession in which a small minority of lawyers engages.

The larger lesson concerning advocacy is precisely that it is based on the lawyer's foremost forensic responsibility to the client or employer. As the leading legal theorist Lon Fuller noted, the lawyer's job is "not to decide but to persuade. He is not expected to present the case in a colorless and detached manner, but in such a way that it will appear in that aspect most favorable to his client."[34] The legal arena is a "grimly combative" business in which lawyers must be "aggressive, combative, cunning, ingenious, required or permitted to employ drama for effect, and, above

---

Prosecutors in criminal cases who uncover evidence that would help the defendant are obligated to make that information available.

[31] Monroe H. Freedman, *Lawyers' Ethics in an Adversary System* (Indianapolis, IN: Bobbs-Merrill, 1975), 27, 43.

[32] Gillers, "The American Legal Profession," 167–68.

[33] American Bar Association Model Rules of Professional Conduct, Sec. 3.8, accessed at http://www.abanet.org/cpr/mrpc/mrpc/rule_3_8.html. See also the ABA's Standards for Criminal Justice, Sec. 3–1.2(c), accessed at http://ethics.iit.edu/codes/. Cases that endorse this special responsibility for prosecutors include *Berger v. U.S.*, 295 U.S. 78 (1935), and *U.S. v. Wade*, 388 U.S. 218 (1967), among others.

[34] Lon L. Fuller, "The Adversary System," in *Talks on American Law*, ed. Harold J. Berman (New York: Vintage, 1971), 35.

all, committed to prevail for their clients and causes."[35] The inherently competitive nature of the adversary process places great emphasis on winning. As Geoffrey Hazard concludes, the inexorable tendency of a lawyer's work "leads him to hold, with Vince Lombardi, that winning is not the most important thing but the only thing."[36] Little wonder that litigation is often compared to a game, a ritual, or a sporting event[37] that often has the effect of driving opposing sides even farther apart,[38] or that the American competitive spirit holds sway in a system where "the fact of guilt or innocence is irrelevant to the role that has been assigned to the advocate."[39] Indeed, the comparison of lawyering to a sporting event dates back a century.[40] As federal judge Marvin F. Frankel wrote, "The gladiator using the weapons in the courtroom is not primarily crusading after truth, but seeking to win."[41]

The aforementioned advocate's loyalty to the client or employer is both long-standing as a trait of the adversarial process and preeminent. In a classic statement, Britain's Lord Henry Brougham argued in 1821 that "An advocate, in the discharge of his duty, knows but one person in the world, and that person is his client. To save that client by all means and expedients, and at all hazards and costs to other persons . . . is his first and only duty; and in performing this duty he must not regard the alarm, the torments, the destruction which he may bring upon others."[42] American law professor Monroe Freedman's contemporary expression voices similar emphatic devotion: "Let justice be done – that is, for my client let justice

---

[35] Marvin E. Frankel, *Partisan Justice* (New York: Hill and Wang, 1980), 11, 21.

[36] Geoffrey C. Hazard, Jr., *Ethics in the Practice of Law* (New Haven, CT: Yale University Press, 1978), 133.

[37] Deborah Rhode, "Ethical Perspectives on Legal Practice," *Stanford Law Review*, 37(January 1985): 604.

[38] Advocates of alternative dispute resolution (ADR) argue that it is a preferable means for resolving certain kinds of disputes, including workplace disputes and divorces, because dispute resolution is less incendiary than advocacy. See, for example, http://www.contilaw.com/adrsyn.html, the Web site of a law firm specializing in ADR, visited May 1, 2007.

[39] Freedman, *Lawyers' Ethics in an Adversary System*, 57.

[40] Roscoe Pound, "The Causes of Popular Dissatisfaction with the Administration of Justice," *Reports of the American Bar Association* 29(1906): 395–417. Pound compared the practice of law to a game of football and referred to "our sporting theory of justice" and the law as "a mere game." 404–405.

[41] Frankel, "The Search for Truth," 1039.

[42] Quoted in David Luban, "The Adversary System Excuse," in *The Good Lawyer: Lawyers' Roles and Lawyers' Ethics*, ed. Luban (Totowa, NJ: Rowman & Allanheld, 1983), 86.

be done – though the heavens fall. That is the kind of advocacy that I would want as a client and that I feel bound to provide as an advocate."[43] Judge Frankel opined that the "ethical standards governing counsel command loyalty and zeal for the client, but no positive obligation at all to the truth."[44]

As these sentiments suggest, advocacy in the adversarial system consists of two elements: zeal and loyalty to the client, with both traits cemented by the pledge of lawyer–client confidentiality. Although one might think of the important and special bond of confidentiality between lawyer and client as a relatively recent development, it dates back hundreds of years: British lawyers were granted this nearly unique privilege as early as 1577, initially to underscore the dignity of the lawyer but even more importantly to facilitate the lawyer's unfettered search for evidence to help the client.[45]

Closely connected to the adversary principle and the elevation of client defense is the conscious separation of law from morality. In his classic essay, Oliver Wendell Holmes wrote in 1897 of the "importance of the distinction between morality and law . . . with reference to a single end, that of learning and understanding the law." Holmes was not arguing that the law was itself immoral or amoral, for "[t]he law is the witness and external deposit of our moral life." Rather, he believed that the separation of law and morals was "of the first importance for . . . a right study and mastery of the law as a business. . . . "[46] Although Holmes's views have long been the subject of debate,[47] they nevertheless represent an important and enduring school of legal thought. Modern legal education places considerable emphasis on ethics; nevertheless, the Holmesian approach "is shared by many legal educators today."[48] Federal judge Harry T. Edwards

---

[43] Freedman, *Lawyers' Ethics in an Adversary System*, 9.
[44] Frankel, "The Search for Truth," 1038.
[45] Landsman, *Readings on Adversarial Justice*, 11.
[46] Oliver Wendell Holmes, "The Path of the Law," *Harvard Law Review* 10(March 25, 1897): 459. Holmes's desire to divorce law from morality was part of the effort to treat the law and legal education as a "science" in which questions of morality simply muddled analytical thinking. This view was shared by Harvard Law School Dean Christopher Langdell. See H. L. A. Hart, "Positivism and the Separation of Law and Morals," *Harvard Law Review* 71(February 1958): 593–629; and James R. Elkins, "Thinking Like a Lawyer: Second Thoughts," *Mercer Law Review* 47(Winter 1996): 532–34.
[47] For example, Lon L. Fuller, *The Law in Quest of Itself* (Chicago: Foundation Press, 1940); Henry M. Hart, Jr., "Holmes' Positivism – An Addendum," *Harvard Law Review* 64(April 1951): 929–37.
[48] Elkins, "Thinking Like a Lawyer," 532.

stated flatly that "a 'strong foundation in ethics' is not being built in legal education."[49]

To some readers, this account of the adversary process and other aspects of legal education might seem draconian or even immoral. As Landsman observes, "it is not hard to understand why onlookers might consider him [the lawyer] to be the enemy of truth."[50] In David Luban's view, the adversary system is arguably nothing less than "an institutional excuse for moral ruthlessness"[51] on the part of lawyers. Indeed, the two most common criticisms of the adversary process are that it slows the wheels of justice and that it places too little value on discovering material or actual truth.[52] Both criticisms are valid, yet the latter is well parried by the counterargument that the judicial system functions as a whole in a manner that is likely to produce a just outcome – or certainly no less likely than any competing system of justice. In fact, I side with defenders of the American system of justice. But I also believe that its traits have other, adverse consequences when removed from the practice of law.

Lawyering versus Scholarship

The logic and consequences of the adversary system have been exhaustively scrutinized and analyzed in much legal writing.[53] I have no quibble with the logic or value of the adversary system, or legal training, when played out between lawyers in the context of a functioning legal system. And there is good reason not only to accept but also to embrace the assertion that "the adversary system is one of the most efficient and fair methods designed for determining [the truth]."[54] Yet, its consequences

---

[49] Edwards, "The Growing Disjunction Between Legal Education and the Legal Profession," 73.

[50] Landsman, *Readings on Adversarial Justice*, 29.

[51] Luban, "The Adversary System Excuse," 90.

[52] Lawyers themselves are among the most frank and harsh of their own profession. Celebrated trial lawyer Roy Grutman said, "A lawyer is like a utensil, like a knife or fork. It makes no difference who ate with it last, only that it was sufficiently sanitized between meals." Quoted in Bonsignore et al., *Before the Law*, 368. See also defense attorney James Mills's *On the Edge* (New York: Doubleday, 1971), "I Have Nothing to Do with Justice."

[53] For example, Frankel, *Partisan Justice*; Freedman, *Lawyers' Ethics in an Adversary System*; Landsman, *Readings on Adversarial Justice*; Luban, *Lawyers and Justice: An Ethical Study* (Princeton, NJ: Princeton University Press, 1988), chaps. 4 and 5.

[54] Freedman, *Lawyers' Ethics in an Adversary System*, 3.

for academic inquiry are not only very different from but also squarely at odds with the goals of that pursuit.

Marvin Frankel makes this point expressly when he observes the following about the consequences of legal education and its practice:

> We become skeptical about, if not indifferent to, the notion of objective truth. Who can know the truth, after all? . . . We are not historians, commissioned to recapture events as they actually happened. Our job is to learn what witnesses will or may say, what evidence exists, who will or won't discover the evidence, who will tell what "story," how much must become known, what may not be discoverable, what "the record" will finally look like. . . . we learn a kind of modulated ignorance, stopping short of final answers, relying enthusiastically on the division of labor that separates lawyers from judging.[55]

In no other academic field of inquiry, whether the natural sciences, the social sciences, or the humanities, is the value of truth-seeking subordinated to the kind of values that are the foundation of legal training: to win an argument, to put the interests of the client/employer above those of the truth, or to maintain confidentiality regardless of its consequences. Law professor Anthony T. Kronman put it succinctly: "Scholarship . . . aims at the truth. Advocacy, by contrast, is concerned merely with persuasion."[56] As lawyer Tracey George notes, "while other academic fields increasingly adopted the scientific method during the twentieth century, law did not. . . . research in the physical and social sciences focused on formulating hypotheses and testing them against relevant data. . . . Most academic law writings, by contrast, concentrated on legal issues and evaluated them in the same way as judges writing opinions."[57]

Writing in 1969, law professor Arthur Selwyn Miller was even more frank in his verdict about the consequences of the adversary system on scholarship: ". . . lawyers, simply because they are trained to be advocates – to take sides – face a particularly difficult task when called upon to shed the habits of their training (and practice) when . . . writing for learned journals. . . . In no other profession or discipline, except theology, can it be said that the very system itself is a hampering effect on the search for

---

[55] Frankel, *Partisan Justice*, 23–24.
[56] Anthony T. Kronman, *The Lost Lawyer: Failing Ideals of the Legal Profession* (Cambridge, MA: Harvard University Press, 1993), vii.
[57] George, "An Empirical Study of Empirical Legal Scholarship," 144.

truth."[58] Miller argues that two key facets of the adversary system explain this: the overarching emphasis the adversary system places on the (partisan) pursuit of the client's interests and the adversary system's reasoning process, which works backward (from conclusion to premise) rather than the reverse.[59] Legal historian Alfred H. Kelly similarly noted "the radical difference in theory and process between the traditional Anglo-American system of advocacy and equally time-honored techniques of the scholar-historian."[60]

Luban makes a similar point in his comparison of the scientific method employed by other disciplines with the tenets of the adversary system. Some defend the adversary system, according to Luban, by saying that science seeks truth through "a wholehearted dialectic of assertion and refutation,"[61] whereby researchers labor to prove their arguments and hypotheses and others attempt to refute these proofs – a description that seems to parallel the adversary process. Yet, Luban rejects the comparison, saying that scientific investigators, unlike clashing lawyers, do not advance arguments they know to be false, or use rules to exclude truthful or factual information, or rely on "privilege" to conceal truth. Nor do scientific investigators present information in a way favorable to their clients[62] or attack the personal credibility of researchers who might produce different or competing theories.

One comparison of traditional research methodology and legal work argues that the latter works in a manner opposite that of the former: whereas researchers examine a problem by collecting information to then

---

[58] Arthur Selwyn Miller, "The Myth of Objectivity in Legal Research and Writing," *Catholic University of America Law Review* 18(1969): 291.

[59] Miller, "The Myth of Objectivity," 291–93.

[60] Alfred H. Kelly, "Clio and the Court," *The Supreme Court Review*, ed. Philip Kurland (Chicago: University of Chicago Press, 1965), 155. Judge Frankel wrote that "we know that others searching after facts – in history, geography, medicine, whatever – do not emulate our adversary system. . . . many of the rules and devices of adversary litigation as we conduct it are not geared for, but are often aptly suited to defeat, the development of the truth." "The Search for Truth," 1036.

[61] Luban, *Lawyers and Justice*, 69. Luban's description of scientific research standards is drawn from Karl Popper, *Conjectures and Refutations: The Growth of Scientific Knowledge* (New York: Harper and Row, 1963).

[62] There are exceptions to this, as when scientific researchers are paid by drug companies to conduct research. In such instances, the research findings may be the property of the companies, and they have been known to suppress findings critical of their products. Yet, such circumstances, although real, are also widely understood to violate the rules and norms of objective scientific inquiry.

draw conclusions, "Lawyers work in reverse. They know their desired outcome at the outset, so they gather arguments to support it." The omission
of contrary evidence is "unethical" in conventional research, but "lawyers
are under no compunction to introduce evidence that hurts their cases;
that's the other side's job."[63]

This does not mean that those trained in the law are incapable of producing sound scholarly analysis any more than it means that scholars in
other disciplines are somehow immunized from defective scholarship by
virtue of their graduate school and disciplinary training. Yet, the difference in values, principles, and training between law and other disciplines
is as stark as it is undeniable. As one critical analysis of legal writing
shrewdly noted, "An attorney who treats a client like a hypothesis would
be disbarred; a Ph.D. who advocates a hypothesis like a client would be
ignored."[64]

Social Sciences and the Rules of Inquiry

By way of comparison, the principles of intellectual inquiry in the arts
and sciences are organized around "the desire for explanations which are
at once systematic and controllable by factual evidence that generates
science.... More specifically, the sciences seek to discover and to formu-
late the general terms the conditions under which events of various sorts
occur...."[65] Whereas one might think that the principles of scientific
inquiry extend only to the "hard" or "natural" sciences – biology, chemistry,
physics, geology, and so on – and not to the "soft" or social sciences –
sociology, psychology, history, economics, geography, political science –
the fundamental rules of inquiry are the same (as are the pitfalls associated with scientific inquiry[66]). Carl Hempel wrote that scientific theory
is composed of general assumptions, connections between theory-based

[63] Cornelia Dean, "When Questions of Science Come to a Courtroom, Truth Has Many
Faces," *New York Times*, December 5, 2006, F3.
[64] Lee Epstein and Gary King, "The Rules of Inference," *The University of Chicago Law
Review* 69(Winter 2002): 9.
[65] Ernest Nagel, *The Structure of Science* (New York: Harcourt, Brace and World, 1961),
4. See also Carl G. Hempel, *Philosophy of Natural Science* (Englewood Cliffs, NJ:
Prentice-Hall, 1966).
[66] Thomas S. Kuhn's seminal critique of the fitful process by which scientific paradigms
are formulated, advanced, and discredited applies no less to the social sciences than to
the natural sciences. See *The Structure of Scientific Revolutions* (Chicago: University
of Chicago Press, 1970).

assertions and observable phenomena, and the testing of these phenomena as measured against the theory.[67] As philosopher of science Abraham Kaplan noted, "What is distinctive of behavioral science . . . is basically its subject-matter. . . . The behavioral scientist seeks to understand behavior in just the same sense that the physicist, say, seeks to understand nuclear processes."[68] The scientific method, generally understood as "a body of logic and methods,"[69] consists of "the primary building blocks of science – concept, law, theory, explanation, and prediction. . . ."[70] These tenets apply as well to the social sciences.

The social sciences continue to debate the extent to which they can or cannot live up to the tenets of scientific inquiry, especially in comparison with the natural sciences. There are, indeed, clear differences between research in the social sciences compared with the natural sciences. Notably, difference arises from the fact that social sciences study "human agents" that are "reflective," meaning that "they contemplate, anticipate, and can work to change their social and material environments and they have long-term intentions as well as immediate desires or wants."[71] As a consequence, social sciences generate fewer law-like propositions; generalizations are more likely to be narrow, qualified, conditioned, and time-bound. Theories in the natural sciences offer explanation and prediction as to both process and outcome, whereas social science theorizing can often explain but rarely predict.[72] And there is a long-standing debate in political science about the question of whether the overarching principles of qualitative and quantitative research are essentially the same, although the proponents of a more unified approach

[67] Carl G. Hempel, *Aspects of Scientific Explanation* (New York: Free Press, 1965), 150–51. See also Richard S. Rudner, *Philosophy of Social Science* (Englewood Cliffs, NJ: Prentice-Hall, 1966).

[68] Abraham Kaplan, *The Conduct of Inquiry* (New York: Chandler Publishing, 1964), 32–33.

[69] E. Terrence Jones, *Conducting Political Research* (New York: Harper and Row, 1971), xi.

[70] Alan C. Isaak, *Scope and Methods of Political Science* (Homewood, IL: Dorsey Press, 1981), 51.

[71] Alexander L. George and Andrew Bennett, *Case Studies and Theory Development in the Social Sciences* (Cambridge, MA: MIT Press, 2005), 129. See also John Gerring, *Case Study Research: Principles and Practices* (New York: Cambridge University Press, 2006).

[72] George and Bennett, *Case Studies and Theory Development in the Social Sciences*, 129–31.

to theorizing and research – whether qualitative or quantitative – have gained the upper hand.[73]

Still, the qualitative principles of inquiry, including objectivity, skepticism, curiosity, gathering and analysis of evidence, and rules of inference, are deeply embedded in the intellectual and professional training of social scientists and certainly in my discipline of political science. The same can even be said of heavily normative fields of inquiry, including political theory, philosophy, and ethics.[74] Philosopher of science Richard S. Rudner argued decades ago that the social or behavioral sciences are, in fact, methodologically indistinct from the natural sciences.[75] Yet, one need not accept Rudner's argument to note that the social and natural sciences share principles of training and instruction on the modes of inquiry that do not extend to and that are very different from law school training.

One may be tempted to argue that the study of law is qualitatively different from all other fields because of the normative or values questions with which it grapples and which, one might argue, do not lend themselves

---

[73] Gary King, Robert O. Keohane, and Sidney Verba, *Designing Social Inquiry: Scientific Inference in Qualitative Research* (Princeton, NJ: Princeton University Press, 1994); "Review Symposium: The Qualitative-Quantitative Disputation," *American Political Science Review* 89(June 1995): 454–81.

[74] See, for example, Fred M. Frohock, *Normative Political Theory* (Englewood Cliffs, NJ: Prentice-Hall, 1974). For texts pertaining to research and theory-building in the social sciences, see, for example, Robert Brown, *Explanation in Social Science* (Chicago: Aldine, 1963); Hubert M. Blalock, Jr., *Causal Inferences in Nonexperimental Research* (New York: W. W. Norton, 1964); Rudner, *Philosophy of Social Science*; Kenneth R. Hoover, *The Elements of Social Scientific Thinking* (New York: St. Martin's Press, 1976); Stanford Labovitz and Robert Hagedorn, *Introduction to Social Research* (New York: McGraw-Hill, 1981); King, Keohane, and Verba, *Designing Social Inquiry*; Richard A. Seltzer, *Mistakes that Social Scientists Make* (New York: St. Martin's Press, 1996); John Gerring, *Social Science Methodology* (New York: Cambridge University Press, 2001); Henry E. Brady, *Rethinking Social Inquiry* (Lanham, MD: Rowman and Littlefield, 2004); George and Bennett, *Case Studies and Theory Development in the Social Sciences*. Texts specific to political science include Lawrence C. Mayer, *Comparative Political Inquiry* (Homewood, IL: The Dorsey Press, 1972); James A. Bill and Robert L. Hardgrave, Jr., *Comparative Politics: The Quest for Theory* (Columbus, OH: Charles E. Merrill, 1973); Jones, *Conducting Political Research*; Isaak, *Scope and Methods of Political Science*; Stephen Van Evera, *Guide to Methods for Students of Political Science* (Ithaca, NY: Cornell University Press, 1997); David Marsh and Gerry Stoker, eds., *Theory and Methods in Political Science* (New York: Palgrave Macmillan, 2002). Some who address these issues in historical research are Terrence J. McDonald, ed., *The Historic Turn in the Human Sciences* (Ann Arbor: University of Michigan Press, 1996); Clayton Roberts, *The Logic of Historical Explanation* (University Park: Pennsylvania State University Press, 1996).

[75] Rudner, *Philosophy of Social Science*, 4–7.

to the methodologies of other disciplines. Yet, all disciplines struggle with matters of morals and values and certainly the social sciences do. Yet, the rules of inquiry apply no less to such areas of study. In fact, when values are most at stake, the rules of inquiry are most important.

The disjunction between law review writing and scholarship in other academic disciplines has begun to receive notice in disciplines including history (where some treatments of history by legal writers have earned the derisive moniker "law office history"[76]) and political science. Jousting between historians and lawyers dates back several decades. In fact, the phrase "law office history" dates to an article published in 1965 by historian Alfred H. Kelly, who defined the term as "the selection of data favorable to the position being advanced without regard to or concern for contradictory data or proper evaluation of the relevance of data proffered."[77] According to legal writer John Phillip Reid, "Law office history is almost completely irresolvable . . . into anything resembling historical truth, in large part because the premises that guided its preparation were radically different from those that should guide a professional historian."[78]

In a recent essay on the relationship among law, legal analysis, and the study of presidential power, political scientist Kenneth Mayer observed that "the legal literature . . . often incorporates simplistic or highly stylized conceptions of politics and government, and legal analyses often do not meet the standards of good social science research. . . ."[79] Mayer's

---

[76] Examples of historians' criticisms of "law office history" are found in J. M. Sosin, "Historian's History or Lawyer's History?," *Reviews in American History* 10(March 1982): 38–43; Martin S. Flaherty, "History 'Lite' in Modern American Constitutionalism," *Columbia Law Review* 95(April 1995): 523–90. Flaherty's verdict is that some lawyers' constitutional historical writing "is replete with historical assertions that are at best deeply problematic and at worst, howlers" (525). Lauren Kalman says that "legal scholars who 'abuse' history undermine their credibility." *The Strange Career of Legal Liberalism* (New Haven, CT: Yale University Press, 1996), 9 (see also chap. 6); Garry Wills, *A Necessary Evil: A History of American Distrust of Government* (New York: Simon and Schuster, 1999), 112–22, 252–60; Jack N. Rakove, "The Second Amendment: The Highest Stage of Originalism," *Chicago-Kent Law Review* 76(2000): 106; Saul Cornell, "A New Paradigm for the Second Amendment," *Law and History Review* 22(Spring 2004): 161–68.

[77] Kelly, "Clio and the Court," 122, note 13. Kelly traces the abuse of history to some of the Supreme Court's earliest cases but notes its full flowering in contemporary cases.

[78] John Phillip Reid, "Law and History," *Loyola of Los Angeles Law Review* 27(November 1993): 201.

[79] Kenneth Mayer, "The Return of the King? Presidential Power and the Law," *PRG Report* 26(Spring 2004): 13.

verdict has found empirical confirmation in the work of political scientists Lee Epstein and Gary King, who authored a landmark article (published in a prominent law journal) in which they examine the methodological soundness of empirically based law review articles. Their study included a reading of every article published in law journals from 1990 to 2000 in which the word *empirical* appeared in the title – 231 articles in all. They found that, without exception, every article they examined violated at least one principle of sound empirical research, leading them to conclude that "serious problems of inference and methodology abound everywhere we find empirical research in the law reviews and in articles written by members of the legal community."[80] Epstein and King argue, too, that at least part of the problem arises from the nature of legal education and training. They note "the markedly different goals" of lawyers as compared with academics of other disciplines. "While a Ph.D. is taught to subject his or her favored hypothesis to every conceivable test and data source, seeking out all possible evidence *against* his or her theory, an attorney is taught to amass all the evidence *for* his or her hypothesis and distract attention from anything that might be seen as contradictory information."[81] They further note that "lawyers and judges, and hence law professors, specialize in *persuasion*. Lawyers need to persuade judges and juries to favor their clients, and the rules of persuasion in the adversary system are different from the rules of empirical inquiry."[82]

Two critics contested elements of Epstein and King's argument, proposing instead the "possibility" that lawyerly advocacy in scholarship might be a virtue instead of a vice: "the contest of 'particular versions' of truth ventilated by legal articles that are tendentious when taken separately may, at the systemic level, produce increasingly accurate approximations of truth, as scholar-advocates criticize the work of opposing camps."[83] In other words, the ability of the adversary system in court to produce a roughly just outcome might also produce "truth" when transposed to the scholarly world in the form of "advocacy scholarship." Epstein and King's response to this notion is to concede that while this might be a "possibility," "we have no examples of academic disciplines making sustained progress

[80] Epstein and King, "The Rules of Inference," 15.
[81] Epstein and King, "The Rules of Inference," 9.
[82] Epstein and King, "The Rules of Inference," 9, note 23.
[83] Jack Goldsmith and Adrian Vermeule, "Exchange: Empirical Research and the Goals of Legal Scholarship," *The University of Chicago Law Review* 69(Winter 2002): 156.

in learning about the world with such an approach."[84] Epstein and King's critics might seize on their small concession that "advocacy scholarship" might, conceivably, provide an alternate way to advance knowledge. But this is a slim reed, indeed; it is also "possible" that space aliens built the Egyptian pyramids. The mere existence of a "possibility," by itself, without supporting evidence or arguments, is an enticing rhetorical ploy but not much more, especially when compared with the decades-long track record of the principles of inquiry embraced by every other academic discipline. What matters is what a hypothesis plausibly suggests, what a fair and full assessment of the available evidence shows, and what then can be logically inferred.

Critics of "advocacy scholarship" are found within the legal community as well. Harvard law professor Mary Ann Glendon condemned the very idea and its increasingly wide acceptance because it "openly or covertly abandons the traditional obligation to deal with significant contrary evidence or arguments. In fact," she concluded more than a decade ago, "advocacy scholarship is not scholarship at all, for its research is not conducted with an open mind and its results are not presented with a view toward advancing knowledge about the subject treated."[85]

In a criminal courtroom, on the other hand, to create a "possibility" that the prosecution's argument might be flawed may also create "reasonable doubt," which in turn may be all that is required to win the case for the defense. But the scholarly enterprise is not and should not be about presenting one-sided or deceptive evidence or, through grand rhetorical flourishes, appealing to a jury's emotions in order to "win" a case. Glendon intimates this very problem when she criticizes "advocacy scholarship" because "it imports the most debased adversarial litigation tactics into the realm of scholarship. Rambo scholars, like Rambo litigators, engage in no-holds-barred attacks on their opponents' positions, and sometimes on the opponents themselves."[86] Later in this book, I present three detailed cases of constitutional analysis to support my argument that

---

[84] Lee Epstein and Gary King, "A Reply," *The University of Chicago Law Review* 69(Winter 2002): 194.

[85] Mary Ann Glendon, *A Nation Under Lawyers* (New York: Farrar, Straus and Giroux, 1994), 208. Glendon dates advocacy scholarship to the 1960s and notes that Justice William O. Douglas was among the first to take note of the "increase in partisan legal literature" (208).

[86] Glendon, *A Nation Under Lawyers*, 209.

"advocacy scholarship" as it is practiced in law reviews is, at least for the cases examined, deeply flawed as a scholarly mode of inquiry regarding the advancement of sane constitutional understanding.

Conclusion

Law is an honorable, noble, and – above all – necessary profession, despite the many slings and arrows it endures both from within its ranks and from outside the profession. Yet, my argument is that lawyers are well equipped by the principles and training of their discipline to function within the professional world for which they are prepared but are poorly equipped to engage in the scholarly world as it pertains to constitutional scholarship. Even setting aside the pedagogical traits of law school education, a curriculum that includes no more than a course or two on constitutional law cannot be taken as a sufficient curricular basis for the average lawyer to claim constitutional law as a scholarly or research specialty. These traits, as discussed later, have profound consequences not only for law as an academic pursuit but even for public policy as well.

To address one example of the suspect link between lawyering run amok and public policy, former State Department policy advisor during the second Bush presidency and Executive Director of the 9/11 Commission, Philip Zelikow, offered a stern warning about this very subject in a 2007 law school presentation. In his paper, Zelikow analyzed the Bush administration's response to the 9/11 attacks by arguing that its new approach to terrorism, while "fundamentally sound," was "developed and implemented in a flawed manner" and that these flaws were magnified because of "the role that law and lawyers played in framing policy choices." Himself a lawyer, Zelikow criticized the administration's reliance on lawyers who were assembled to "consider and approve the legality" of actions that the administration had already decided to take to fight the war on terror. In other words, a political and policy debate "became framed as a legal debate. Legal opinions became policy guides." Worse yet, in Zelikow's words, *"The legal defense then became the public face of the policies."* This was deeply problematic because it circumvented the normal policy-vetting processes that a presidential administration might otherwise use to arrive at policy decisions. Instead, the lawyers chosen to justify and ratify the second Bush administration's policy decisions did what lawyers do for their clients: prepare the equivalent of briefs to justify the actions of the client.

These legal opinions were used "to provide formal policy cover for Agency [i.e., CIA] operations. . . . Thus the public debate was decisively framed – and deformed." A further problem, according to Zelikow, is the fact that lawyers are not normally taught moral reasoning. Therefore, problems are framed "less as a detailed analysis of what *should* be done, and more as a problem of what *could* be done."[87] No wonder the Bush administration found itself defending policies pertaining to matters including justifications for torture, rendition, and prisoner detainment that seemed plainly illegal, politically corrosive, and strategically unnecessary.

All of this does not mean that trained lawyers cannot be good public servants or, for that matter, good scholars; obviously, that is not so. But the core principles of legal training and practice discussed in this chapter, encapsulated in the adversarial system, extending to the elevation of client loyalty – even at the expense of the truth – the separation of law and morality, and the emphasis on winning all function effectively and well in the practice of law in America but operate at right angles to the fundamental tenets of academic inquiry (and, perhaps, good public policy), including the scientific method, hypothesis formation and testing, and other elements of scholarly investigation. And, "adversary scholarship," I argue, is an oxymoron. But the nature of professional legal training is only part of the explanation for wayward legal theorizing about the Constitution. The other part of the explanation lies in the unique characteristics of the primary breeding ground for this theorizing: law reviews.

[87] Philip Zelikow, "Legal Policy for a Twilight War," Annual Lecture, *Houston Journal of International Law*, April 26, 2007, accessed at http://www.hnn.us/articles/39494.html on May 30, 2007.

2 . . . . . The Law Journal Breeding Ground

Like every other academic discipline, the field of law publishes the research of its scholars in disciplinary journals, and that body of writing serves as the primary arena for the explication of the discipline's scholarly work. Yet, two features of law reviews set this body of writing apart from every other academic discipline: first, most of the nation's two hundred–plus law schools[1] publishes at least one such journal (and most larger schools publish multiple journals), producing an incomparably vast publishing realm; and second, nearly all of these publications are controlled by students rather than by academics or professionals in the field. Faculty involvement is minimal, generally limited to an advisory role. Law students alone review, accept, reject, and edit the articles published in their journals, most of which come from law school faculty who, like faculty in other disciplines, seek and obtain promotion, tenure, pay increases, and status within their institutions and profession through their records of publication. Even though this arrangement "turns the academic hierarchy upside down,"[2] it is an old and firmly entrenched feature in the world of law schools. Further, with a few exceptions, article submissions are not subject to the process of blind peer review, meaning that no review

---

[1] In 2006, the law-based Web site Findlaw listed 213 law schools in America. See www.stu.findlaw.com/schools/fulllist.html/, accessed on June 15, 2006. The legal guide Web site Hieros Gamos lists 204 law schools. See www.hg.org, accessed on June 15, 2006.

[2] Lawrence M. Friedman, *American Law in the 20th Century* (New Haven, CT: Yale University Press, 2002), 497.

or "refereeing" of manuscripts by experts in the field normally occurs. Publishing decisions almost always rest with students alone.

The consequences of these pivotal traits for law review content, and the profession, have been extensively discussed and debated within the law school community but are little known outside of it. For example, historian Garry Wills has noted that scholars in other fields are "astonished" when they learn that students are the gatekeepers to most legal publications.[3] Law professor James Lindgren reports that "Scholars elsewhere frequently can't believe that, for almost all our major journals, we let students without advanced degrees select manuscripts."[4] Legal writer Bernard Hibbitts observes that in academic fields other than law, "student control of academic publishing is unknown. . . ."[5] To be sure, academics in specialized research fields, such as constitutional historians and political scientists who study the Constitution, are aware of these traits. And, from time to time, the unusual traits of law reviews have received attention outside of the legal community; yet, the matter of student control, if mentioned at all, rarely receives more than passing comment.[6] Yet, the most important question for this book pertains to the consequences of student control, not the degree to which law's unusual publication practices and principles are or are not known outside of the profession.

Whatever else might be said of legal writing, at least three traits stand out: its publishing realm is huge; its influence – over court rulings, the legislative process, public discourse regarding America's legal system, and the public policy process itself – is significant; and further, no other

---

[3] Garry Wills, "To Keep and Bear Arms," *New York Review of Books*, September 21, 1995, 62.

[4] James Lindgren, "An Author's Manifesto," *University of Chicago Law Review* 61(Spring 1994): 535.

[5] Bernard J. Hibbitts, "Last Writes? Reassessing the Law Review in the Age of Cyberspace," *New York University Law Review* 71(June 1996), 647.

[6] For example, an article in the *New York Times* about the shopping of manuscripts to law journals noted that "law students are the gatekeepers of scholarly journals" but failed to note the unusual nature of this fact. Lisa Anderson, "Law Journals Attack 'Shopping' of Manuscripts," *New York Times*, July 12, 1995, B6. See also Patricia B. Gray, "Harvard's Faculty Stirs a Tempest with Plans for a New Law Journal," *Wall Street Journal*, May 28, 1986, 37. Exceptions are found in publications that specialize in higher education: Christopher Shea, "Students v. Professors," *The Chronicle of Higher Education*, June 2, 1995, A33–34; Rosa Ehrenreich, "Look Who's Editing," *Lingua Franca* (January/February 1996): 58–63.

discipline possesses such a vast publishing hole. In 2006, the Current Law Index listed more than 1,100 legal publications.[7] This list includes publications of law schools as well as bar associations and commercial publishers. My primary concern, however, is with the hundreds of student-edited publications attached to law schools because these are the ones generally considered most prestigious and influential and which publish the brunt of legal scholarship.[8] In this chapter, I discuss the evolution, traits, and consequences of this huge, student-controlled publishing realm and argue that its unique traits provide a fertile breeding ground for the cultivation of wayward constitutional theorizing.

History

The origins of student-run law reviews coincide with the institutionalization and professionalization of the legal profession in the late nineteenth century, although the need fulfilled by these publications predated their appearance.[9] Even in the early 1800s, the American legal profession recognized the need to establish a system of publications that could inform it of the latest developments in the burgeoning common law, as well as other matters related to the profession. These needs prodded the establishment of a succession of legal publications, the earliest of which was the *American Law Journal and Miscellaneous Repertory*, first published in 1808. It included excerpts of judicial opinions, descriptions of recently published law books, and editorializing about legal matters of the day. Although it lasted only nine years, it was succeeded by an array of

---

[7] My count is taken from LegalTrac, the electronic version of the Current Law Index listing, which is produced by the American Association of Law Libraries (accessed at www.gale.com/tlist/sb5008.html on May 28, 2006). The *Index to Legal Periodicals* indexes "nearly 1,000 law reviews." It is published by H.W. Wilson (accessed at www.hwwilson.com/sales/printindexes.htm on June 6, 2006). LexisNexis's law review Source List listed 683 journals in 2006. The terms *law journal* and *law review* are treated as synonyms.

[8] The student-run law reviews have been long understood as the fountainhead of the discipline's scholarship: ". . . the law reviews affiliated with the law schools are the principal ones devoted primarily to scholarship." Albert J. Harno, *Legal Education in the United States: A Report Prepared for the Survey of the Legal Profession* (Westport, CT: Greenwood Press, 1953), 193.

[9] Robert Stevens, *Law School: Legal Education in America from the 1850s to the 1980s* (Chapel Hill, NC: University of North Carolina Press, 1983), 20.

similarly short-lived legal publications that cropped up around the country. One such publication, the *American Law Register*, was founded in 1852 and was notable for two reasons. First, it presaged in form and content modern academic and professional legal publications; second, it survived because of its adoption by the University of Pennsylvania Law School in 1895, when students there assumed editorial tasks related to its publication. In 1908, its title was changed to the *University of Pennsylvania Law Review and American Law Register*, with the latter portion of the title dropped in 1945. It continues to publish up to the present and is therefore the oldest continuously published law journal.[10]

Yet, the origins of the modern student-run law journal are usually traced to Harvard Law School,[11] where in 1886 a small group of third-year law students who had formed a club called the Langdell Society (named after pathbreaking Harvard Law School dean Christopher Columbus Langdell[12]) decided to produce a publication to provide an outlet for legal essays written by the student club members. The plan was presented to the faculty for approval, and most of them encouraged the students to proceed. From the outset, the *Harvard Law Review* served as an outlet for faculty publications, providing a welcome means to spread the faculty's scholarship and the institution's reputation. Yet, it was also designed to serve as a mode of student training and development because students would not only contribute articles but also organize and edit the publication's content. The publication proved to be a great success and, in the years to come, most law schools mimicked Harvard and established their own law reviews. Seven law reviews were published by law schools

---

[10] Michael I. Swygert and Jon W. Bruce, "The Historical Origins, Founding, and Early Development of Student-Edited Law Reviews," *The Hastings Law Journal* 36 (May 1985): 750–57.

[11] Harvard's student-run law review was not, in fact, the first. Students at Albany Law School published a legal periodical in 1875, and Columbia University's Law School founded one in 1885. Neither survived, but the Columbia publication served as a model for Harvard's. Swygert and Bruce, "The Historical Origins, Founding, and Early Development of Student-Edited Law Reviews," 764–69.

[12] Langdell introduced what came to be known as the Harvard system of legal instruction, emphasizing the case method, incorporating the use of casebooks instead of standard legal texts, and Socratic dialogue instead of lectures in the classroom. These methods swept law classrooms throughout the country in the early twentieth century. Swygert and Bruce, "The Historical Origins, Founding, and Early Development of Student-Edited Law Reviews," 774–76.

in 1900; by 1927, the number had grown to thirty-three; by 1937, there were fifty.[13] In 1972, 138 of the nation's then 149 law schools published at least one journal.[14] Nearly all were run by students.

Almost from the start, modern law journals began to have an impact on the public policy process. Among the earliest and most compelling examples was the seminal article by Samuel Warren and Louis Brandeis, "The Right to Privacy," published in the *Harvard Law Review* in 1890.[15] A year after its publication, the article was the keystone of a judicial decision that relied heavily on it. Soon thereafter, other courts drew on the article, and eventually the right to privacy became a cornerstone of individual rights.[16] The first Supreme Court decision to cite a law review article in its opinion (although it happened to be a dissenting opinion) was in 1897. By the early twentieth century, law review articles were being regularly cited in legal briefs and court decisions. They also began to exert influence among legislators in Washington and around the country. Even if the content or arguments of the articles did not sway the outcome of a court decision or the content of a statute, the very mention of such articles lent credibility and prestige to the publications.[17] Noted jurists also praised the publications. Writing in 1931, Supreme Court Justice Benjamin Cardozo referred to their "conspicuous utility" in his work.[18] Supreme Court Chief Justice Charles Evans Hughes wrote approvingly in 1941 of law reviews' "prestige and influence."[19] And, Supreme Court

[13] Hibbitts, "Last Writes?," 629. In 1900, there were 101 law schools in the United States. See Kermit L. Hall, *The Magic Mirror* (New York: Oxford University Press, 1989), 218.

[14] Olavi Maru, "Measuring the Impact of Legal Periodicals," *American Bar Foundation Research Journal* 1(1976): 227.

[15] Samuel D. Warren and Louis D. Brandeis, "The Right to Privacy," *Harvard Law Review* 4(December 1890): 193–216.

[16] Swygert and Bruce, "The Historical Origins, Founding, and Early Development of Student-Edited Law Reviews," 787–88; Andrea L. Bonnicksen, *Civil Rights and Liberties* (Palo Alto, CA: Mayfield Publishing, 1982), 194–95; Friedman, *American Law in the 20th Century*, 369–70.

[17] Swygert and Bruce, "The Historical Origins, Founding, and Early Development of Student-Edited Law Reviews," 789–90; Douglas B. Maggs, "Concerning the Extent to Which the Law Review Contributes to the Development of the Law," *Southern California Law Review* 3(1930): 181–207; Michael L. Closen and Robert J. Dzielak, "The History and Influence of the Law Review Institution," *Akron Law Review* 30(Fall 1996): 26–27.

[18] Benjamin Cardozo, *Selected Readings on the Law of Contracts* (New York: Macmillan, 1931), 186.

[19] Charles E. Hughes, "Foreword," *Yale Law Journal* 50(March 1941): 737.

Chief Justice Earl Warren wrote of the American law review in 1953 that it was "the most remarkable institution of the law school world."[20]

Students in Charge?

To the contemporary academic world, the decision to allow students to create and run an academic publication, especially at a flagship university, might seem puzzling, even inexplicable. But the explanation arises from the evolving nature of legal education and occupational training in the late nineteenth century. In 1890, fifty law schools attached to universities operated in America.[21] Those institutions produced a minority of the nation's practicing lawyers, however, because the majority still received their training by apprenticing themselves to practicing lawyers and law firms.[22] Apropos of this occupational pattern, most law school professors were practicing attorneys who found their time and talents outside the classroom better spent in profitable legal practice rather than pursuing what would today be considered the more appropriate academic pursuits of research and writing. According to a law student at the University of Pennsylvania in 1887, "The race of full-time professors of law was in its infancy. In almost all cases the lecturers in the schools were active practitioners who had a flair for teaching."[23]

Most law school faculty were not, therefore, academics of the sort found in most other academic disciplines even by late-nineteenth-century university standards, and the editorial and writing responsibilities assumed by student editors were considered more clerical than scholarly. At Harvard, one of the faculty's most enthusiastic proponents of the new publication was James Barr Ames, whose initial appointment to the law school in 1873 was considered "a milestone" because he was the first faculty member appointed for his academic (scholarly and teaching), as opposed to practical, skill and potential. Ames's lack of legal experience was no drawback given the new Langdellian view that law was a "science" better learned in the library than in the courtroom.[24] Langdell notwithstanding,

[20] Earl Warren, "Messages of Greeting to the U.C.L.A. Law Review," *U.C.L.A. Law Review* 1(December 1953): 1.

[21] Hibbitts, "Last Writes?," 619.   [22] Stevens, *Law School*, 24.

[23] Quoted in Hibbitts, "Last Writes?," 620, note 15.

[24] Michael Ariens, "Modern Legal Times: Making a Professional Legal Culture," *Journal of American Culture*, 15(March 1992): 25–35; Stevens, *Law School*, 38.

the legal profession at this time was viewed as more of a "mechanical trade" than a "liberal science,"[25] an attitude that likely fortified faculty members' disinclination to involve themselves directly in law reviews and to justify student control based on its educational value for students. Further, law faculty were reportedly reluctant to assume leadership positions with the new, university-based journals because they would be competing with already established commercial legal journals.[26]

Indeed, the overriding reason given for establishing law reviews at law schools was the belief that students' legal education would be importantly advanced through such work. In his survey of founding rationales for the establishment of law reviews, Harvard law faculty member John Jay McKelvey concluded in 1937 that "no law school review has been free from the idea of service to the student body as a medium of extracurricular training."[27] In a report prepared for the Survey of the Legal Profession in 1953, Albert J. Harno noted approvingly that "the common vehicle of legal scholarship in America is the law review." Its two purposes, according to Harno, were "education for the students" and providing a means "through which legal scholars can make the results of their research available to the public."[28]

Further insight into this phenomenon can be seen in the few instances of law reviews initially placed under the control of faculty but then later shifted to student control. The *Michigan Law Review* was one such publication. Founded in 1902 after the unsuccessful publication of a student-produced "pamphlet," faculty at Michigan initially controlled the publication, with students retained as assistant editors. Over time, however, faculty yielded more work – and, therefore, control – to students, so that by the late 1930s, the faculty role was reduced to an advisory capacity.[29] The Michigan case and the larger trend toward student-run publications buttress the view that such responsibilities were not considered by the faculty to be sufficiently important or desirable for them to intervene in

---

[25] Quoted in Stevens, *Law School*, 24.
[26] Hibbitts, "Last Writes?," 625–26, note 45.
[27] John Jay McKelvey, "The Law School Review," *Harvard Law Review* 50(April 1937): 871. McKelvey was a student founder of the *Review* in 1887.
[28] Harno, *Legal Education in the United States*, 192.
[29] Swygert and Bruce, "The Historical Origins, Founding, and Early Development of Student-Edited Law Reviews," 784–86. A similar pattern unfolded at Northwestern University Law School, where the faculty initially controlled the publication but yielded to full student control by 1932.

more than an advisory capacity. In the words of one legal scholar, "The faculty may have decided that law reviews were simply unimportant."[30] From the 1960s through the 1980s, faculty involvement and influence declined even further.[31]

The typical content of early law review writing also helps clarify an understanding of the law review past and the pivotal role of students. At its founding, the *Harvard Law Review* student editors stated two primary (and very practical) purposes for the publication: to spread news and information about their institution and to provide assistance to practicing lawyers.[32] The format of this and other reviews consisted of lead articles, usually written by faculty or other legal professionals (subject to editing by student editors), and student-authored case notes. Over time, various types of essays, comments, and book reviews became staples as well.[33]

Further, the tradition in legal writing throughout the nineteenth century consisted of two types of writing: *doctrinal* and *case*. Doctrinal writing involved extended exposition on some theory, body, or principle of law (i.e., doctrine); case writing included summaries of court decisions and opinions, with accompanying commentary. Both types of writing were of great use to practicing lawyers.[34] Top law students, chosen to serve as law review editors because of their academic excellence and trained from the outset of a law school education to explicate such doctrine, were logical choices to assume responsibility for such writing, which became for them the singular honor of "making law review." In the words of federal judge and law professor Richard A. Posner, the main purpose of legal writing in the nineteenth century was "to serve judges and practicing lawyers, rather

---

[30] Afton Dekanal, "Faculty-Edited Law Reviews: Should the Law Schools Join the Rest of Academe?" *University of Missouri at Kansas City Law Review* 57(1989): 235.

[31] Dekanal noted that before the late 1960s, "faculty members played a major, although not dominant, role in the processing of articles as well as student notes and comments. Faculty advice was sought and often, although certainly not always, taken." "Faculty-Edited Law Reviews," 237. See also Cramton, "'The Most Remarkable Institution,'" 6–7.

[32] Richard S. Harnsberger, "Reflections About Law Reviews and American Legal Scholarship," *Nebraska Law Review* 76(1997): 691.

[33] Closen and Dzielak, "The History and Influence of the Law Review Institution," 17–19.

[34] Swygert and Bruce, "The Historical Origins, Founding, and Early Development of Student-Edited Law Reviews," 742–50. Much of the legal writing from the nineteenth century known well today, including that produced by the important constitutional scholars James Kent, Joseph Story, and Thomas Cooley, is doctrinal.

than other professors, by offering careful doctrinal analysis. . . . activities organized around legal doctrine to which the students had been introduced on their first day in law school and in which the best of them had become fairly expert by the end of their first year of study." Such writing was thus "primarily a professional rather than an academic product."[35]

A Scholarly Enterprise?

In the twentieth century, law schools, legal writing, and the law itself changed dramatically. Entry to the legal profession increasingly came through the law schools rather than apprenticeship, partly in an effort "to upgrade the intellectual quality of law and lawyers and thus enhance their professional status."[36] Law school training shifted from an undergraduate to a graduate education as it also integrated itself more fully into the maturing American university system. Intellectual perspectives from other disciplines, especially including the social sciences, began to infuse approaches to the law.[37] Law school faculty increasingly consisted of teaching professionals instead of practitioners, many of whom had served as law review editors as students, and institutional pressures on them to publish accelerated by the 1950s, in part because of the growing appetites of an ever-expanding number of law journals. Yet, even at this point, most law review writing still focused on relatively orthodox doctrinal and case writing.[38]

As for the law reviews, they continued to proliferate such that no self-respecting law school could now afford to be without one or even several. This single fact explains the explosion in numbers of these publications. No other academic discipline hosts an academic journal at each and every one of its graduate institutions, and multiple publications have, in fact, become the norm at most larger law schools. In 2006, for example, Harvard Law

[35] Richard A. Posner, "Against the Law Reviews," *Legal Affairs* (November/December 2004), accessed at http://www.legalaffairs.org/issues/November-December-2004/toc. html. Accessed June 1, 2006. See also Harnsberger, "Reflections About Law Reviews and American Legal Scholarship," 691–92.

[36] Stevens, *Law School*, 24.

[37] Ariens, "Modern Legal Times"; Samuel Nirenstein, "The Law Review and the Law School," *New York University Annual Review* 1(1924): 31.

[38] Stevens, *Law School*, 58, 73–84, 134–41, 271. See also Harno, *Legal Education in the United States*; Lyman P. Wilson, "The Law Schools, the Law Reviews and the Courts," *Cornell Law Quarterly* 30(1945): 493.

School published thirteen journals, Yale published twelve, Cornell eight, Stanford seven, and Michigan and Chicago six each.

Law reviews continued to publish doctrinal analysis but, increasingly, an eclectic, even dizzying array of articles on every imaginable subject, drawing on a variety of disciplinary perspectives (sometimes called "law and..." writing[39]), began to fill legal publications, encompassing such areas as history,[40] economics, critical theory, feminism, philosophy, postmodernism and deconstructionism, gay and lesbian studies, game theory, literature, critical race theory, anthropology, sociology, and many others.[41] Both feeding and responding to this trend toward publishing what law historian Lawrence Friedman dubbed "a bewildering kaleidoscope of every form and mutation of scholarship"[42] was the growth of specialty journals and symposium journal publications devoted to specific topics. Among mainstream journals, the decline of doctrinal analysis was matched by an increase in constitutional law analysis and an ever-greater focus on the very small number of Supreme Court rulings handed down annually. The "vast expansion in constitutional law"[43] in law reviews occurred for at least two related reasons. First, from the New Deal period on, the courts injected themselves ever more into political controversies, from the constitutionality of New Deal programs to civil rights, reapportionment, abortion, affirmative action, and a host of other issues, both hot-button and mundane. This ever-growing corpus of court decisions helped move America's courts more centrally into the American polity, a trend that, by

[39] See Laura Kalman, *The Strange Career of Legal Liberalism* (New Haven, CT: Yale University Press, 1996), chap. 2. Kalman dates the "law and..." phenomenon to the 1970s.

[40] The link between law and history is both the strongest and longest. Alfred H. Kelly apparently coined the phrase "law-office" history in his 1965 article, in which he took the courts to task for their persistent misuse and distortion of history in court cases dating to the late eighteenth century. Kelly concludes his article with this sweeping indictment: "The Court, I submit, has attempted to sit on two stools at once and has fallen between them. It has confused the writing of briefs with the writing of history." "Clio and the Court: An Illicit Love Affair," *The Supreme Court Review*, ed. Philip Kurland (Chicago: University of Chicago Press, 1965), 155.

[41] Friedman, *American Law in the 20th Century*, 499; Richard A. Posner, "The Future of the Student-Edited Law Review," *Stanford Law Review* 47(Summer 1995): 1133; Harry T. Edwards, "The Growing Disjunction Between Legal Education and the Legal Profession," *Michigan Law Review* 91(October 1992): 50; George L. Priest, "Triumphs or Failings of Modern Legal Scholarship and the Conditions of Its Production," *University of Colorado Law Review* 63(1992): 726.

[42] Friedman, *American Law in the 20th Century*, 499.

[43] Posner, "The Future of the Student-Edited Law Review," 1133.

its nature, invited greater examination in the pages of law reviews. Second, constitutional law "mesmerized students"[44] who controlled the gateways to law reviews – hardly a surprising development given the compelling import, not to mention drama, of court (and especially Supreme Court) rulings. And, the subject undoubtedly had a similar effect on law faculty who increasingly won tenure and professional advancement through law journal publications addressing these matters.

Even within the realm of constitutional law, law review articles focus disproportionately on the relative handful of Supreme Court rulings (i.e., about seventy to eighty per year), neglecting by comparison the thousands of lower federal court rulings where law review articles might offer a more welcome and useful contribution to the legal profession.[45] Law professor James Lindgren reports that constitutional law is the topic most frequently addressed in law reviews (both in faculty- and student-authored articles), followed by corporate law. Yet, this contrasts starkly with the areas of greatest concern to practicing lawyers, whose work normally centers on domestic law, wills, criminal law, and real estate – subjects that receive virtually no attention in law reviews.[46]

In sum, the student-run law review system began at a time when law professors were practitioners, not scholars, and when the more narrow and orthodox nature of legal writing justified student authorship and editorship. The proliferation of law reviews soon made the student-run system nearly indispensable because law academia lacked the human resources necessary to effectuate any kind of wholesale transfer of control over to faculty. Moreover, there was little incentive to do so because law faculty benefited from the system, both as students who had served on law reviews and advanced their careers through such service and as faculty who then published in them. And, as Friedman, noted, "the system became encrusted with honor and antiquity and prestige."[47] Further, law faculty of the nineteenth and early twentieth centuries simply could not predict the prominent role that such publications would play by the latter part of the century or the ways in which their profession would evolve. And, there was certainly no incentive for students to voluntarily relinquish control, especially because law review service was and is viewed

---

[44] Ibid.   [45] Posner, "Against the Law Reviews."
[46] Lindgren, "An Author's Manifesto," 532–33.
[47] Friedman, American Law in the 20th Century, 498.

as an important benchmark of student academic excellence, leading to better jobs and prestige within the legal community. The end result is the paradoxical student-run publishing system of law reviews. Law reviews' evolution also laid bare an ever-growing "division – indeed, a tension – between the aims of legal scholarship and the requirements of law teaching that has no analogue in disciplines such as history and philosophy."[48]

How the System Works

The mechanics of the law review system may vary from one law school to another but, in general, students selected to serve as members of a law review are chosen by the current editors on a merit-based system at the end of their first year of study (out of a three-year course of study). The merit criterion is usually based on grades, submission of a writing sample, or some combination of the two. The senior editorial positions are generally held by third-year students. Students may earn academic credit and sometimes a stipend for editorial service, as well as the prestige of having "made" law review. Although students may consult faculty members (those consulted are usually limited to faculty affiliated with the law review's law school), the student editorial board controls the publication process. Articles that are accepted for publication are carefully edited for content and style. Citations are checked for accuracy, and authors may be asked to revise their work or to submit additional information.[49] Article authors typically submit their manuscripts to multiple reviews simultaneously, a practice discouraged in other disciplines. Multiple submissions mean that student editors, especially at higher-prestige journals, must wade through a great many manuscripts, and do so quickly.

According to a study of law review practices, high-status (called "high-impact") journals received 600 to 1,200 manuscripts per year; medium-impact journals about 300 to 750 per year; and low-impact journals about 50 to 300 per year. The volume and competitiveness factors resulted in rapid reported turnaround times of one to two weeks for low-impact

---

[48] Anthony T. Kronman, *The Lost Lawyer: Failing Ideals of the Legal Profession* (Cambridge, MA: Harvard University Press, 1993), 265.

[49] Closen and Dzielak, "The History and Influence of the Law Review Institution," 43–49; Harnsberger, "Reflections About Law Reviews and American Legal Scholarship," 685–86.

journals, two to four weeks for medium-impact journals, and two to six weeks for high-impact journals. Once accepted, an article may appear within a few months of acceptance.[50]

Much has been written about the criteria students employ in selecting articles for publication. An intensive study of student-edited law journal publication decisions involved interviews with student law journal editors at forty-three law schools. This study found that student editors' adoption decisions were influenced not only by editors' judgments of quality but also by whether the submissions dealt with a new topic, as opposed to a subject about which much had already been written. In addition, submissions from well-known – that is, famous or prestigious – authors (as well as the prestige of those thanked by the author in the "Acknowledgments" footnote), who had established publishing records and who came from more elite institutions, were also favored, as were authors on the faculty of the editors' institution. Student editors admitted feeling pressure to accept such home-team submissions.[51] As the authors of the study noted, most student editors interviewed "simply conceded that famous authors are granted a presumption of excellence," although editors also said that even these submissions would be rejected if their manuscripts were considered "inferior."[52] Others who have written on this subject also agree that student editors favor articles that adhere to the seemingly contrary trends of being safely orthodox, on the one hand, or faddish on the other.[53] As to subject matter, student editors are especially drawn to submissions pertaining to constitutional law and corporate law, subjects of great

---

[50] The study was based on onsite, in-depth interviews conducted at 43 law schools around the country, based on a target population of 153 generalist or "principal" student-edited law journals (omitting specialty publications). Jordan H. Liebman and James P. White, "How the Student-Edited Law Journals Make Their Publication Decisions," *Journal of Legal Education* 39(March 1989): 387–425. See also Lee Epstein and Gary King, "The Rules of Inference," *University of Chicago Law Review* 69(Winter 2002): 48, 125–27.

[51] Liebman and White, "How the Student-Edited Law Journals Make Their Publication Decisions," 404–405.

[52] Liebman and White, "How the Student-Edited Law Journals Make Their Publication Decisions," 405. See also Ronald J. Krotoszynski, Jr., "Legal Scholarship at the Crossroads," *Texas Law Review* 77(November 1998): 330.

[53] Roger C. Cramton, "'The Most Remarkable Institution': The American Law Review," *Journal of Legal Education* 35(1986): 5; Hibbitts, "Last Writes?," 641; Leo P. Martinez, "Babies, Bathwater, and Law Reviews," *Stanford Law Review* 47(Summer 1995): 1142–43.

interest to them. Further, longer and more heavily footnoted articles generally find greater favor, especially at more prestigious journals.[54]

Criticisms

The student-run law review system has indisputably flourished in the last century. Even from their initial founding, however, law reviews have had their critics, who focused specifically, although not exclusively,[55] on the fact that they were student-run. Supreme Court Justice Oliver Wendell Holmes referred to such publications dismissively as the "work of boys."[56] Writing in the 1920s, one law professor argued that law review publications should be edited by faculty, not students, because the latter "will scarcely be sufficiently well prepared" to make editorial decisions.[57]

In a legendarily scathing, sarcastic, and caustic essay, Yale law professor Fred Rodell published an article in 1936 titled "Goodbye to Law Reviews." In it, he launched into his explanation of "why I do not care to contribute further to the qualitatively moribund while quantitatively mushroom-like literature of the law." His reason was this: "There are two things wrong with almost all legal writing. One is its style. The other is its content."[58] Rodell proceeded to unload, excoriating law reviews' dull sameness, poor and obtuse writing, humorlessness, excessive footnoting, and unimportant content. The motives of faculty and student writers he attributed to, respectively, the desire for pay raises and the hunt for good jobs. Although not laying the blame exclusively or even primarily at the feet of the student editors, Rodell noted that student writers were "just as superficial" as faculty authors but were "even more assiduously stilted."[59] His essay's conclusion was suitably pessimistic: law reviews would continue to print articles "not fit to read, on subjects that are not worth the bother of writing about them."[60] Rodell's complaints would resonate throughout the

---

[54] Lindgren, "An Author's Manifesto," 532–33; Posner, "The Future of Student-Edited Law Reviews," 1133–34.

[55] For example, as early as 1906, some in the legal field complained that the publishing field was being swamped by too many publications, calling it "overcrowded." Hibbitts, "Last Writes?," 629.

[56] Quoted in Hughes, "Foreword," 737.

[57] Clarence M. Updegraff, "Management of Law School Reviews," *University of Cincinnati Law Review* 3(1929): 119.

[58] Fred Rodell, "Goodbye to Law Reviews," *Virginia Law Review* 23(1936): 38.

[59] *Ibid.*, 43.   [60] *Ibid.*, 45.

profession from that time to the present, and the intensity of the debate has not diminished in recent years.[61]

Contemporary criticisms of the law review system include complaints that the publishing realm is too vast, resulting in much that is of poor quality or that is never read;[62] that articles are too long – and pointlessly so – often running more than a hundred pages per article;[63] that there are far too many footnotes (a 1989 article reported that the record for the law review article with the most footnotes was 4,824[64] – a record likely surpassed since that time);[65] that law review writing is increasingly divorced from the interests, needs, and concerns of the legal profession;[66] that the writing is poorly edited by student editors;[67] and that students are not competent to judge the content of articles submitted to them, with the result that they often publish articles that are unworthy of publication, and that either repeat the prevailing orthodoxy or, contrarily, embrace the

[61] See Rodell's book-length indictment of lawyers and the legal profession: *Woe Unto You Lawyers!* (New York: Reynal and Hitchcock, 1939). The law school community's soul-searching on this issue is reflected in several symposia issues. See "Symposium on Law Review Editing: The Struggle Between Author and Editor Over Control of the Text," *Chicago-Kent Law Review* 61(1994); "Special Issue," *Stanford Law Review* 47 (1995); "Special Issue," *Akron Law Review* 30(Winter 1996). See also Carl T. Bogus, "The Death of an Honorable Profession," *Indiana Law Journal* 71(Fall 1996): 911–47.

[62] Alan W. Mewett, "Reviewing the Law Reviews," *Journal of Legal Education* 8(1955): 188; Margaret A. Goldblatt, "Current Legal Periodicals: A Use Study," *Law Library Journal* 78(1986): 55–72; Kenneth Lasson, "Scholarship Amok: Excesses in the Pursuit of Truth and Tenure," *Harvard Law Review* 103(February 1990): 926–29; Hibbitts, "Last Writes?," 629.

[63] Elyce Zenoff, "I Have Seen the Enemy and They Are Us," *Journal of Legal Education* 36(1986): 21; Lasson, "Scholarship Amok," 942–43; Lindgren, "An Author's Manifesto," 531–32; Friedman, *American Law in the 20th Century*, 498; Robert C. Berring, "Less is More. Really." *Green Bag* 8(Spring 2005): 231–34.

[64] David Margolick, "The Law: At the Bar," *New York Times*, June 9, 1989, B5.

[65] John E. Nowak, "Woe Unto You, Law Reviews!" *Arizona Law Review* 27(1985): 318; Cramton, "'The Most Remarkable Institution,'" 5; David Margolick, "At the Bar: The Fetish of Footnotes, or the Folly of Trying to Eradicate the Profession's Enduring Weeds," *New York Times*, June 8, 1990, B16; Arthur Austin, "The Reliability of Citation Counts in Judgments on Promotion, Tenure, and Status," *Arizona Law Review* 35(Winter 1993): 829–39; Posner, "The Future of the Student-Edited Law Review," 1134.

[66] Harry T. Edwards, "The Growing Disjunction Between Legal Education and the Legal Profession," *Michigan Law Review* 86(August 1988): 1835–1905; Posner, "The Future of the Student-Edited Law Review," 1133–34.

[67] Carol Sanger, "Editing," *Georgetown Law Journal* 82(December 1993): 513–27; Lindgren, "An Author's Manifesto," 528–31; Posner, "The Future of the Student-Edited Law Review," 1134–35.

latest fads, including approaches distinctive primarily for their novelty.[68] On this latter point, law professor James Lindgren minces no words: "Our scholarly journals are in the hands of incompetents."[69]

What defense is mounted against this withering attack of the law review system? A spirited one, to be sure. Defenders of the current system argue that the fault for poor quality articles lies with the faculty authors because student editorial boards can only publish what is submitted;[70] that students are, in fact, capable judges who can improve faculty submissions because students are unencumbered by the academic baggage of faculty and can therefore reduce conceptual or linguistic obtuseness, and that many excellent and important articles are published, especially in the most prestigious journals;[71] that faculty are hypocrites for criticizing a system from which they benefit and continue to buttress;[72] that the system allows for short turnaround time between submission and publication, allowing for quick response on developing issues;[73] and that review editorship is an important and valuable learning experience that provides benefits for top students both in law school and after graduation (this latter proposition is one on which even law review critics generally agree).[74]

---

[68] Daniel A. Farber and Suzanna Sherry "describe a phenomenon that has come to pervade legal scholarship – the idea that novelty is the ultimate test of the worth of an idea." They do not specifically attribute this to the nature of law reviews, but it lends support to that thesis. *Desperately Seeking Certainty: The Misguided Quest for Constitutional Foundations* (Chicago: University of Chicago Press, 2002), 6. See also Mewett, "Reviewing the Law Reviews," 190; Cramton, "'The Most Remarkable Institution,'" 8; Posner, "The Future of the Student-Edited Law Review," 1134.

[69] Lindgren, "An Author's Manifesto," 527.

[70] Phil Nichols, "A Student Defense of Student Edited Journals," *Duke Law Journal* (December 1987): 1124–25; James W. Harper, "Why Student-Run Law Reviews?" *Minnesota Law Review* 82(May 1988): 1274–76; The Articles Editors, "A Response," *University of Chicago Law Review* 61(Spring 1994): 554.

[71] Michael W. Dowdle, "The Case Against Law Reviews Rebutted," *New York Times*, December 21, 1990, A38; Wendy J. Gordon, "Counter-Manifesto: Student-Edited Reviews and the Intellectual Properties of Scholarship," *University of Chicago Law Review* 61(Spring 1994): 544–45; Richard S. Harnsberger, "Reflections About Law Reviews and American Scholarship," *Nebraska Law Review* 76(1997): 693; Harper, "Why Student-Run Law Reviews?" 1274–76, 1279–82.

[72] Nichols, "A Student Defense of Student Edited Journals"; Ehrenreich, "Look Who's Editing," 62; C. Scott Andrews, "Law Review Under Review," *Legal Affairs* (March/April 2005), 6.

[73] Lisa Anderson, "Law Journals Attack 'Shopping' of Manuscripts," *New York Times*, July 12, 1995, B6.

[74] Scott M. Martin, "The Law Review Citadel: Rodell Revisited," *Iowa Law Review* 71(May 1986): 1100–1101; Michael Vitiello, "In Defense of Student-Run Law Reviews," *Cumberland Law Review* 17(1987): 862; Harper, "Why Student-Run Law Reviews?,"

Interesting as this debate is, my purpose is to focus on those characteristics of law reviews that explain how law reviews, as a body of academic literature, differ from the academic literature of every other field of academic inquiry, and why that difference matters. To draw out those differences, it is useful to compare law with the publishing principles and practices of other disciplines, which rely on the process of peer review.

Professional Peer Review: The Academic Gold Standard

Legal writers are by no means unacquainted with peer review. A few legal publications do use peer review,[75] and some legal writers also publish in the peer-reviewed journals of other disciplines or publish books that undergo peer review. But this project's concern is with the publishing venue of the academic legal profession, and law reviews continue to be the place where most law faculty publish most of the time.

Some legal writers defend the law review system by arguing that peer review is no better as an alternative, charging, for example, that "While the peer-review process sounds good, its reliability and validity is questionable" and it "has shown itself to be wanting."[76] Another law review defender cautions the legal community to avoid the "unhealthy imitation of other traditional academic disciplines."[77] The question is not whether peer review is "questionable" or "wanting," for it undoubtedly has its

---

1272–74; Nathan H. Saunders, "Student-Edited Law Reviews: Reflections and Responses of an Inmate," *Duke Law Journal* 49(April 2000): 1670–73; Ben Potter, "Law Review Under Review," *Legal Affairs* (March/April 2005), 6.

[75] For example, the *Journal of Law and Economics*, the *Journal of Law, Economics, and Organization*, the *Journal of Legal Studies*, and the *Law and Society Review*. *Law and Contemporary Problems* has significant faculty control through a faculty board of editors, although there is also a student executive board. The *Supreme Court Review* and *Constitutional Commentary* are also controlled by faculty.

[76] Frank Cross, Michael Heise, and Gregory C. Sisk, "Above the Rules," *University of Chicago Law Review* 69(Winter 2002): 148, note 97. For similar objections to peer review, see Jack Goldsmith and Adrian Vermeule, "Empirical Methodology and Legal Scholarship," *University of Chicago Law Review* 69(Winter 2002): 156; Bernard Hibbitts, "Yesterday Once More," *Akron Law Review* 30(Winter 1996): 292. Phil Nichols even argues that student control is superior to peer review because it operates more quickly and because the annual turnover of student editorial control means that no single point of view can predominate. One may thus conclude that speed and ignorance become virtues in deliberations over scholarly merit. "A Student Defense of Student Edited Journals," 1127.

[77] Vitiello, "In Defense of Student-Run Law Reviews," 861. Vitiello argues that imitating the practices of other disciplines would reduce the number of publishing possibilities and that faculty editors can be poor judges of article quality as well (872–73).

problems, as I discuss herein. Rather, the key question is whether peer review offers a more sound and reliable alternative.

Academic research and publishing in every other discipline – whether the natural sciences, social sciences, or fine arts and humanities – follow some version of peer review and have done so for many decades. In broad outline, the academic publications process involves the submission of manuscripts to journal editors, who are themselves trained in the field of specialty coinciding with the subject of the publication and who often have prior experience or training in the editorial process. These editors then send the manuscripts for review to one or more other experts in the field who read and evaluate the suitability of the work for publication. They may recommend immediate publication, publication subject to revisions, or rejection. The names of the reviewers are customarily not revealed to the authors (referred to as "blind review"; if the authors' names are also shielded from the reviewers, it is "double-blind" review). This is done to encourage reviewers to be frank in their evaluations. Editors normally abide by the judgments of the reviewers, but final decisions nevertheless rest with the editors. Just as there are some law reviews in which publication decisions do not rest with students, so too there are some professional publications that do not rely on independent peer review, but these are the exceptions.[78]

The logic of peer review is self-evident: scholarly work, by its nature, is designed to advance knowledge. Field specialists are most likely to be able to judge the relative merits of often complex work that is aimed at a small and specialized field of study. Does the work deal with an important subject? Does it employ sound methods? Does it demonstrate appropriate knowledge of the existing research and literature of the field? Does it represent a new contribution or merely duplicate that which has already been published? Does the work present concepts and facts accurately? These and other similar questions guide peer review in every field, from anthropology to zoology, from literature to political science. In short, peer review is "the gold standard" of scientific inquiry.[79]

Peer review is not without its critics or faults. In fact, peer review has taken a battering in recent years, as highly publicized incidents of scientific

[78] In political science, for example, the editors of the journal *Presidential Studies Quarterly* made publishing decisions when it was first founded, a fact that tarnished its reputation. When it converted to peer review, its reputation rose.

[79] Daniel Engber, "Quality Control: The Case Against Peer Review," *Slate Magazine*, April 5, 2005. Accessed at http://slate.msn.com/id/2116244/ on April 6, 2005.

fraud in the natural sciences and fraud in disciplines like history have shaken disciplinary confidence. In 2005, for example, the international scientific establishment was euphoric when it was revealed that a team of South Korean scientists who claimed to have cloned human embryos and extracted their stem cells, all with relative ease, was reported in the pages of the prestigious publication *Science*. Shortly after the article's publication, however, the results were found to be fraudulent, a devastating and humiliating revelation especially for *Science*'s editors, who were forced to withdraw the article.[80] Fraud in scientific research is nothing new.[81] Indeed, modern peer review was first established in the 1700s in order to improve the reliability of scientific research; it finally became a uniform scientific standard after World War II.[82] In recent decades, concerns about fraud, especially as a result of increasing competition for lucrative government and private research grants, have prompted an increase in safeguards.[83]

The social sciences have experienced their own highly publicized instances of fraud and misconduct in recent years. Celebrated and award-winning historians Stephen E. Ambrose and Doris Kearns Goodwin were both discovered to have committed plagiarism in their writings. Although their cases were hardly the first, their notoriety (i.e., both appeared frequently on national television and served as consultants for politicians and Hollywood moviemakers, among others) drew national attention.[84] Historian Michael Bellesiles resigned from his academic position after a university inquiry concluded that he misrepresented data he cited in an article and a book concerning early probate records pertaining to gun

---

[80] Gina Kolata, "A Cloning Scandal Rocks a Pillar of Science Publishing," *New York Times*, December 18, 2005, A28.

[81] A famous historical example of scientific fraud was the case of "Piltdown Man," an allegedly prehistoric human "discovered" by an amateur anthropologist in 1908. It was eventually proven to be a fraud in 1953. Boyce Rensberger, "Fraud in Research Is a Rising Problem in Science," *New York Times*, January 23, 1977, A1.

[82] Engber, "Quality Control."

[83] Rensberger, "Fraud in Research Is a Rising Problem in Science"; Lawrence K. Altman and William J. Broad, "Global Trend: More Science, More Fraud," *New York Times*, December 20, 2005, F1; Horace F. Judson, *The Great Betrayal: Fraud in Science* (New York: Harcourt, 2004).

[84] David Greenberg, "School for Scandal," *Slate Magazine*, December 10, 2004. Accessed at http://slate.msn.com/id/2110907/ on December 20, 2004. See also Ron Robin, *Scandals and Scoundrels: Seven Cases That Shook the Academy* (Berkeley, CA: University of California Press, 2004). The Ambrose and Goodwin cases involved book publishing, not articles in scholarly journals. But book publishing normally relies on peer review as well.

ownership.[85] Another researcher on gun control, economist John Lott, was charged with inventing poll data regarding the frequency with which citizens used guns to protect themselves. Lott's humiliation escalated when he admitted to inventing a fictional defender, "Mary Rosh," whose comments appeared widely on the Internet extolling his work and criticizing his detractors.[86]

Leaving aside the serious problem of fraud or other types of willful misconduct, peer review has also been criticized for its tendency to favor institutional conservatism; that is, reviewers and editors tend to support the intellectual status quo and are sometimes reluctant to approve publications that are innovative or controversial. The secretiveness of the review process has also raised objections because it places much discretion in the hands of people who are able to hide behind anonymity. Peer review is also often slow, especially given the problems of enlisting reviewers (who are almost never paid for their services) and getting them to respond promptly. And, of course, any biases on the part of editors and reviewers, whether intellectual or personal, may hold sway over the review process.[87]

Such incidents and concerns, especially in the scientific community, have prompted calls for reforms of the peer review system. Among the proposals for change are calls to open up the peer review process – that is, to reveal the names of reviewers to those whose work is being reviewed; open-source reviewing, whereby drafts of work would be posted on the Internet, where anyone with expertise and interest could offer commentary; encouraging greater data sharing and experimental replication; and increasing the professional staffs of publications in order

[85] Peter Charles Hoffer, *Past Imperfect: Facts, Fictions, Fraud – American History from Bancroft and Parkman to Ambrose, Bellesiles, Ellis, and Goodwin* (New York: Public Affairs Press, 2004). Bellesiles's book, *Arming America: The Origins of a National Gun Culture* (New York: Alfred A. Knopf, 2000), won the Bancroft Prize in history in 2001, but the prize was later withdrawn. Other analyses of objectivity and fraud in the study of history include Peter Novick, *That Noble Dream: The 'Objectivity Question' and the American Historical Profession* (New York: Cambridge University Press, 1988); Joyce Appleby, Lynn Hunt, and Margaret Jacob, *Telling the Truth About History* (New York: W. W. Norton, 1994).

[86] Donald Kennedy, "Research Fraud and Public Policy," *Science* 300(April 18, 2003): 393; Richard Morin, "Scholar Invents Fan to Answer His Critics," *Washington Post*, February 1, 2003, C1. For a fuller chronicle of Lott's ethical and other lapses, see http://timlambert.org/lott/.

[87] Liora Schmelkin, "Weaknesses of Peer Reviewing and Peer Refereeing," Presidential Address to the American Psychological Association, accessed at http://knowledge-and-communication.org/inquiry4/inquiry6.asp on March 27, 2006.

to have more in-house experts trained and experienced in research evaluation.[88]

Yet, for all its problems, no one has ever suggested that the review process would be improved by placing it in the hands of students. In fact, the thrust of peer review reform efforts has advocated moving in a direction opposite of that found in law reviews: that is, reforms emphasize efforts to draw on *more, not less*, professional expertise. The title of one article on the peer review process encapsulates the situation this way: "Peer Review: Crude and Understudied, but Indispensable."[89] Political scientists Lee Epstein and Gary King state the case succinctly, referring to the law's adversary system and student-run law reviews: "there exists no serious basis for thinking it would work better in academia than the system – indeed the only system – that has worked so well for learning about the world in so many other disciplines."[90]

The existence of fraud within the system of peer review lends no support to the idea of abandoning expertise-based review of academic writing and publication, any more than the persistence of murder in society would support the proposition that laws against murder should be repealed. However imperfect, peer review is a standard and a practice of expertise-based evaluation. Leaving aside the few rare exceptions, law reviews are alone among all academic disciplines in having no such standards.

The Problems with Student Control

It is difficult to fully disentangle the consequences of student editorial control from other traits of legal writing. For example, the great importance given to footnotes stems from a long tradition, dating to the early nineteenth century and before, of their important role in court

---

[88] Engber, "Quality Control"; David Dobbs, "Trial and Error," *New York Times Magazine*, January 15, 2006, 18–19. Since the 1980s, the International Congress on Biomedical Peer Review and Scientific Publication has held conferences every four years on this subject. The most recent such conference was in 2005. See http://www.ama-assn.org/public/peer/peerhome.htm.

[89] Jerome P. Kassirer and Edward W. Campion, "Peer Review: Crude and Understudied, but Indispensable," *Journal of the American Medical Association* 272(July 13, 1994): 96–97.

[90] Lee Epstein and Gary King, "A Reply," *University of Chicago Law Review* 69(Winter 2002): 195. Epstein and King urge legal writers "to follow the norms in the dozens of academic disciplines that have decades of experience making progress in learning about the world" (195).

decisions.[91] And, legal writing by law scholars has a tradition of using "the same assumptions, vocabulary, and methods of argument and proof as found in judicial opinions," a trait that distinguishes the method and content of their writing from "colleagues in other departments of their university."[92] Yet, it is the fact of student control that, above all, distinguishes law reviews from the professional publications found in every other discipline.

The problem is not difficult to summarize. One may readily concede at the outset that law review service is highly valuable as a learning experience for law students. Would anyone similarly doubt that second-year medical students would reap enormous educational benefits from the chance to perform open-heart surgery on live patients? Medical school administrators and faculty (not to mention the patients!) would recoil at such a suggestion, however, for the obvious reason that students do not yet possess the requisite knowledge to perform such a delicate procedure and, therefore, the risks to the patients would simply be too great, even though the learning experience for the students would be considerable. The operating room is no place for trainee trial-and-error. Admittedly, the stakes are not as high in the legal profession but neither are they trivial.

Although intelligent and hard-working student editors may be able to discern the meaning of manuscript submissions, they do not and cannot be expected to possess the knowledge and expertise of those who have researched and published in a field, and who therefore are best suited to provide a substantive evaluation of the merits of a piece of work. Whereas some law students may also possess other advanced degrees or training, the normal law school admissions educational prerequisite is only a bachelor's degree from an undergraduate institution. Further, student editors and editorial assistants are second- and third-year law students who are working on a part-time basis for law reviews (even if they put in full-time hours) for which they receive little or no formal training, limited or no monetary compensation, and while they are also meeting the other demands imposed on law students, including coursework. And,

---

[91] Lasson, "Scholarship Amok," 939–40; Fred R. Shapiro, "Origins of Bibliometrics, Citation Indexing, and Citation Analysis: The Neglected Legal Literature," *Journal of the American Society for Information Science* 43(1992): 337–39.

[92] Richard A. Posner, "Law, Knowledge, and the Academy: Legal Scholarship Today," *Harvard Law Review* 115(March 2002): 1315.

normal student turnover means that law reviews undergo constant personnel change. As political scientists Epstein and King noted in their important study of the methodological problems found in empirical law journal articles, "While it is easy to fool oneself (or law students, as the case may be) into believing that one has produced an important research result, it is a good deal more difficult to 'fool,' however inadvertently, a community of experts spending their lives working on related problems."[93]

Without question, law reviews publish a great deal of important, interesting, stimulating, and significant scholarship. In that respect, the law review system functions effectively. But, while it functions without a ceiling on excellence, it also functions without a floor or barrier to writing that is incompetent, bad, and wrong. The mischief that may (and does) result cannot be blithely accepted or dismissed as a reasonable or benign consequence of the law journal system. As Epstein and King caution, academics are well advised to follow the physicians' maxim of "first, do no harm."[94] Subsequent chapters provide detailed examples of just such damaging writing in constitutional law. As noted previously, disciplines in which peer review is the norm are not insulated against defective or wrong-headed writing, but the peer review firewall is at least a functioning barrier; no comparable barrier exists in the world of law reviews.

Stated differently, the flaws of peer review are flaws of implementation, not of concept. No one in any field outside of law has proposed abandoning the principle that the judgments of experts should be used to judge other experts. In the modern era of law review publishing, the flaw of student-run law reviews is, at bottom, a flaw of concept. To say that student-run law reviews publish some excellent writing, although true, is not an adequate defense. Given the competitive nature of publishing in top law journals, any method of selection – including random selection – would produce some excellent publications. Even more important, to deny the superiority of peer review is to deny that knowledge and experience matter in the academic world. Winston Churchill's oft-quoted aphorism about democracy as a system of governance applies with equal vigor to peer review: "Democracy is the worst form of Government except all those other forms that have been tried from time to time."[95]

[93] Epstein and King, "The Rules of Inference," 48.
[94] Epstein and King, "A Reply," 195.
[95] The Oxford Dictionary of Quotations (New York: Oxford University Press, 1979), 150.

Length, Redundancy, and Footnotes

Before concluding this subject, three particular symptoms of law review problems, often discussed by critics and supporters alike, are particularly germane for this analysis: length, redundancy, and footnoting. As I have noted, many have commented on the sheer length of law journal articles, often running to well over a hundred pages per article.[96] To cite one measure of the acceleration of the trend toward ever-increasing length, one study reports that the average length of lead articles in the *Yale Law Journal* and *Harvard Law Review* was fifteen pages in the 1890s, thirty-three pages in the 1950s, and sixty pages by the 1980s.[97] This is significant because the typical academic journal places a far greater premium on relative brevity. Medical and scientific articles often run only a few printed pages. In the social sciences, a standard limit on manuscript length is on the order of around thirty manuscript pages (typed, double-spaced). Such standard length limitations impel authors to synthesize, economize, and emphasize that which is more important, and it thwarts the tendency of academics to excessively rhapsodize or duplicate that which has already been published. Few outside of the law would dispute the value of such a standard, and its universality in every other discipline speaks adequately well to its utility and wisdom.

A partial explanation for excessive length in law reviews is redundancy. I have engaged in several research projects (including this one) that involved extensive reading of many hundreds of law review articles and have consistently noted "the nearly unbelievable degree of repetition to be found in that writing."[98] Although some recapitulation of existing knowledge or literature is standard in academic writing, it does not begin to explain or justify the "mind-numbing" degree of repetition, which serves

---

[96] An extreme symptom of the obsession with length is a survey conducted more than once by the Chicago-Kent College of Law, which ranks laws schools' scholarly productivity by the number of pages published in leading law reviews per faculty member. In its 1992 survey, the University of Chicago Law School ranked first with 101.58 pages per faculty member. That length, rather than number or quality of articles, was offered as a serious yardstick of scholarship speaks to the faculty's obsession with sheer volume, although it was touted by its authors as a "more objective measure of law schools' quality" than other rankings. "Ranking Law Schools by Faculty Publishing Rate," *New York Times*, July 17, 1992, A23.

[97] Kalman, *The Strange Career of Legal Liberalism*, 95.

[98] Robert J. Spitzer, "Lost and Found: Researching the Second Amendment," *Chicago-Kent Law Review* 76(2000): 382.

no other purpose than to duplicate what has already been published. Even in the research for this chapter, I have discovered duplicative articles that do little more than repeat the arguments of previous authors. It is almost unimaginable that so many repetitive publications would find their way into print in other disciplines because redundancy is an obvious, typical, and eminently sensible ground for manuscript rejection.[99] In the case of law reviews, however, students have no such knowledge of the literature (and can only hope to acquire it by consulting experts in the field), so it cannot play a role in their decisions.

Finally, article length is also partly a function of the extravagant foot-noting found in many articles. Many critics in the legal community have complained about the "voluminous and largely meaningless citations for every proposition"[100] so often found in law review articles. Yet, for all the debate about excessive footnoting,[101] surprisingly little of it specifically addresses the central question: when, and under what circumstances, are footnotes necessary?

According to one expert on footnotes, they exist to serve two purposes: (1) to persuade the reader that the writer has conducted the necessary degree of work on the subject, and (2) to present the primary sources relied on most heavily by the writer.[102] These two purposes translate into explanatory footnotes that elaborate on some point of insufficient centrality to justify bringing it into the main text (this can take the form of either additional discussion inserted in the footnote or referring the reader to other sources) and footnotes that provide the direct sourcing from which information is taken. As for the question of what information needs footnoting, a standard English composition book recommends this: "Cite all facts, statistics, and pieces of information unless they are common

---

[99] *Ibid.*, 376–77.

[100] Cramton, "'The Most Remarkable Institution,'" 8.

[101] The *University of Pennsylvania Law Review* (123[1975]: 1474–81) published a legendary parody of law footnotes, titled "The Common-Law Origins of the Infield Fly Rule." Its first sentence was: "The(1) Infield Fly Rule(2) is neither a rule of law nor one of equity; it is a rule of baseball.(3)" The numbers appearing in the quote correspond to the three footnotes inserted just in that first sentence. Margolick, "At the Bar."

[102] Anthony Grafton, *The Footnote: A Curious History* (Cambridge, MA: Harvard University Press, 1997), 22. Grafton is writing specifically about the use of footnotes by historians, although he is well aware of the "exhaustive footnotes for the legal journals," as he further observes that legal writers "have an especially good excuse for regarding footnotes with dislike. . . ." (25)

knowledge and are accessible in many sources."[103] At their worst, law review articles go far over the top in both instances. Student editors do this when they ignore the common-knowledge rule, when they insert more footnotes than are necessary to provide proper attribution, and when they adhere to conventions such as liberal insertions of "supra," a footnote that refers the reader to another section of the article. Many of these arcane, superfluous, and anachronistic practices are traceable to the reference source for legal writing, *A Uniform System of Citation*, also known as the "Bluebook." It is difficult to chastise student editors for adhering to a style manual they did not create (although students do play a role in its revision); yet, it is symptomatic of the larger problem with law reviews that major reform of the Bluebook system has not occurred, especially because other disciplines have successfully revamped their rules of style.[104]

To those who have taught students, it should come as little surprise that they are likely to be uniquely impressed by and amenable to ever-more lengthy articles with ever more footnotes. But no serious argument can be made that more footnotes or greater length equal more or greater quality. It is the very emphasis on, even mania for, length and footnotes that underscores how manifestly unqualified students are to judge what matters most: the substantive merit of arguments made and the quality of the evidence offered.

Conclusion

Student-run law reviews made sense when a relatively small number of law schools struggled to professionalize legal training in the late nineteenth and early twentieth centuries and when legal writing was narrowly doctrinal and case-oriented. Yet, as the field grew, matured, and diversified, the tenets of legal training (see Chapter 1) left students ever further behind in terms of possessing the requisite knowledge (never mind the absence of appropriate editorial skills) at the very time that the number of law reviews exploded. Aside from the obvious limitations of students, law reviews on the whole failed to compensate for these problems with any

---

[103] Ann Raimes, *Universal Keys for Writers* (Boston: Houghton Mifflin, 2004), 744.
[104] The Modern Language Association's (MLA) Handbook has undergone a series of major revisions in the last several decades. In the discipline of political science, its flagship journal, the *American Political Science Review*, changed from endnotes to in-text citations in 1978.

expertise-based standard or mechanism. The result is a vast publication hole that retains unwarranted academic legitimacy and public prestige.

Yes, law reviews publish many excellent articles, but in a realm of more than 1,100 publications, some excellent articles would be published if the criterion for selection were by Ouija board, astrology, or random selection. The one irrefutable and insurmountable fact of the law review publishing realm, taken as a whole, is that the critical publishing and related editorial decisions are made by people who do not and cannot possess the knowledge or judgment to evaluate submissions on their academic merits. This is not an effort to "blame the victim" but rather to identify a problem that has visible and important adverse consequences. There may be no limit to high quality, but there is also no substantive barrier to dross. Add to the fact of student control another – the vastness of the publishing realm – and one may readily realize that the sheer volume of publishing possibilities provides a uniquely wide and fertile opportunity for the cultivation and propagation of wayward constitutional theories. The next three chapters examine three such wayward constitutional theories, pertaining to the president's veto power, the executive's CIC power, and the right to bear arms. As historian Garry Wills noted in his analysis of a particular body of law journal writing, "It seems as if our law journals were being composed by Lewis Carroll using various other pseudonyms."[105]

[105] Wills, "To Keep and Bear Arms," 71.

3 . . . . . The Inherent Item Veto

On June 15, 1994, the U.S. Senate Judiciary Committee, Subcommittee on the Constitution, held hearings on a constitutional theory that might be alternately labeled stunning or bizarre – that the Constitution as written in 1787 provides the president not only with the power to veto bills but also parts of bills when they cross the chief executive's desk.

For more than 160 years, scholars and political figures have debated the desirability of granting the president item veto powers.[1] This debate took on new life in the 1980s with President Reagan's repeated calls for such a power. During the Clinton administration, Congress enacted legislation to give the president limited item-veto–type powers (actually called "enhanced rescission"), which gave to the president the power to, in effect, cancel certain types of spending provisions. The law took effect in 1997, whereupon Clinton exercised the power against eighty-two provisions embedded in ten pieces of legislation,[2] only to have the power challenged in court. In 1998, the Supreme Court struck down the Line Item Veto Act of 1996, arguing that it violated the Constitution's Presentment Clause.[3]

---

[1] Members of Congress first debated an item veto for the president in the 1840s; Ulysses S. Grant was the first president to formally request the power in 1873. See Robert J. Spitzer, *The Presidential Veto* (Albany, NY: SUNY Press, 1988), chap. 5; "Symposium on the Line-Item Veto," *Notre Dame Journal of Law, Ethics, and Public Policy*, 1(1985); Philip G. Joyce and Robert D. Reischauer, "The Federal Line-Item Veto: What Is It and What Will It Do?," *Public Administration Review* 57(March/April 1997): 95–104.

[2] Robert J. Spitzer, "The Item Veto Dispute and the Secular Crisis of the Presidency," *Presidential Studies Quarterly* 28(Fall 1998): 799–805. The total dollar amount of spending blocked by these vetoes, had they been sustained, was about $1.9 billion.

[3] *Clinton v. City of New York*, 524 U.S. 417 (1998).

In 2006, Congress again moved to give the president a limited item-veto–type power through regular legislative means when the House of Representatives passed such a measure, at the urging of President George W. Bush (the measure stalled in the Senate).

Yet, this enduring debate over the item veto took an odd twist during the George H. W. Bush presidency when he made it known in 1989 that he already possessed a constitutionally based item veto, was actively considering its unilateral exercise, and then invited Congress to take him to court if it objected.[4] Both the House and the Senate took up this cause as well, with some lawmakers supporting Bush's claim.[5]

Since the end of the first Bush presidency, no president has embraced the idea that the president already possesses an item veto, and legislative attempts to create some version of the power in the Clinton and second Bush administrations seem to have closed the door on such a theory. Why, then, devote space and effort to this arcane and obscure dispute? The answer is because the consequences of this debate are anything but arcane and obscure.

First, this dispute over the nature of the president's veto power actually bundles together several vitally important constitutional issues and practices regarding presidential–congressional powers, including impoundment, the legal status of legislative riders and omnibus legislation, the Presentment Clause, the boundaries of statutory discretion, the efficacy and limits of the veto, and the very definition of law. Second, stated in simplest terms, constitutionalists should be both interested and

---

[4] "A Bush Line-Item Veto?," *CQ Weekly Report*, October 28, 1989, 2848; Gerald Seib, "If Bush Tests Constitutionality of Line-Item Veto, Reverberations Could Transform Government," *Wall Street Journal*, October 30, 1989, A12.

[5] This idea won partisan endorsement in the 1988 Republican Party Platform, under the section on "Controlling Federal Spending," which said: "We will use all constitutional authority to control congressional spending. This will include consideration of the inherent line-item veto power of the president" (17).

On November 20, 1989, six members of the House of Representatives introduced a resolution (i.e., H.R. Res. 297) urging Bush to apply such a power. Even though Bush announced in 1992 that he now no longer accepted the validity of this argument (see "Address to Republican Members of Congress," *Weekly Compilation of Presidential Documents* 28[March 23, 1992]: 512), the Senate took up the cause in 1994 when Senator Arlen Specter (R-PA) introduced a resolution (i.e., S. Res. 195) calling on the president to exercise a unilateral item veto in order to create a test case for the courts. See U.S. Congress, Senate, "Remarks of Arlen Specter on S. Res. 195," 103rd Cong., 2d sess., *Congressional Record*, March 24, 1994, S3751–54. No bill was reported out of committee during the 103rd Congress, but it engendered the previously mentioned hearings.

skeptical when an entirely new theory of the exercise of constitutional powers emerges two centuries after the document's construction. More specifically, it illustrates how a constitutional confrontation – indeed, one might well think of it as a constitutional crisis – was nearly precipitated based on a theory that arose almost entirely from the legal community. The fact that the first President Bush never actually tried to use this power by no means minimizes its significance for the constitutional balance of power between the executive and legislative branches. More important for this study is the fact that this flight of constitutional fancy was born and legitimized in the pages of law reviews.

The inherent item veto argument first appeared in an article published in the *Temple Law Quarterly* in 1965.[6] The idea received an important boost in 1987 when lawyer Stephen Glazier published a widely noted and quoted op-ed piece in the *Wall Street Journal* that advocated the inherent item veto.[7] The following year, a Washington, DC–based conservative law center, the National Legal Center for the Public Interest, published proceedings of a conference held in 1988 that included a paper by historian Forrest McDonald, who offered what appeared to be sound historical evidence in support of the inherent item veto thesis. As I discuss herein, that research turned out to be defective, and McDonald later abandoned the argument. Other articles appeared in legal publications, peaking in the early 1990s when the first Bush administration proved receptive to the idea. But the inherent item veto was planted, cultivated, and legitimated in the pages of legal publications, eventually yielding a notable list of supportive (and also critical) articles.

Setting aside the obvious fact that no president until the first Bush ever claimed or exercised an item veto based on executive powers enumerated in the Constitution,[8] it is nevertheless at least theoretically possible

---

[6] Richard A. Givens, "The Validity of a Separate Veto of Non-germane Riders to Legislation," *Temple Law Quarterly* 39(Fall, 1965): 60–64.

[7] Steven Glazier, "Reagan Already Has Line-Item Veto," *Wall Street Journal*, December 4, 1987, 14. Glazier was a New York securities lawyer who was credited with reviving the idea. David Rapp, "Does Reagan Already Have a Line-Item Veto?" *CQ Weekly Report*, May 14, 1988, 1284.

[8] Glazier's argument was met with skepticism by the Reagan administration. See Rapp, "Does Reagan Already Have a Line-Item Veto?," 1284–85. In a fifty-four-page memorandum prepared by Charles Cooper, head of Reagan's Office of Legal Counsel, the inherent item veto argument was rejected. See "Memorandum for the Attorney General Re: The President's Veto Power," U.S. Department of Justice, Office of Legal

that such a power lies concealed, like an unexploded bomb, within the confines of the Constitution. Yet, what are we to make of such a claim? Is it indeed, as its proponents claimed, a shocking discovery, akin to an archeological discovery of a new link between modern humans and their distant ancestors? Is the debate more in the nature of an academic intellectual exercise that happened to catch the attention of the president and some in Congress? Was it a ruse, a stalking horse for other agendas, or a sincere – if misguided – effort to plumb the depths of the Constitution? To understand the inherent (also sometimes called unilateral or implicit) item veto argument and discern the pivotal role of law reviews, I examine, in considerable detail, the constitutional and historical case for the power. Only by examining the veracity of law journal article research on this subject can a judgment be made regarding its role in constitutional theorizing.

Colonial Precedents

Much of the support for the inherent item veto is based on the argument that an item veto was a common component of colonial government and that these practices, if they indeed existed, would therefore support the idea that the Constitution's founders meant an item veto to be a part of the modern veto power described in Article I, sec. 7. This argument is itself a slim reed upon which to read into the president's constitutional power an item veto. Nevertheless, the claims merit scrutiny.

Counsel, July 8, 1988. Past presidents have at times exercised considerable veto creativity, as when President Andrew Jackson signed a bill in 1830 but at the same time sent a message to Congress (after the House had recessed) that restricted the scope of the bill. President Tyler did something similar. See Louis Fisher, *Constitutional Conflicts Between Congress and the President* (Lawrence, KS: University Press of Kansas, 1997), 132–33. President George W. Bush has used presidential signing statements to, in effect, exercise an item veto by announcing in such statements his refusal to implement provisions he deemed unconstitutional or otherwise in violation to his executive powers. This breathtaking power grab by Bush is unprecedented as to both quality and quantity: from George Washington to the end of the Clinton administration, presidents have issued fewer than six hundred signing statement challenges to aspects of legislation; in his first six and a half years in office, Bush has issued more than eleven hundred such challenge statements. See American Bar Association, "Task Force on Presidential Signing Statements and the Separation of Powers Doctrine," August 2006, accessed at www.abanet.org/op/signingstatements/ on August 9, 2006; Charlie Savage, *Takeover: The Return of the Imperial Presidency and the Subversion of American Democracy* (New York: Little, Brown, 2007), 230.

It is well understood that colonial and early state political structures and practices had an important influence on the thinking of the Constitution's founders. Therefore, it is reasonable to examine those experiences for any light they may shed on the meaning of the modern Constitution. Yet, any such examination is constrained by two vital principles: first, interpretation of colonial experiences cannot and should not supersede the words and intentions of the Constitution's founders because this is the more direct, immediate, and relevant source of information for constitutional analysis; and second, although earlier practices fed into the thinking of the Constitution's framers, the government they constructed in 1787 was different from any other that came before it, especially as to the construction of the American presidency.[9]

Several governing structures operated to control colonial lawmaking. Ironically, the colonial governors and the British monarch were not the most important decision makers, although they took the brunt of blame for colonial frustrations as expressed, for example, in the Declaration of Independence. All laws emanating from colonial legislatures were transmitted to the Board of Trade (which operated to review colonial laws from 1696 to 1776), which in turn passed its recommendations for approval or disallowance on to the monarch's Privy Council. The Board's recommendations were based on entirely sensible criteria, given America's colonial status, including whether the new laws were within the proper legal domain of colonial legislatures, such laws encroached on royal prerogative, harmed relations between the colonies, or otherwise involved ill-advised legislative adventurism.[10] The Board's recommendations were almost always adopted by the Privy Council. Even though the disallowance or disapproval of colonial laws was referred to as being "disallowed by the King

---

[9] Robert J. Spitzer, *President and Congress* (New York: McGraw-Hill, 1993), chap. 1.

[10] The reasonableness of most of the Board's vetoes is illustrated by Dickerson's detailed account of vetoed laws, ranging from bills that might have harmed America's ability to defend itself, to settling legal differences between parliamentary law and the needs of the colonies, to laws that restricted religious freedom or otherwise persecuted Catholics or other minority religious groups. See Oliver Morton Dickerson, *American Colonial Government, 1696–1765* (New York: Russell and Russell, 1962; first published in 1912), chap. 5. All of this occurred under the operating principle that the "colonies did not exist primarily for their own benefit, but rather for that of the mother country which fostered and protected them." See Leonard Woods Labaree, *Royal Government in America* (New York: Frederick Ungar, 1930), 234.

and Council," this actually meant that the Board's recommendations had been disapproved by the Privy Council; the monarch was almost never personally involved in Privy Council decisions.[11]

In his search for support for the argument that the modern Constitution provides for an inherent item veto, McDonald cites as precedent the actions of the British Board of Trade. Of the more than eight thousand pieces of legislation passed to the British monarch during the colonial period, the Crown, according to McDonald, "vetoed all or part of 469 pieces of legislation in the eighty years in which the Board of Trade oversaw the colonies."[12] Speaking of the Board's actions, McDonald concludes that "the veto that they were exercising in the name of the Crown was a selective veto, a line-item veto."[13] Writing six years later, McDonald cites a selective veto exercised by Governor Francis Bernard in 1767 of the appropriations for one of two military fortifications found in a single bill passed by the Massachusetts legislature to illustrate that colonial governors exercised "what would come to be called a 'line-item' veto...."[14] Gordon Crovitz[15] and Diane-Michele Krasnow[16] embrace McDonald's argument that this was an item veto as it is understood today and use it to support the inherent item veto theory.

Yet, this line of argument, indirect though it is as support for an inherent item veto in the modern Constitution, is fatally flawed because (1) the actions of the Board of Trade and the Privy Council were not vetoes at all;

[11] Oliver Morton Dickerson, *American Colonial Government, 1696–1765* (New York: Russell and Russell, 1962; first published in 1912), 227.

[12] Forrest McDonald, "The Framers' Conception of the Veto Power," in *Pork Barrels and Principles* (Washington, DC: National Legal Center for the Public Interest, 1988), 2–3.

[13] McDonald, "The Framers' Conception," 2.

[14] Forrest McDonald, *The American Presidency* (Lawrence, KS: University Press of Kansas, 1994), 106. McDonald's source is John F. Burns, *Controversies Between Royal Governors and Their Assemblies in the North American Colonies* (New York: Russell and Russell, 1969; first published in 1923), who wrote: "The one thing worthy of mention during this session was the Governor's objection to the novelty of combining in one appropriation bill two distinct items, 6– somewhat after the manner of the more modern 'rider.' In a bill providing support for Castle William and Fort Pownal, Governor Bernard disapproved the latter on grounds of insufficiency; and the House immediately objected to the separation of parts of the same bill" (174).

[15] Gordon Crovitz, "The Line-Item Veto: The Best Response When Congress Passes One Spending 'Bill' a Year," *Pepperdine Law Review* 18(1990): 47.

[16] Diane-Michele Krasnow, "The Imbalance of Power and the Presidential Veto: A Case for the Item Veto," *Harvard Journal of Law & Public Policy* 14(Spring, 1991): 586–87.

(2) the colonial governors' role was, in toto, far greater than anything contemplated or desired by the Constitution's founders; and (3) the mechanics of this legislative process were very different from the lawmaking process and veto power established in 1787, in that colonial legislatures were, as a matter of British law, legal creatures of their British rulers. As Ronald Moe points out, "the term 'veto' . . . was generally inaccurate as it applied to the actions of the Board of Trade. Technically, the Board did not 'veto' an act; it recommended 'disallowance' of an act to the Privy Council."[17] As Frank Prescott and Joseph Zimmerman note in their definitive work on the New York veto, "the disallowance of colonial legislation [by the Board of Trade] was technically neither a repeal nor a veto" but was "analogous to the invalidation of laws by the United States Supreme Court."[18]

One distinctive element of the colonial legislative process was that the measures passed on to the Board of Trade were not bills but rather laws, once they were signed by the royal governor. Technically speaking, then, the action was a "disallowance," not a veto. As Dickerson noted, the "royal disapproval of such a law is very different, both in form and effect, from what is usually known as a veto. . . . The royal disapproval . . . had the effect of a legislative repeal. . . ."[19]

In addition, assemblies were directed to follow Crown-designed gubernatorial guidelines regarding the style and content of colonial legislation – that is, what they could and could not enact. Colonial legislatures were given some discretion, however, to redraft legislation to their liking, subject to final Crown approval. Notably, they were directed to treat different subjects as separate bills in order to avoid the "rider" or "tacking" strategy that had been used in the British House of Commons as early as the seventeenth century to frustrate the wishes of the House of Lords or the monarch.[20] In addition, laws were to have indefinite duration (except for circumstances when a date certain was obviously needed); tax laws had to extend for at least a year; lapsed laws were not to be reenacted without permission; no taxes were to be imposed on European goods brought to

---

[17] Ronald Moe, "The Founders and Their Experience with the Executive Veto," *Presidential Studies Quarterly* 17(Spring, 1987): 416. See also Louis Fisher, "The Presidential Veto: Constitutional Development," in *Pork Barrels and Politics*, 18.

[18] Frank W. Prescott and Joseph F. Zimmerman, *The Politics of the Veto of Legislation in New York State*, 2 vols. (Washington, DC: University Press of America, 1980), I, 5.

[19] Dickerson, *American Colonial Government*, 226.

[20] Labaree, *Royal Government in America*, 222.

America in British ships; and so on.[21] If they disobeyed, the governor could dissolve the assembly or exercise his absolute veto. If the governor yielded to colonial wishes, he could be subject to removal and other penalties.

Further, the British sometimes required the insertion of a "suspending clause" in legislation. The purpose of such a provision was to delay implementation of a duly enacted law until royal consent could be obtained – a process that could easily take years. The concern was that a law objectionable to the Crown might not be disallowed for a period of three years or more because of the slow and uncertain communications link stretching across the Atlantic and also because of bureaucratic delays or royal foot-dragging. Indeed, the average time span between law enactment in the colonies and disallowance of the 437 laws repealed by the Crown during the colonial period and examined by Russell was three years and five months. In one instance, a Virginia law that barred importation of North Carolina tobacco was disallowed in 1731 – twenty-six years after enactment.[22] In the case of Massachusetts, Governor Burnet was directed that routine laws should have a time line of at least two years.[23]

This time lag might mean that a legislature could obtain gubernatorial consent (by bribery, coercion, or persuasion) of an objectionable bill and implement the terms of the law for an extended period before royal disapproval could be transmitted. According to Leonard Labaree, this suspension procedure had the effect of changing "the royal allowance or disallowance from an act of executive prerogative to a direct participation in the process of legislation itself. The king in council became, in such cases, a part of the colonial legislature. . . ." Using these powers, the British "were able to prescribe fairly effectively the method by which laws should be passed."[24] In short, actions taken by the Board of Trade and the Privy Council were not, by definition, vetoes. Only the colonial governors exercised vetoes. Even so, the sweeping powers of the governors, the Board of Trade, and the Privy Council were such that colonial legislatures were prevented from exercising legislative functions in a manner consistent with contemporary thinking about what constitutes legislative power. In

[21] Elmer Beecher Russell, *The Review of American Colonial Legislation by the King in Council* (Buffalo, NY: William S. Hein, 1981; first published in 1915), 505–506.

[22] Russell, *The Review of American Colonial*, 222–23.

[23] Burns, *Controversies Between Royal Governors*, 77.

[24] Labaree, *Royal Government in America*, 225.

fact, the rest of the British government shared, even controlled, colonial legislative power.

Two observations merit special attention. First, despite these many restrictions, colonial legislatures still found ways to wrangle concessions from the British government and its representatives.[25] Some of these were discussed during the debates at the Constitutional Convention.[26]

Second, and more important to this analysis, these colonial structural relationships bear little relation to the operation of Congress and the president under the modern Constitution. As mentioned previously, the actions of the Board of Trade and Privy Council were not vetoes at all. Responding to McDonald's claims to having discovered gubernatorial item vetoes, an exhaustive study of colonial practices by President Reagan's Office of Legal Counsel concluded that there were no instances when colonial governors used an item veto (the one instance cited earlier in McDonald seems to be a single exception).[27] In any case, colonial governors possessed far greater power over colonial legislatures than anything included or contemplated for the modern Constitution, including an absolute veto[28] (also including instances in which the rest of the British government could direct the actions of the governors).

Just as clearly, the founders were aware of the idea that parts of laws could be vetoed. Yet, the very fact that no wording in the Constitution, or debate surrounding it, contemplated such a power for the president militates against the inherent item veto argument. Moreover, because the actions of the Board of Trade and the Privy Council were not vetoes, nothing in the colonial period can be taken as lending support to the theory that an item veto was included in the 1787 Constitution.

[25] Thomas Stefan Schroeder, "Original Understanding and Veto Power: Are the Framers Safe While Congress Is in Session?" *Journal of Law and Politics* 7(Summer, 1991): 769–71.

[26] Benjamin Franklin, for example, described how colonial governors sometimes insisted on bribes or other inducements to obtain gubernatorial assent: "The negative of the Governor was constantly made use of to extort money. No good law whatsoever could be passed without a private bargain with him." See Max Farrand, *The Records of the Federal Convention of 1787*, 4 vols. (New Haven, CT: Yale University Press, 1966), I, 98–99. These infringements on colonial legislatures by the British government undoubtedly contributed to the legislative-centered nature of early American governments.

[27] Cooper, "Memorandum for the Attorney General," 21–25.

[28] An absolute veto was proposed for the president at the Constitutional Convention, but it was soundly and overwhelmingly rejected on several occasions. Spitzer, *The Presidential Veto*, 12.

Defining the Veto

Many actions that occurred before and after the writing of the Constitution have been identified as the *de facto* or *de jure* exercise of item veto powers. For example, McDonald cites the circumstance of state legislatures during the revolutionary period passing on appropriations that were "permissive, not mandatory" in that the governor/executive then could spend at his discretion.[29] Yet, such an arrangement flies in the face of the modern legislative process.

What is Law?

The keystone power of Congress is lawmaking, meaning the enactment of legally binding decisions. According to Henry Black, law "is a body of rules of action or conduct prescribed by controlling authority, and having binding legal force.... Law is a solemn expression of the will of the supreme power of the State."[30] Of the many purposes served by Congress, lawmaking is "first and foremost."[31] Speaking more generally about American legislatures, Keefe and Ogul observe that "The principal task of the American legislature is to make law."[32] With respect to law and appropriations, the Constitution notes in Article I, sec. 9, that "No Money shall be drawn from the Treasury, but in Consequence of Appropriations made by Law."

Therefore, an act passed by a legislature that does not include a legal mandate – McDonald's "permissive" appropriations – does not normally carry the force of law, obviating any question of a veto, item or otherwise. If Congress grants spending discretion to the executive, the subsequent exercise of that discretion by the president is not in law an item veto, even though the decisions arising from the discretion over spending may have an item veto effect.

Impoundment

This principle becomes even clearer in the case of impoundments. McDonald and Stephen Glazier cite instances when Presidents

[29] McDonald, "The Framers' Conception of the Veto Power," 3.
[30] Henry C. Black, *Black's Law Dictionary* (St. Paul, MN: West Publishers, 1991), 612.
[31] Alan L. Clem, *Congress: Powers, Processes, and Politics* (Pacific Grove, CA: Brooks/Cole, 1989), 7.
[32] William J. Keefe and Morris S. Ogul, *The American Legislative Process* (Englewood Cliffs, NJ: Prentice-Hall, 1985), 13.

Washington, Adams, and Jefferson refused to spend funds duly appropriated by Congress (and as signed into law by these respective presidents) or diverted money that had been appropriated for one purpose to another purpose. "Ceding this power not to spend funds once appropriated amounted to a grant or acknowledgment by Congress of a form of 'line-item veto,'" said Glazier, "even though that term itself was not coined until around the Civil War."[33] Sidak and Smith say that "The practice of impoundment . . . can be seen as a line-item veto under a different name."[34] McGowan makes the same argument.[35]

Leaving aside the fact that presidential impoundment was eliminated in the Budget and Impoundment Control Act of 1974 (with the practices of deferrals and rescissions substituted for it), impoundment and item veto powers are vitally different, even if their political or fiscal consequences might be the same. By definition, a veto can only be exercised on a bill before it is enacted into law because its very purpose is to block enactment. Any action or decision that occurs subsequent to the enactment of legislation into law is not a veto, although actions such as impoundment may have an item veto effect. To indiscriminately blend these two types of powers as though they were the same is to vitiate foundational legal principles about how legislation is enacted, and where institutionally defined powers begin and end.

Krasnow argues that the elimination of impoundment has "drastically weakened" the president's power over appropriations, thus necessitating implementation of the inherent item veto because, absent impoundment, the item veto is "consistent with the Framers' intentions."[36] Krasnow's linking of impoundment and item veto extends beyond their fiscal similarities. The weakening or absence of the first, she argues, provides a constitutionally based justification for the second.

This analysis is built on several false suppositions. First, although impoundments date back to Washington, they have never constituted a primary means of fiscal control by presidents, especially when compared

---

[33] Stephen Glazier, "The Line-Item Veto: Provided in the Constitution and Traditionally Applied," in *Pork Barrels and Principles*, 12.

[34] J.Gregory Sidak and Thomas A. Smith, "Four Faces of the Item Veto: A Reply to Tribe and Kurland," *Northwestern University Law Review* 84(Winter, 1990): 447.

[35] Carl McGowan, "The President's Veto Power: An Important Instrument of Conflict in Our Constitutional System," *San Diego Law Review* 23(July–August, 1986): 810.

[36] Krasnow, "The Imbalance of Power and the Presidential Veto," 605, 612.

to the wide array of other formal and informal fiscal-budgetary controls and powers available to presidents. Curtailing impoundment use
has hardly eviscerated presidential influence over budgeting. Second,
impoundment powers were regulated by Congress in 1974 precisely
because presidents – although primarily Nixon – were using the power
with greater frequency and under circumstances that stretched far beyond
traditional historical purposes. Congress imposed restraints because of
presidential abuse of power, not because of newfound congressional
aggrandizement or arrogance.[37] Stated another way, impoundment was
predicated on interbranch comity. When that comity broke down under
Nixon, the practices were altered.[38] Third, the Constitution makes no
provision for executive impoundment; instead, it vests the power of the
purse squarely in the hands of Congress, including the powers to lay and
collect taxes, deal with indebtedness and bankruptcy, impose duties, and
borrow and coin money. The presence or absence of impoundment bears
no relationship to whether the Constitution already provides for an item
veto.

This line of argument is further undercut by comparison with the
fact that the regular veto may have an item veto effect. From George
Washington to the present, presidents have vetoed legislation because
they objected to a single provision within the vetoed bill. Such vetoes
often persuade Congress to repass the legislation with the offending provision removed.[39] These instances do not mean that a regular veto is
somehow also an item veto.

Finally, Crovitz argues that the first President Bush "has already exercised the line-item veto."[40] His evidence is several instances when Bush, in
his signing statements, announced that he would refuse to enforce certain
provisions of several bills. Leaving aside the legality of such declarations,

---

[37] Louis Fisher, *Presidential Spending Power* (Princeton, NJ: Princeton University Press, 1975).

[38] James P. Pfiffner, *The President, the Budget, and Congress: Impoundment and the 1974 Budget Act* (Boulder, CO: Westview Press, 1979).

[39] To mention the earliest example of this phenomenon, President Washington's second and final veto was of a bill that included a reduction of America's already small army by two dragoon companies. In his veto message, Washington argued on behalf of retaining the two companies. Congress re-passed the bill, this time with the offending provision excised. Washington signed that bill into law on his last day in office. See Spitzer, *The Presidential Veto*, 28–29.

[40] Crovitz, "The Line-Item Veto," 52.

no veto – item or otherwise – was applied in these instances because there was no veto announcement or statement and no bill return. All of the bills (and provisions thereof) in question were signed into law. The failure to enforce provisions in legislation is just that; it is not an item veto.

What the Founders Understood about the Veto

As Glazier observed, the term *item veto* did not arise until around the time of the Civil War, when the president of the Confederacy was given an item veto[41] (although Jefferson Davis never used the power; the term *item veto* does not actually appear in the Confederate Constitution). And, there was no discussion of an item veto at the Constitutional Convention of 1787. Yet, this does not mean that the founders were unaware of the idea. The man who presided over the convention, George Washington, offered this definitive comment on the item veto question and existing presidential powers to veto in 1793:

> You do me no more than Justice when you suppose that from motives of respect to the Legislature (and I might add from my interpretation of the Constitution) I give my Signature to many Bills with which my Judgment is at variance. In declaring this, however, I allude to no particular Act. *From the nature of the Constitution, I must approve all parts of a Bill, or reject it in toto*. To do the latter can only be Justified upon the clear and obvious ground of propriety; and I never had such confidence in my own faculty of judging as to be over tenacious of the opinions I may have imbibed in doubtful cases [emphasis added].[42]

President Benjamin Harrison opined similarly that "many laws contain more than one proposition . . . and the President must deal with them as thus associated."[43] President and Supreme Court Chief Justice William H. Taft noted that the president "has no power to veto parts of the bill and allow the rest to become a law. He must accept it or reject it, and his rejection of it is not final unless he can find one more than one-third of one of the Houses to sustain him in his veto."[44] These presidents certainly had no inkling of a unilateral item veto.

[41] Glazier, "The Line-Item Veto."

[42] John C. Fitzpatrick, ed., *The Writings of George Washington*, 39 vols. (Washington, DC: GPO, 1940), XXXIII, 94.

[43] Benjamin Harrison, *This Country of Ours* (New York: Charles Scribner's Sons, 1897), 132.

[44] William Howard Taft, *The President and His Powers* (New York: Columbia University Press, 1916), 14.

State Precedent?

McDonald claims that some state precedents buttress the case for the inherent item veto because he argues that state actions after the adoption of the federal Constitution reflected their understanding of the federal document and because most governmental spending in the nation's first century occurred at the state rather than the federal level, suggesting that nineteenth-century state actions are roughly analogous to the federal government of this century because this is where most governmental spending now occurs. McDonald asserts that states that revised their constitutions at the end of the eighteenth century (including Georgia, Pennsylvania, Delaware, Kentucky, and Vermont) copied wording from the federal Constitution, and that "the governors began immediately to exercise the veto in a line-item fashion."[45] McDonald provides no evidence or source for this assertion.

McDonald does assert, with attribution, that three northern states adopted line-item veto provisions for their constitutions before the Civil War, a startling discovery if true because sources until now always cite the Confederate Constitution of 1861 as the first American document to codify the power. Such a discovery might suggest a hitherto uncovered item veto trail, perhaps even leading back to 1787. The three state constitutions, with the years of alleged item veto inclusion, are New Jersey (1844), Ohio (1851), and Kansas (1859).[46] McDonald's source is an authoritative work edited by Francis Newton Thorpe that compiles all charters and constitutions from colonial times to the date of the seven-volume set's publication. Yet, McDonald's discovery turns out to be fool's gold. In each of these three instances, McDonald has misread Thorpe. All three states adopted the item veto after the Civil War, not before.[47]

---

[45] McDonald, "The Framers' Conception of the Veto Power," 6.

[46] Ibid., 7, note 5.

[47] Francis Newton Thorpe, ed., *The Federal and State Constitutions, Colonial Charters, and other Organic Laws of the States, Territories, and Colonies*, 7 vols. (Washington, DC: GPO, 1909). In the case of the New Jersey Constitution, it is presented in Thorpe's alphabetical listing of state constitutions as dated 1844. It does include an item veto provision but with a note saying "as amended" in 1875 and 1897. (The description of veto powers appears in Article V, sec. 7.) In Thorpe's "Appendix" section, the unamended 1844 New Jersey Constitution is reprinted; it makes no mention of an item veto (VII, 4193). Following it is a separate listing of amendments to the 1844 constitution, ratified in 1875. It is here that the first mention of an item veto appears (VII, 4203). The Ohio Constitution is dated 1851, but the paragraph describing item veto powers for the governor (Article II, sec. 16, para. 3) has a note at the end saying, "As amended November, 1903." The Kansas Constitution dated 1859 describes item veto powers in Article II,

The "Rider" Problem

Much has been made of the fact that Congress has sought to circumvent presidential vetoes by attaching objectionable "riders" onto legislation in the hopes of winning enactment of such provisions that might not otherwise survive on their own. The practice gained attention in America in the 1840s and prompted no little acrimonious debate in Congress and elsewhere.[48]

Some have argued that the congressional penchant for attaching (often non-germane) riders was unanticipated by the Constitution's founders. Zinn concluded that "since the subject was not raised in the [Constitutional] Convention we may infer that the delegates did not foresee omnibus bills and legislative riders to appropriation bills."[49] Clineburg states flatly that "There is no evidence that the invention of non-germane riders and omnibus bills was foreseen at the time the Constitution was being written and debated."[50]

Leaving aside for the moment the "omnibus" problem, many have seized on this point to argue that presidents might possess a unilateral

---

sec. 14. But a footnote at the end of the description says "Adopted November, 1904." (V, 2607 [New Jersey]; V, 2917 [Ohio]; II, 1246 [Kansas].) According to a committee print prepared for the Rules Committee, House of Representatives, the New Jersey item veto provision was added in 1875, the Ohio provision in 1903, and the Kansas provision in 1904. Thorpe confirms these dates. The committee print also provides a detailed history of the item veto, confirming its Civil War–era origins. See U.S. Congress, House of Representatives, Committee on Rules, "Item Veto: State Experience and its Application to the Federal Situation," 99th Cong., 2d sess., December, 1986: Appendix A, 201. McDonald evidently failed to examine the footnotes and appendix in Thorpe, leading him to an erroneous conclusion.

In his subsequent book on the presidency, McDonald says only that "it has also been argued that the president actually has an item veto if he will but exercise it." See *The American Presidency*, 352. He repeats none of his earlier arguments but does cite the writings of proponents of the inherent item veto – but not his own. One might reasonably infer that McDonald lost faith in the veracity of his analysis, owing to his failure to cite his own prior arguments and writing on the subject. Had McDonald submitted his article printed in *Pork Barrels and Politics* to a refereed history journal, its flaws might well have caught the eye of a reviewer and been corrected.

[48] Spitzer, *The Presidential Veto*, 55–56, 124.

[49] Charles J. Zinn, *The Veto Power of the President* (Washington, DC: GPO, 1951), 34.

[50] William A. Clineburg, "The Presidential Veto Power," *South Carolina Law Review* 18(1966): 752. Schroeder says, "The attachment of non-germane riders and amendments to bills is discussed nowhere in the records of the Constitutional Convention." See "Original Understanding and Veto Power," 767. Ronald D. Rotunda and John E. Nowak concur: "At the time of the Constitutional Convention, the term 'line-item' veto did not exist because the problem of unrelated bills and riders did not then exist." See *Treatise on Constitutional Law*, 4 vols. (St. Paul, MN: West Publishers, 1992), I, 757.

item veto because the legislative linking of disparate subjects through the attachment of riders under the heading "bill" would be viewed by the founders as an artifice for confounding an otherwise finely wrought legislative process. As early as 1965, Givens used this argument to propose that presidents should simply try an item veto and let the courts resolve the dispute.[51] Clineburg asserts flatly that presidents may veto non-germane riders.[52] Writing more recently, Schroeder adapted this argument to propose that the courts had the power and standing to strike down laws containing "measures topically or operationally unrelated to the bills carrying them into law."[53] Riggs makes the same claim.[54]

Clineburg,[55] Glazier,[56] Haswell,[57] Crovitz,[58] Sidak and Smith,[59] Krasnow,[60] Schroeder,[61] and Rotunda and Nowak[62] all rely on the argument that the founders' lack of knowledge of the rider problem justifies an item veto to restore the more pure and simple legislative process they allegedly envisioned. These writers further assert that the rider practice, in effect, has vitiated the potency of the regular veto.[63] If this assumption about what the founders knew is correct, it could be construed as support for the unilateral item veto. In fact, however, the founders were not only aware of the rider problem but also discussed it at considerable length in the Federal Convention.

The antecedents of the rider problem trace back to the British Parliament in the seventeenth and eighteenth centuries. As early as 1667, the House of Commons engaged in a process then referred to as "tacking." Based on the rule that the House of Lords could not amend money bills,

---

[51] Givens, "The Validity of a Separate Veto of Non-germane Riders to Legislation." See rejoinder to Givens by Richard A. Riggs, "Separation of Powers: Congressional Riders and the Veto Power," *University of Michigan Journal of Law Reform* 6(Spring, 1973): 735–59.

[52] Clineburg, "The Presidential Veto Power," 753.

[53] Schroeder, "Original Understanding and Veto Power," 760.

[54] Riggs, "Separation of Powers," 738.

[55] Clineburg, "The Presidential Veto Power," 752–53.

[56] Glazier, "The Line-Item Veto," 10.

[57] Anthony Haswell, "Partial Veto Power – Does the President Have It Now?" *Federal Bar News and Journal* 36(March/April, 1989): 142, 144.

[58] Crovitz, "The Line-Item Veto," 43.

[59] Sidak and Smith, "Four Faces of the Item Veto," 467.

[60] Krasnow, "The Imbalance of Power and the Presidential Veto," 584, 601.

[61] Schroeder, "Original Understanding and Veto Power," 759, 784–85.

[62] Rotunda and Nowak, *Treatise on Constitutional Law*, I, 757.

[63] Judith A. Best also makes this argument. See "The Item Veto: Would the Founders Approve?," *Presidential Studies Quarterly* 14(Spring, 1984): 183–88.

the Commons would include in such bills non-germane riders that would not otherwise win acceptance from the Lords. The practice was used in 1692, 1698, and 1701.[64] In 1700, the House of Commons attached to a tax bill a rider annulling King William III's Irish land grants. Despite the resistance of the House of Lords, not to mention the displeasure of the king, the bill was approved.[65] As keen students of British history and politics, the founders were fully aware of this history, as the federal debates make clear.[66]

The practice of tacking extended to the colonies as well. As discussed previously, colonial governors were instructed not to approve any colonial legislation that included riders. Even so, many legislatures attempted to attach such riders, which resulted in protracted political disputes that often delayed the allocation of funding for the colonies.[67]

During the Federal Convention, Pierce Butler argued on June 13 that both houses of Congress should have equal say over money bills because a failure to do so "will lead the latter [i.e., the House] into the practice of tacking other clauses to money bills."[68] Colonel George Mason discussed a proposal by fellow Virginia delegate, Edmund Randolph, to mimic the British system, whereby the upper house (i.e., the Senate) would similarly be denied the ability to alter or amend money bills (as was true of the British House of Lords). Such a proposal, Mason said on August 13, would mean that "the Senate could not correct errors of any sort, & that it would introduce into the House of Reps. the practice of tacking foreign matter to money bills."[69] (Note that Butler and Mason used the British term *tacking*.)

[64] Thomas Pitt Taswell-Langmead, *English Constitutional History* (Boston: Houghton-Mifflin, 1946), 613–14.

[65] Paul R. Q. Wolfson, "Is a Presidential Item Veto Constitutional?" *Yale Law Journal* 96(March, 1987): 841.

[66] Indeed, one convention delegate, John Rutledge, complained that the convention relied too much on British law and practice, exhibiting "a blind adherence to the British model." See Farrand, *The Records of the Federal Convention*, II, 279.

[67] Wolfson, "Is a Presidential Item Veto Constitutional?," 843. Prescott and Zimmerman note that New York's colonial governor was forbidden by royal instruction from approving acts that included riders on appropriations bills. See *The Politics of the Veto of Legislation in New York State*, I, 2.

[68] Farrand, *The Records of the Federal Convention of 1787*, I, 233.

[69] Farrand, *The Records of the Federal Convention*, II, 273. Much of the subsequent discussion on that August day dealt with the extent to which the founders should or should not follow the British example. That discussion alone makes clear that the founders well understood the British system. In comments offered the same day, James Wilson expressed a similar concern that "The House of Reps. will insert the other things in

James Madison described the essence of the problem of trying to restrict amendments by subject matter: "The words *amend or alter*, form an equal source of doubt & altercation. When an obnoxious paragraph shall be sent down from the Senate to the House of Reps it will be called an origination under the name of an amendment. The Senate may actually couch extraneous matter under that name. In these cases, the question will turn on the *degree* of connection between the matter & object of the bill and the (alteration or) amendment offered to it."[70]

Thus, the founders were familiar with the rider problem, although it was as controversial then as it is today. Zinn, Clineburg, Schroeder, and Rotunda and Nowak are simply and demonstrably wrong in saying that the founders were unaware of this practice.[71]

The manual prepared by Thomas Jefferson during his vice presidency under John Adams (1797–1801) to guide congressional procedures not only acknowledges but also condones non-germane riders: "Amendments may be made so as totally to alter the nature of the proposition; and it is a way of getting rid of a proposition by making it bear a sense different from what it was intended by the movers, so that they vote against it themselves."[72]

The Bill Definition and "Omnibus" Problems

Critics similarly argue that, aside from the possibilities and consequences of riders just discussed, early legislation was limited to single subjects.[73] Modern legislation, by contrast, is often a complex conglomeration of diverse topics housed under the single title "bill." More significantly, modern appropriations often take the form of enormous omnibus

---

money bills, and by making them conditions of each other, destroy the deliberate liberty of the Senate" (II, 275).

[70] Farrand, *The Records of the Federal Convention of 1787*, II, 276.

[71] Schroeder actually presents evidence undercutting his own argument when he reports several instances of the attachment of non-germane riders in the early years of the country's history, including the attachment of a rider "for building a light-house on Cape Henry, in the state of Virginia" added to a 1790 appropriations bill. "Original Understanding and the Veto Power," 778.

[72] Lewis Deschler, *Constitution, Jefferson's Manual, and Rules of the House of Representatives* (Washington, DC: GPO, 1973), 229 (sec. 467). The note to this section observes that "This was the rule of Parliament, which did not require an amendment to be germane."

[73] Clineburg, "The Presidential Veto Power," 753; Russell M. Ross and Fred Schwengel, "An Item Veto for the President?," *Presidential Studies Quarterly* 12(Winter, 1982): 67–68; Krasnow, "The Imbalance of Power and the Presidential Veto," 601.

appropriations bills when, many argue, early appropriations were limited to single subjects.

Although it is certainly true that modern legislation is more likely to be composed of diverse elements, such legislation constitutes a single bill as much as a bill dealing with a single subject. Contrary to the claim that "separate legislative proposals in substance contained in the same Act are separately vetoable 'bills' regardless of the format or timing of introduction . . . ,"[74] a bill quite simply is "any singular, entire piece of legislation in the form in which it was approved by the two Houses [of Congress]."[75]

In addition to history and past practices, to restrict the definition of "bill" to single subjects is to raise two serious problems. One is the practical problem of deciding which items do and do not belong together. The making of law and policy follows no simple formula, and the interconnectedness of matters addressed in legislation would render chaotic any effort to meaningfully enact a one-subject-per-bill rule (a fact noted previously by James Madison). Edmund Randolph directly contradicted modern critics advancing the one-subject bill definition when he described how bills might be defined as single-subject in nature (of course, no such restriction appeared in the final Constitution, except for the provision in Article I, sec. 7, stipulating that all revenue bills were to originate in the House): "As to Commercial regulations which may involve revenue, the difficulty may be avoided by restraining the definition to bills for the *mere* or *sole,* purpose of raising revenue."[76]

Luther Martin's address to the Maryland state legislature on November 29, 1787, evinced a similar awareness that *bill* could have been defined narrowly in the Constitution but was not. Speaking about possible controversies between the Senate and the House, Martin predicted problems

[74] Haswell, "Partial Veto Power," 142.

[75] Anthony Gressman, "Observation: Is the Item Veto Constitutional?" *North Carolina Law Review* 64(April, 1986): 819. According to *Black's Law Dictionary*, a bill in legislation is "The draft of a proposed law from the time of its introduction in a legislative house through all the various stages in both houses. . . . The form of a proposed law before it is enacted into law by a vote of the legislative body" (Black, 114). Rappaport's examination of the meaning of bill in the eighteenth century in both Britain and America supports the conclusion that, even then, *bill* meant "a draft of a law containing whatever provisions the author deemed desirable." Michael B. Rappaport, "The President's Veto and the Constitution," *Northwestern University Law Review* 87(Spring, 1993): 762.

[76] Farrand, *The Records of the Federal Convention of 1787*, II, 279.

over "what are or are not revenue bills, and the more so as they are not *defined* in the constitution."[77] Randolph's and Martin's stated awareness that bills could be defined in such a way as to limit their scope or purpose disproves the assertions that *bill* necessarily meant a single subject to the founders, and that the founders had a very limited, naive, or narrow understanding of bill construction when compared with the behavior of the modern Congress. As with riders, the omnibus problem was as controversial in the eighteenth century as it is today, but it was both known and used.

The second problem with narrow bill definition is the principled one that any effort to impose restrictions on the definition of a bill from the outside would amount to nothing less than improper interference in the legislative process. The Constitution gives to Congress alone the power to regulate its internal affairs, including all matters pertaining to the handling of legislation (subject to constitutional guidelines and existing congressional rules; Congress always retains the option of dissecting complex, multi-subject bills into smaller, distinct bills, should it decide to do so). Thus, one cannot justify a unilateral item veto on a narrow definition of *bill*.

As for the use of omnibus appropriations bills, contrary to much erroneous supposition, this practice is not a modern one. Indeed, the nation's first appropriations bill, passed in 1789, was an omnibus measure that incorporated the entire budget, consisting of four lump-sum dollar amounts for the Department of War, the "civil list," pensions for invalid individuals, and prior government expenditures. This omnibus appropriations process was used in 1790, 1791, 1792, and 1793. In 1794, appropriations were split between two bills – one for the military and the other for the rest of the government.[78]

The Presentment Clause

The Presentment Clause of the Constitution (Article I, sec. 7) provides no basis for the president to approve or disapprove a bill in anything other than the form in which it is presented.[79] Clause 2 of this section says simply

---

[77] Farrand, *The Records of the Federal Convention of 1787*, III, 202.
[78] Louis Fisher, "The Item Veto – A Misconception," *Washington Post*, February 23, 1987; Fisher, "The Presidential Veto," 22.
[79] The Supreme Court ruled as much in *Clinton v. City of New York* (524 U.S. 417; 1998) when it struck down the Line Item Veto Act of 1996, stating that such a power could

that "Every bill" passing the House and Senate shall go to the president for final action. Yet, if Clause 2 is so clear, why, critics have asked, does the next paragraph (Clause 3) repeat this same directive by saying again that "Every Order, Resolution, or Vote to which the Concurrence of the Senate and House of Representatives may be necessary ... shall be presented to the President...."? This question takes on added significance because the framers were parsimonious and careful in their final construction of the Constitution in order to produce a stylistically cleaner and neater document. This included the excision of extraneous words and phrases.[80]

The answer is provided in the federal debates. Clause 3 "was added to avoid a situation in which Congress might seek to avoid presidential review of legislation by giving it some other name."[81] Considerable attention was focused at the convention on the concern that Congress might try to duck a veto by calling a bill something other than a bill to avoid presentment entirely. Such ploys had been used repeatedly by colonial legislatures to duck vetoes by the British monarch's appointed governors. As Madison said at the convention, "if the negative of the President was confined to *bills*; it would be evaded by acts under the form and name of Resolutions, votes, &c."[82] (The specific reference to "the negative" – that is, the veto – arose because the veto clause was under discussion at the time.) Edmund Randolph concurred by offering a motion the next day "putting votes, Resolutions &c. on a footing with Bills."[83] There is no reason to believe that this wording means presidents can veto the constituent parts of legislation passed on for signature or veto.

only be given to the president by constitutional amendment. See Spitzer, "The Item Veto Dispute and the Secular Crisis of the Presidency."

[80] Max Farrand, *The Framing of the Constitution of the United States* (New Haven, CT: Yale University Press, 1913), 179.

[81] Robert J. Spitzer, "Presentation Clause," *Encyclopedia of the American Presidency*, 4 vols. (New York: Simon & Schuster, 1994), III, 1193.

[82] Farrand, *The Records of the Federal Convention of 1787*, II, 301.

[83] *Ibid.*, 304. This is logical because the second paragraph of sec. 7 begins "Every bill...shall, before it becomes a Law, be presented to the President...." The next paragraph in the section begins with the "Every order" language to resolve the bill-ambiguity problem. Madison had offered a hurried motion late in the day on August 15 to resolve the problem, but the impromptu attempt engendered confusion and was defeated. Early the next day, probably after consulting with Edmund Randolph the previous night, Randolph offered the language that was included in the Constitution. As Randolph stated, the reference to orders, resolutions, and votes applied not just to bills to be vetoed but also to all legislation presented to the president for final review (as, indeed, the clause reads).

Yet, according to Glazier, Clause 3 authorizes an item veto because "Congress may not subvert the veto by bunching legislation into something it calls 'one' bill."[84] Such a "bunching gambit" is, in effect, the ducking of presentment barred by Clause 3, Glazier asserts. Crovitz makes the same argument.[85] This argument fails, first, because the proposition that a bill was meant to be only a single subject is false. Thus, presidents have no basis for subdividing that which is presented to them by Congress. Second, presentment is not ducked at all because presidents are indeed presented with omnibus bills and bills with riders.

Beyond this, there is another important distinction justifying the separation of the two paragraphs. Clause 2 is written as a set of directions *to the president*, carefully explaining executive options for dealing with legislation sent to the president. Quite simply, it is the president's "how-to" guide for handling enrolled bills. Clause 3, however, serves a different purpose, in that it speaks not to the president but *to Congress*. The whole thrust of the paragraph is to caution Congress against using subterfuge of the sort used by colonial legislatures to thwart the executive's role in the legislative process laid out in the Constitution. In other words, it is a "thou shalt not" aimed at Congress (as is much of the succeeding sec. 9 in Article I).

The Veto as a "Revisionary" Power

The odious connotations surrounding the word *veto* prompted the founders to use such synonyms as *negative, qualified negative, revisionary power*, and *restraining power*.[86] Aside from avoiding the stigmatized word *veto*, these other terms were significant for another reason. Throughout their discussion of the veto at the convention, the founders repeatedly emphasized that the veto was not – as we think of it today – merely a negative to block or thwart action. Rather, they viewed it as a creative, positive means to revise and improve legislation by giving Congress a final opportunity to review it after the bill is returned by the president.[87]

---

[84] Glazier, "The Line-Item Veto," 11.   [85] Crovitz, "The Line-Item Veto," 45–46.

[86] Vernon L. Wilkinson, "The Item Veto in the American Constitutional System," *Georgetown Law Journal* 25(November, 1936): 108, note 11.

[87] Spitzer, *The Presidential Veto*, 18–20. This positive construct is revealed in constitutional debate (see Farrand, *The Records of the Federal Convention of 1787*, II, 73–79, 161, 568–69; III, 133, 385) and in the stipulation that the president must state his objections

Reflecting this view, the veto paragraph was worded this way until September 10 (the convention adjourned September 17):

> Every bill . . . shall, before it become a law, be presented to the President of the United States, *for his revision*; if, *upon such revision*, he approve of it, he shall signify his approbation by signing it: But if, *upon such revision*, it shall appear to him improper for being passed into a law, he shall return it, together with his objections against it, to that House in which it shall have originated. . . . [emphasis added][88]

Similar wording is found in the New York Constitution of 1777, which reflects the fact that New York's strong gubernatorial model served as important precedent for construction of the presidency.[89] With respect to the veto power, the New York Constitution of 1777 diverged from the federal document in that it provided for the veto to be exercised by a Council of Revision (this group included the governor, the judges of the state supreme court, and the chancellor of the court of chancery). The Massachusetts Constitution of 1780 was similarly patterned on New York, minus the Council of Revision. Neither constitution used the word *veto* and both used the revision language.

Advocates of the inherent item veto have cited the revisionary language of the debates and these early constitutions to propose that the revision process amounted to "a selective veto, a line-item process"[90] on the assumption that vetoed bills were somehow rewritten by the state legislatures of New York and Massachusetts at the instruction of the governors. Krasnow cites sec. III of the New York Constitution of 1777 to support her claim that under its terms, a vetoed bill "was returned to the chamber from which it originated with comments. The legislature would then enact the bill into law, incorporating the proposed revisions."[91] In other words, the governor exercised an item veto. If this were true, a similar logic might apply to the similar wording in the 1787 Constitution.

to vetoed bills in writing and return them to the house of origin. See Josiah H. Benton, *The Veto Power in the United States: What Is It?* (Boston: Addison C. Getchall, 1888), 35–36.

[88] Farrand, *The Records of the Federal Convention of 1787*, II, 568–69.

[89] Charles C. Thach, *The Creation of the Presidency, 1775–1789* (New York: DaCapo Press, 1969; first published in 1923), 53–54, 176.

[90] McDonald, "The Framers' Conception of the Veto Power," 4. See also Sidak and Smith, "Four Faces of the Item Veto," 442–45.

[91] Krasnow, "The Imbalance of Power and the Presidential Veto," 590.

The problem with this claim is that Krasnow has misrepresented the wording of the New York Constitution. Sec. III says:

> ...all bills which have passed the senate and assembly shall, before they become laws, be presented to the said council for their revisal and consideration; and if, upon such revision and consideration, it should appear improper to the said council...they return the same, together with their objections thereto in writing, to the senate or house of assembly...who shall enter the objection sent down by the council at large in their minutes, and proceed to reconsider the bill. But if, after such reconsideration, two-thirds of the said senate or house of assembly shall, notwithstanding the said objections, agree to pass the same, it shall...be sent to the other branch of the legislature, where it shall also be reconsidered, and, if approved by two-thirds of the members present, shall be a law.[92]

The wording of the Massachusetts Constitution of 1780 is almost precisely the same.[93] Neither constitution supports Krasnow's claim. The wording simply says that the legislature shall consider the Council's objections and vote by two-thirds to override the veto.[94]

The process and discussion of revision in both state constitutions constituted a review of all bills presented for signature, with a return to the legislature of those subject to veto, just as it did in the federal Constitution. The revision language was not a reference to any kind of selective or item veto. If the state legislatures decided to rewrite a vetoed bill, it would then be a new bill, requiring a simple majority to pass and again subject to a gubernatorial veto. This becomes even plainer when this wording is compared to that of subsequent constitutions (beginning with the Confederate Constitution) that did incorporate an item veto. Although the term *item veto* was not used in the eighteenth century, the concept itself was known from colonial days.

---

[92] Thorpe, *The Federal and State Constitutions*, V, 2629.

[93] Thorpe, *The Federal and State Constitutions*, III, 1893–94.

[94] Further, Prescott and Zimmerman's analysis of New York's Council of Revision provides no support for the assertion that an item veto was exercised in New York at any time until its inclusion in the state constitution in 1874. (The New York item veto was first proposed but rejected in a state constitutional convention in 1867.) See *The Politics of the Veto of Legislation in New York State*, I, 143, 173. The item veto power was not added to the Massachusetts Constitution until 1918. See U.S. Congress, House, "Item Veto," 202.

An Eviscerated Veto?

Claims have been made repeatedly that the modern veto power is somehow a shell of its once formidable self.[95] Having been thus eviscerated by congressional riders, amendments, and omnibus bills, the veto is now but a pathetic, limp instrument in the hands of modern presidents, or so say critics. Yet, none of these claims to veto impotency is based on any systematic empirical or historical analysis of actual veto use and effectiveness.

First and foremost, presidents have applied more than 2,500 vetoes from 1789 to the present. Of these, about 96 percent have been upheld. When private bills are eliminated from the tally in order to consider only public bills, less than 20 percent have been overridden. Surely, a presidential batting average of more than 80 percent in any area outside of direct executive command authority is no inconsiderable accomplishment. Second, the claim of progressive veto evisceration over time flies in the face of the simple fact that presidents have used the power more, not less, often over time. Fewer than sixty vetoes were applied from Washington to Lincoln. Beginning with Grant, veto use grew almost exponentially.

Third, two modern presidents – Ford and the first Bush – relied on a veto strategy as linchpins of their dealings with Congress.[96] Reagan did so

[95] A recent example of the stubborn persistence of the claim that the modern veto is somehow eviscerated because of riders or omnibus legislation is seen in an article by Duke law professor and former Clinton administration head of the Office of Legal Counsel, Walter Dellinger, who opined that presidents needed to have the right to use signing statements so that they could "decline to enforce unconstitutional laws." Why would Dellinger not simply advise presidents to veto such suspect laws? Because, according to Dellinger, "most laws today are passed as part of multiprovision omnibus legislation," and "the Constitution does not force the president to choose between two starkly unpalatable options: veto the entire bill or enforce an unconstitutional provision." "A Slip of the Pen," *New York Times*, July 31, 2006, A17. Dellinger has this exactly backward: the sign-all-or-veto-all choice is precisely what the Constitution imposes on every president. It is the adventurous use of signing statements (which are mentioned nowhere in the Constitution) that is beyond constitutional bounds. Dellinger's arguments about signing statements date to his service in the Clinton administration when he defended the practice, providing yet another instance when lawyer advocacy translates into defective constitutional theorizing.

[96] Spitzer, *The Presidential Veto*, 85–87; Robert J. Spitzer, "Presidential Prerogative Power: The Case of the Bush Administration and Legislative Power," *PS: Political Science and Politics* 24(March, 1991): 38–42; Robert J. Spitzer, "The Veto King: The 'Dr. No' Presidency of George Bush," in *Honor and Loyalty: Inside the Politics of the Bush*

as well but in a more symbolic and, therefore, less risky fashion.[97] Whereas such a strategy incorporates considerable political risks for the president, it also betokens a weapon that is, if nothing else, effective. Fourth, the mere threat of a veto has been and continues to be a vital tool for presidents, especially as a way to compel Congress to alter or remove offending provisions.[98] Fifth, as mentioned previously, presidents from Washington to the present have used the veto effectively to force Congress to alter or eliminate disputed provisions from bills. In short, although not a perfect tool, the veto has been effective since the days of George Washington.[99] And, if the founders had wanted the president to exercise perfect control over the legislative process, they would have vested lawmaking power in the executive rather than the legislative branch.

Conclusion: Rescuing Constitutional Interpretation

The inherent item veto argument is predicated on a veritable parade of erroneous assumptions and assertions. As this chapter has shown, there are no applicable colonial or early state precedents for the inherent veto argument, including the actions of the Board of Trade and Privy Council; the founders were indeed aware of the rider and omnibus phenomena in the construction of legislation; they were also aware that bill construction could be limited to single subjects but chose not to codify such a narrow definition; the interpretation of the "revisionary" language related to veto use had nothing to do with describing an item veto; and the modern veto is hardly an eviscerated power.

To be sure, one may still argue that the president ought to be able to exercise some form of item veto. One may not argue, however, that the

---

White House, eds. Leslie Feldman and Rosanna Perotti (Westport, CT: Greenwood Press, 2002), 233–53.

[97] Robert J. Spitzer, "The Disingenuous Presidency: Reagan's Veto and the 'Make-My-Day' President," *Congress & the Presidency* 21(Spring, 1994): 1–10.

[98] Spitzer, *The Presidential Veto*, 100–103; Spitzer, "The Disingenuous Presidency," 6–7; John B. Gilmour, *Strategic Disagreement: Stalemate in American Politics* (Pittsburgh, PA: University of Pittsburgh Press, 1995); Charles M. Cameron, *Veto Bargaining: Presidents and the Politics of Negative Power* (New York: Cambridge University Press, 2000).

[99] Richard A. Watson, *Presidential Vetoes and Public Policy* (Lawrence, KS: University Press of Kansas, 1993).

Constitution somehow already incorporates an item veto for the president. Although it is certainly true that presidents have exercised and do exercise an array of powers that have an item veto effect (the rescission power is an obvious example), an item veto is a precisely defined instrument to which no sitting president may now legally lay claim based on any sane reading of the Constitution. How, then, do we explain the strength and depth of this argument, and what are its consequences?

First, the tale of the inherent item veto exemplifies wayward constitutional theorizing from lawyers and law journals. More specifically, constitutional gamesmanship seems to find singularly free rein in this case. For example, Haswell argues that – regardless of the validity of the inherent item veto theory – it is good for the presidency to attempt such a procedure. "Win or lose, the President stands to gain by attempting a partial veto. The 'bully pulpit' of the Presidency would be illuminated by the glow of publicity arising out of the constitutional litigation which would likely ensue. . . ."[100] This anticonstitutional recommendation is troubling not only because it comes from a lawyer but also because it treats proper or successful exercise of executive power as directly proportionate to the amount of litigation it generates. Absent a bona fide emergency, action should be predicated *only* on a firm legal basis, which Haswell himself admits is absent in this case. If it is good for the presidency to claim and exercise a constitutional power for which the justification is at best tenuous, why stop with the veto? Why not encourage the president to devote the resources of the Justice Department to the development and implementation of new theories for more expansive use of other presidential powers and let the courts arbitrate if challenges arise? In fact, the nation has undergone just such presidential experimentation. Its consequences precipitated such crises as Watergate (constitutionally justified as a feasible use of executive authority and executive privilege), Iran–Contra (constitutionally justified as a proper use of presidential foreign policy power), and the second President Bush's unprecedented use of signing statements to rewrite laws with which he disagrees (based on the tendentious "unitary executive" theory; see Chapter 4).[101] The

---

[100] Haswell, "Partial Veto Power," 145.

[101] See Christopher S. Kelley, "The Significance of the Presidential Signing Statement," in *Executing the Constitution: Putting the President Back into the Constitution*, ed. Kelley (Albany, NY: SUNY Press, 2006), 73–89.

constitutional paradigm suggested by Haswell is nothing less than an application of chaos theory to the Constitution. The only "glow" arising from such suspect executive action would be the brief light accompanying the Constitution's immolation.

Sidak and Smith propose a different – if parallel – justification for their advocacy of the inherent item veto. At the start of their article, they note that because the courts have never ruled on this matter, it is still an open legal question: "reasonable minds differ on this constitutional question – as they do on abortion, the War Powers Resolution, affirmative action, the death penalty, and many other constitutional issues."[102] By indiscriminately blending these issues together, they attempt to reduce and thus equalize a wide mix of political and policy disputes using the "reasonable minds differ" standard.[103] Yes, reasonable people may differ over whether affirmative action or the death penalty is or is not good public policy. But this approach obliterates objective analysis that may and should proceed aside and apart from normative questions of policy. As a question of public policy, reasonable people may differ about whether the president should have item veto powers. But, no such standard is useful or appropriate for the empirical research question of whether Article I, sec. 7, of the Constitution actually *gives* such a power to the president, for this is a matter to be resolved by a careful weighing of legal, historical, and political evidence. In this instance, the facts in this case speak clearly about what is true. Can "reasonable minds" differ about whether Darwinian evolution or intelligent design better explains the development of complex planetary life? Can "reasonable minds" differ about whether the Earth is flat or round? It is simply the wrong question.

The "reasonable minds" standard has an added pernicious consequence. It implies that a social–scientific weighing of evidence cannot lead to a clear conclusion as long as people dubbed "reasonable" (note: not reasonable arguments) stand against that conclusion. The law review articles cited in this chapter that defend the inherent item veto theory are

---

[102] Sidak and Smith, "Four Faces of the Item Veto," 439.

[103] During the Senate Judiciary Committee hearings on S. Res. 195 on June 15, 1994, Sen. Specter repeatedly asked those testifying against the inherent item veto if they could at least agree that "reasonable people may differ" on the question, presumably as a way of constructing some kind of consensus to justify support for the inherent item veto proposal.

full of waffling phrases like the "reasonable minds" touchstone. All seek to find cracks of daylight by raising the lawyer's reasonable-doubt questions to chip away at the prevailing wisdom, as in "since we do not know for sure what the founders knew, our interpretation is as valid as any other." These writers argue and write not as scholars but rather as lawyers arguing a case before a jury. Their argument style is designed to create doubt (see the discussion of the adversarial system in Chapter 1) rather than find some approximation of the truth by amassing and weighing evidence cast in broader historical–political perspective.

The pages of law reviews may contain a panoply of other misbegotten constitutional theories but which have failed to generate a similar national debate. But, in this instance, the inherent item veto theory garnered national attention because it had obvious appeal to politicians. The reason for this appeal is not complicated. Any tactic that offers as a prize the exercise of greater authority at little or no political risk or cost represents a political temptation of the first order. When that authority carries with it the mantle of constitutional legitimacy, the value of the prize increases. Other examples of such a temptation arose during the first Bush administration, including adoption of an expansive interpretation of the pocket-veto power (a view also accepted at the end of the Clinton presidency)[104] and the second President Bush's expansive use of signing statements mentioned previously.

To respond to the questions posed at the beginning of this chapter, the inherent item veto theory is not a shocking new discovery; it poses a debate inspiring no little intellectual curiosity, but its central argument does not stand up to scrutiny; there is no evidence that it is a ruse or stalking horse; rather, it can be taken as a case of misguided constitutional scholarship. Its flaws assume more damaging proportions to the extent that political leaders, including a president and several members of Congress, seized on this writing to support a means to grab some added constitutional authority on the cheap.

This case also proves to be an exemplar of constitutional theorizing gone awry. Arguments built on a plain misreading of history, on distortions and omissions of fact, accumulated systematically in law reviews to provide

---

[104] See Robert J. Spitzer, "The 'Protective Return' Pocket Veto: Presidential Aggrandizement of Constitutional Power," in *Executing the Constitution*, 109–25.

an utterly unwarranted degree of legitimacy for a theory undeserving of such elevation. It is a clear case of defective research supporting an untenable theory. Yet, it is a logical – perhaps inevitable – consequence of legal training applied to academic inquiry that flowers in the law journal breeding ground.

4 . . . . . The Unitary Executive and the Commander-in-Chief Power

During the summer of 2004, a series of internal Bush administration memoranda and reports became public detailing a variety of justifications for the administration's detention, handling, and interrogation of various suspects and combatants captured in the war on terrorism and the war in Iraq. Most of these documents were authored or supervised by administration lawyers including then–White House Counsel Alberto Gonzales; William J. Haynes II, General Counsel to the Department of Defense; David Addington, Counsel to Vice President Dick Cheney; Timothy E. Flanigan, Deputy White House Counsel; Assistant Attorney General Jay Bybee, head of the Department of Justice's Office of Legal Counsel; and John Yoo, Deputy Assistant Attorney General in the Office of Legal Counsel.

The release of these documents prompted considerable criticism aimed at the George W. Bush administration, focusing chiefly on arguments offered in these documents to justify the use of torture by the government. These revelations stood in stark contrast to long-standing American policy rejecting the use of torture. The position articulated by President Bush in June 2003, for example, regarding the use of torture was this: "Freedom from torture is an inalienable human right. . . . The United States is committed to the worldwide elimination of torture and we are leading this fight by example."[1] Within a year, however, the administration

---

[1] Quoted in James P. Pfiffner, "Torture and Public Management: The Ethics of Interrogation." Paper presented at the Conference on Ethics and Integrity of Governance, Leuven, Belgium, June 2–5, 2005, 1.

was reeling not only from release of documents seeking to justify torture but also from revelations of the use of torture by American forces in Afghanistan, at the American-controlled Guantánamo Base on the island of Cuba, and most vividly at the Abu Ghraib prison in Iraq, where video-tapes and photographs of prisoners being subjected to a wide variety of "sadistic, blatant, and wanton criminal abuses"[2] by American captors made worldwide news.

In the aftermath of these revelations, most public attention was focused on the legal, military, strategic, political, and moral consequences of tor-ture. Almost entirely overlooked in this important public debate, however, was one of the key legal props advanced in some of the Bush administra-tion documents: the administration's aggressive assertions regarding the scope and reach of presidential power – specifically, the CIC power.

A digest of what became the Bush administration's view of presidential power related to military actions under the Constitution appeared initially in a lengthy memorandum authored by John Yoo two weeks after the 9/11 attacks, titled "The President's Constitutional Authority to Conduct Mili-tary Operations Against Terrorists and Nations Supporting Them."[3] Sub-sequently, at least two documents later made public amplified this analysis: a fifty-page August 2002 memorandum signed by Assistant Attorney Gen-eral Jay Bybee and sent to White House Counsel Alberto Gonzales;[4] and an initially classified report prepared for Secretary of Defense Donald

---

[2] From Antonio M. Taguba, "Article 15–6 Investigation of the 800th Military Policy Brigade," February 26, 2004, Part I, Sec. 2, No. 5; quoted in Pfiffner, "Torture and Public Management," 2.

[3] John C. Yoo, "The President's Constitutional Authority to Conduct Military Opera-tions Against Terrorists and Nations Supporting Them," Memorandum Opinion for the Deputy Counsel to the President, September 25, 2001, accessed at http://www.usdoj.olc/warpowers925.htm on September 12, 2006.

[4] Jay S. Bybee, Assistant Attorney General, U.S. Department of Justice, "Memoran-dum for Alberto R. Gonzales," August 1, 2002. Accessed at http://www.washingtonpost.com/wp-srv/nation/documents/dojinterrogationmemo20020801.pdf. On December 30, 2004, the Justice Department issued a new memorandum, authored by Acting Assis-tant Attorney General Daniel Levin, which repudiated the administration's August 2002 memorandum, specifically rejecting the earlier, narrow view of torture that attempted to defend some acts otherwise considered under the rubric of torture. News reports attributed the change, at least in part, to Alberto Gonzales's impending confirmation hearings for attorney general. There was, however, no refutation or reconsideration of the administration's views on presidential power in the seventeen-page memo. R. Jeffrey Smith and Dan Eggen, "Justice Expands 'Torture' Definition," *Washington Post*, December 31, 2004, A1.

Rumsfeld, titled "Working Group Report on Detainee Interrogations in the Global War on Terrorism: Assessment of Legal, Historical, Policy, and Operational Considerations," completed in April 2003.[5] Buried in this latter report's eighty-seven pages of analysis is a five-page section on "Commander-in-Chief Authority," which is a primary focus of this chapter. The ambitious claims regarding the extent and nature of the CIC power discussed in these documents are a subset of a larger and even more sweeping theory of executive power called the "unitary theory," which itself is arguably the most sweeping claim to executive power ever penned by an administration.

To understand the context of how the CIC power was defined by the second Bush administration, this chapter begins with a brief treatment of the unitary executive theory, a notion that has relied heavily on law journal publications to frame and legitimize the theory. It then turns to the traditional understanding of the CIC power found in Article II, sec. 2, of the Constitution and compares that with the Bush administration view – a view that emerged from a single law journal article and which played a crucial role in its elevation and legitimization. The focus then turns to the case analysis of this power as it arose in these writings and the numerous problems with that analysis.

The Unitary Executive Theory: Article II on Steroids[6]

The unitary theory of executive power emerged in the 1980s in the Justice Department's Office of Legal Counsel under President Ronald Reagan. Under office heads Theodore Olson and Charles Cooper, and Attorney General Edwin Meese, staff lawyers, including future Supreme Court

---

[5] "Working Group Report on Detainee Interrogations in the Global War on Terrorism: Assessment of Legal, Historical, Policy, and Operational Considerations," April 4, 2003. Accessed at http://www.defenselink.mil/news/Jun2004/d20040622doc8.pdf. The Report (hereafter "Working Group Report") was to be declassified in 2013 but was declassified on June 21, 2004, after an earlier draft of the report, dated March 6, 2003, had been leaked to the *Wall Street Journal*. The working group organized to write the Report was appointed by Department of Defense General Counsel William J. Haynes II. It was headed by Air Force General Counsel Mary Walker and included "top civilian and uniformed lawyers" from the military branches, who in turn consulted with the Justice Department, the Joint Chiefs of Staff, and intelligence agencies." Jess Bravin, "Pentagon Report Sought to Justify Use of Torture," *Wall Street Journal*, June 7, 2004, A1.

[6] Richard A. Epstein, "Executive Power on Steroids," *Wall Street Journal*, February 13, 2006, A16.

Justice Samuel Alito, formulated the unitary executive theory. With coordinate support from the newly formed organization of conservative lawyers, the Federalist Society, these young legal thinkers were looking for a way to limit federal power and curb, if not dismantle, the modern regulatory state. In the words of the Federalist Society, it is "a group of conservatives and libertarians dedicated to reforming the current order."[7] The phrase *unitary executive* was derived from references in the Federalist Papers to "unity" in the executive.[8] Departing from the traditional conservative view that sought limited executive power,[9] the unitary view argued for even greater presidential power as a means of attacking and routing power in the rest of the government.

Key to the unitary theory is the contrarian and counter-factual assumption that presidential power has declined, not increased, since the enactment of the Constitution in 1789.[10] In an essay published in 1989, Olson

---

[7] The Federalist Society was formed in 1982. See http://www.fed-soc.org/AboutUs/ourbackground.htm, accessed on October 5, 2006.

[8] Jeffrey Rosen, "Power of One: Bush's Leviathan State," *The New Republic*, July 24, 2006, 8. The phrase appears most famously in Alexander Hamilton's *Federalist Paper 70*, in which he wrote that the "unity" of the executive was one of the important advantages of the executive office proposed in the new Constitution. But, Hamilton's reference was far more straightforward than that ascribed to it by the unitary theorists: Hamilton was simply comparing the presidency as an office occupied by a single individual with competing proposals of the day for a "plural executive," whereby the office would be composed of two or more people who would function as a kind of executive committee. Alexander Hamilton, James Madison, and John Jay, *The Federalist Papers* (New York: New American Library, 1961), 423–31.

[9] James Burnham, *Congress and the American Tradition* (Chicago: Regnery, 1959); Willmoore Kendall, *The Conservative Affirmation* (Chicago: Regnery, 1963); Alfred DeGrazia, *Republic in Crisis* (New York: Federal Legal Publications, 1965). See also Raymond Tatalovich and Thomas S. Engeman, *The Presidency and Political Science* (Baltimore: Johns Hopkins University Press, 2003), chap. 7.

[10] Bush's Vice President, Dick Cheney, has been that administration's foremost proponent of the corollary notion that presidential power was gutted in the 1970s, and that it had not recovered its proper powers from then up to the present. Jane Mayer, "The Hidden Power," *The New Yorker*, July 3, 2006, 44–55. This notion has been challenged from all political quarters. For example, as Reagan Justice Department official Bruce Fein commented about the Bush administration's and Cheney's views of presidential power, "They're in a time warp. If you look at the facts, presidential powers have never been higher." Dana Milbank, "In Cheney's Shadow, Counsel Pushes the Conservative Cause," *Washington Post*, October 11, 2004, A21.

The proposition that presidential power has significantly increased in the last two centuries, yielding a "modern strong presidency" in the twentieth century, is one of the most well-established and widely accepted tenets of the institutional presidency. Many contemporary analysts argue that presidents of recent decades have found that

(who also served as solicitor general in the second Bush administration) asserted that the presidency had endured "two centuries of unrelenting encroachments by Congress," during which time Congress has "adeptly and persistently eroded and disassembled executive power. . . . "[11] To rectify this alleged imbalance and recapture presumably latent or dormant constitutional presidential powers, the unitary theory stakes out two sets of aggressive power claims.

The first is that presidents have sole and complete control over the executive branch. As then–federal judge Alito said in a 2000 speech to the Federalist Society, "The president has not just some executive powers, but *the* executive power – the whole thing."[12] This power claim might seem unexceptionable on its face, but it presumes to extend presidential powers beyond the well-established understanding of the president's role as chief executive.

As applied during the George W. Bush presidency, it deigns to empower the president to exercise sole control over the removal of executive branch officials, to direct the actions of such officials, and to nullify the decisions or actions of others that are believed to impede the president's full control over the executive. In practice, this has meant that Bush has felt at liberty to ignore provisions of laws with which he disagrees (most prominently by relying on signing statements[13]), interpret or set aside treaties unilaterally,

the demands and expectations placed on the office outstrip its powers, placing modern presidents in an often untenable political situation, but this assertion does not contradict the truism of the long-term rise of presidential powers. A small sampling of such writing includes Edward S. Corwin, *The President: Office and Powers* (New York: NYU Press, 1957); Clinton Rossiter, *The American Presidency* (New York: New American Library, 1960); Theodore J. Lowi, *The Personal President* (Ithaca, NY: Cornell University Press, 1985); Richard E. Neustadt, *Presidential Power* (New York: Free Press, 1990); Stephen Skowronek, *The Politics Presidents Make* (Cambridge, MA: Harvard University Press, 1993); Robert J. Spitzer, *President and Congress* (New York: McGraw-Hill, 1993); Gordon Silverstein, *Imbalance of Powers: Constitutional Interpretation and the Making of American Foreign Policy* (New York: Oxford University Press, 1997); and Michael A. Genovese, *The Power of the American Presidency* (New York: Oxford University Press, 2001). A superb synthesis of competing arguments about presidential power is found in Tatalovich and Engeman, *The Presidency and Political Science*.

[11] Theodore B. Olson, "The Impetuous Vortex: Congressional Erosion of Presidential Authority," in *The Fettered Presidency: Legal Constraints on the Executive Branch*, eds. L. Gordon Crovitz and Jeremy Rabkin (Washington, DC: American Enterprise Institute, 1989), 231.

[12] Jess Bravin, "Bush's Power Play Has Key Ally," *The Wall Street Journal*, January 5, 2006, 12.

[13] A typical invocation of unitary executive power in a signing statement to void a part of a law was that issued by Bush in his signing statement of H.R. 2863 on December 30,

determine the fate of enemy combatants, use tactics generally considered to be torture against enemy combatants despite strictures against such actions in federal and international law, allow warrantless surveillance of domestic telephone calls contrary to existing law, and curtail judicial oversight, among other actions. Further, the unitary view questions the very constitutionality of government agencies (and the rules they issue) created to be independent of the president by law – that is, independent regulatory agencies, commissions, and other similar entities[14] (the first of which, the Interstate Commerce Commission, was created in 1887), notwithstanding the undisputed fact that presidents are empowered to appoint the heads of these agencies, and that these agencies' constitutionality has been upheld since their creation. In fact, the legal basis for the modern bureaucracy, including independent agencies, is one of the most well-established features of modern governance.[15]

2005. This bill to provide emergency supplemental appropriations included an amendment, sponsored by Republican Senator John McCain (AZ) to bar cruel, degrading, and inhumane treatment of prisoners being held by the United States. Bush had opposed the amendment but dropped his opposition when it became clear that the measure had overwhelming congressional support. Yet, his signing statement included this phrase: "The executive branch shall construe Title X in Division A of the Act, relating to detainees, in a manner consistent with the constitutional authority of the President to supervise the unitary executive branch and as Commander in Chief and consistent with the constitutional limitations on the judicial power. . . . " McCain protested the implication that Bush might decline to enforce this provision of the law, but the White House refused to explain Bush's intentions. Yet, the just-quoted phrase was typical of hundreds inserted in prior and subsequent pieces of legislation. The arcane, mantra-like wording ("to supervise the unitary executive . . . ") raised little attention in the first several years of Bush's presidency until the intent behind it came into public view. "President's Signing Statement of H.R. 2863," December 30, 2005. See http://www.whitehouse.gov/news/releases/2005/12/20051230–8.html, accessed on January 17, 2006; Elisabeth Bumiller, "For President, Final Say on a Bill Sometimes Comes After the Signing," *New York Times*, January 16, 2006, A11.

[14] Bravin, "Bush's Power Play Has Key Ally"; "How Bush Has Asserted Powers of the Executive," *USA Today*, June 6, 2002, 2A; R. Jeffrey Smith and Dan Eggen, "Justice Expands 'Torture' Definition," *Washington Post*, December 31, 2004, A1; Stuart Taylor, Jr., "The Man Who Would Be King," *Atlantic Monthly*, April 2006, 25–26.

[15] The voluminous and decades-old literature on the American bureaucracy, nearly all of which is ignored by advocates of the unitary view, confirms the constitutional, legal, and political place for agencies. Good summaries are found in Robert E. Cushman, *The Independent Regulatory Commissions* (New York: Oxford University Press, 1941); Theodore J. Lowi, *The End of Liberalism* (New York: W.W. Norton, 1979); Richard J. Stillman II, *The American Bureaucracy* (Chicago: Nelson-Hall, 1987). Peter Woll addressed these issues decades ago in his standard work on bureaucracy when he noted that Hamilton's reference to unity in the presidency was cited by early critics as an impediment to the development of independent agencies. Woll's analysis was: "the

The second claim of the unitary theory is that the other branches of government may not interfere with presidential actions arising from these executive powers. It is on this basis that Bush has argued that he may ignore laws or provisions of laws that, in his view, impinge on his so-called unitary power as chief executive. From 2001 to mid-2007 alone, Bush used signing statements to void or refuse to enforce laws or provisions of laws in more than eleven hundred instances (almost twice as many as all of his predecessors combined), asserting that these provisions infringed on his unitary executive power.[16] In addition, Bush administration lawyers have also argued that the courts may not adjudicate in areas the president deems within his executive power. Administration lawyers have made these arguments in such recent court cases as *Hamdi v. Rumsfeld* (2004),[17] *Rasul v. Bush* (2004),[18] and *Hamdan v. Rumsfeld* (2006).[19] To date, courts have largely rejected the argument that they do not have a right to rule.

As mentioned previously, the provenance of the unitary theory dates to Justice Department lawyers and the Federalist Society in the 1980s. Yet, central to the theory's legitimacy was the predicate that its roots were founded in 1787, not the 1980s. As one architect of the unitary view

fact is that the system they [the Framers] constructed supported in many particulars bureaucratic organization and functions independent of the President. It was the role they assigned to *Congress* in relation to administration that assured this result, as well as the general position Congress was to occupy in the governmental system.... Congress can not only set up an administrative agency on an independent basis, but it can see to it that the agency remains independent." Woll, *American Bureaucracy* (New York: W.W. Norton, 1977; first published 1963), 62–63.

[16] Charlie Savage, "Bush Challenges Hundreds of Laws," *Boston Globe*, April 30, 2006, A1; Savage, "Bush Cites Authority to Bypass FEMA Law," *Boston Globe*, October 6, 2006, A1; Savage, *Takeover: The Return of the Imperial Presidency and the Subversion of American Democracy* (New York: Little, Brown, 2007), 230. These data come from the work of political scientists Christopher S. Kelley and Phillip J. Cooper. For more on signing statements, see Kelley and Ryan J. Barilleaux, "The Past, Present, and Future of the Unitary Executive," a paper presented at the Annual Meeting of the American Political Science Association, Philadelphia, PA, August 31–September 3, 2006; Cooper, *By Order of the President* (Lawrence, KS: University Press of Kansas, 2002); Cooper, "George W. Bush, Edgar Allen Poe, and the Use and Abuse of Presidential Signing Statements," *Presidential Studies Quarterly* 35(September 2005): 515–32; Louis Fisher, "Signing Statements: What to Do?" *The Forum* 4(2006): 1–10. Bush II is not the first president to use signing statements to balk at the enforcement of provisions of bills. But all of Bush's predecessors combined used signing statements in such a manner in about six hundred instances. Moreover, no president has ever overlain these actions with a theory in the nature of the grandiose unitary theory.

[17] 542 U.S. 507 (2004).   [18] 542 U.S. 466 (2004).

[19] 165 L.Ed. 2d 723 (2006).

admitted, "What the idea had lacked was an intellectual justification and defense."[20] Enter the law reviews.

Articles referencing the unitary executive began to appear in law journals in the mid-1980s,[21] but the first full-blown and sustained explication and defense of the idea was published in 1992.[22] Thereafter, a lengthy series of articles appeared debating the merits of the unitary theory.[23] Capping the unitary argument was a series of four law review articles, amounting to nearly five hundred published pages and all authored by Steven Calabresi, Christopher S. Yoo, and other associates, that provide a chronological account of what they claim shows the infusion of the unitary executive throughout American history under the modern Constitution.[24] The sweep and ambition of this unitary-view writing is nicely encapsulated by legal writer Gary Lawson, whose breathtaking argument in his article

[20] "Yoo Presidency, The," *The New York Times Magazine*, December 11, 2005, 106.

[21] Peter L. Strauss, "The Place of Agencies in Government: Separation of Powers and the Fourth Branch," *Columbia Law Review* 84(April 1984): 599–602; Geoffrey P. Miller, "Independent Agencies," *Supreme Court Review* (1986): 41–97; Harold J. Krent, "Fragmenting the Unitary Executive: Congressional Delegations of Administrative Authority Outside the Federal Government," *Northwestern University Law Review* 85(Fall 1990): 62–112.

[22] Steven G. Calabresi and Kevin H. Rhodes, "The Structural Constitution: Unitary Executive, Plural Judiciary," *Harvard Law Review* 105(April 1992): 1153–1216. Calabresi is a co-founder of the Federalist Society and also worked as a lawyer in the Reagan administration.

[23] Articles defending the unitary view include Gary Lawson, "Changing Images of the State: The Rise and Rise[AU: is this correct? Yes] of the Administrative State," *Harvard Law Review* 107(April 1994): 1231–54; Steven G. Calabresi and Saikrishna B. Prakash, "The President's Power to Execute the Laws," *Yale Law Journal* 104(December 1994): 541–665. Critics of the unitary view include Lawrence Lessig and Cass R. Sunstein, "The President and the Administration," *Columbia Law Review* 94(January 1994): 1–120; Abner S. Greene, "Checks and Balances in an Era of Presidential Lawmaking," *University of Chicago Law Review* 61(Winter 1994): 123–96; Martin S. Flaherty, "The Most Dangerous Branch," *Yale Law Journal* 105(May 1996): 1725–1839; Neil Kinkopf, "Of Devolution, Privatization, and Globalization: Separation of Powers Limits on Congressional Authority to Assign Federal Power to Non-Federal Actors," *Rutgers Law Review* 50(Winter 1998): 331–96.

[24] Steven G. Calabresi and Christopher S. Yoo, "The Removal Power: The Unitary Executive During the First Half-Century," *Case Western Reserve Law Review* 47(Summer 1997): 1451–1561; Steven G. Calabresi and Christopher S. Yoo, "The Unitary Executive During the Second Half-Century," *Harvard Journal of Law and Public Policy* 26(Summer 2003): 667–801; Christopher S. Yoo, Steven G. Calabresi, and Lawrence D. Nee, "The Unitary Executive During the Third Half-Century," *Notre Dame Law Review* 80(November 2004): 1–109; Christopher S. Yoo, Steven G. Calabresi, and Anthony J. Colangelo, "The Unitary Executive in the Modern Era, 1945–2004," *Iowa Law Review* 90(January 2005): 601–731.

on the subject is that, as per the unitary theory, "The post–New Deal administrative state is unconstitutional. . . ."[25]

A detailed critique of the unitary theory itself is beyond the scope of this chapter because its purpose is to examine the unitary theory as applied specifically to the president's CIC power. Yet, this overarching unitary literature found in law reviews suffers from at least four problems[26] endemic to the law journal writing discussed in this book: it cherry-picks its evidence, often misrepresents the historical record, and ignores pertinent literature in other disciplines; it attempts to manufacture a constitutional pedigree for a purely contemporary political construct; it seeks to configure a constitutional basis for overturning existing case law that has long accepted the constitutionality of (in this case) the modern regulatory state; and it is a paradigmatic example of lawyerly advocacy scholarship – which is to say, it is not scholarship at all. Perhaps the best example of this latter criticism is the fact that the unitary theory turns the related principles of separation of powers and checks and balances on their head. Any power identified as belonging to the president or the executive branch is, by unitary theory definition, beyond the reach of the other two branches, despite the fact that the essence of the three-branch relationship is one of overlapping and interconnected powers (which does not deny that each branch does retain exclusive control over some aspects of its respective branch). One need go no further than James Madison, who wrote in *Federalist Paper 51* that "Ambition must be made to counteract ambition." To effectuate such a governing system, " . . . the constant aim is to divide and arrange the several offices in such a manner as that each may be a check on the other. . . ."[27] As constitutional scholar Louis Fisher concludes, "The model of the Unitary Executive was never adopted or intended, nor does it have any wholesale application today either in theory or practice."[28]

---

[25] Lawson, "Changing Images of the State," 1231.
[26] Particularly effective critiques of the unitary view are found in Lessig and Sunstein, "The President and the Administration"; Kelley and Barilleaux, "The Past, Present, and Future of the Unitary Executive"; and Louis Fisher, "The 'Unitary Executive': Ideology Versus the Constitution," a paper presented at the Annual Meeting of the American Political Science Association, Philadelphia, PA, August 31–September 3, 2006.
[27] Alexander Hamilton, James Madison, and John Jay, *The Federalist Papers* (New York: New American Library, 1961), 322.
[28] Fisher, "The 'Unitary Executive,'" 1.

The Constitutional Commander-in-Chief

Unanimity is rare in any matter of constitutional interpretation, and it is not to be found in the interpretation of the CIC power. Disagreement persists, for example, regarding the question of whether the CIC power makes the president merely the titular head of the military establishment or extends to specific, operational decision making. Analysts also continue to disagree about the extent of the president's discretionary powers in limited, undeclared military conflicts. There is, however, a high degree of consensus among scholars, including political scientists, historians, and legal writers, regarding this power's constitutional genesis and construction.

This understanding is first framed by an asymmetry underlying the separation of powers: that the legislative branch was to be the first, most important, and most powerful branch among the three. The three-branch system was emphatically not one of three co-equal branches but rather was to be legislative-centered.[29] This principle applies to foreign as well as domestic powers.[30] The manifestation of this congressional-dominant relationship is seen in the country's first one hundred years, when, as political scientist Theodore J. Lowi noted, American governance more nearly resembled a parliamentary system typified by "congressional dominance."[31] To be sure, the modern three-branch relationship would appear to little resemble anything like a legislative-dominant system (and one might certainly argue that such a development was desirable, even necessary), but that is a consequence of more than two hundred years of institutional evolution.

The CIC power that made its way into Article II traces back to seventeenth-century Britain, where from the outset the title possessed two specific traits: that the CIC was "the highest office in a particular chain of command"[32] and that that officer was to function under the command of a political superior, whether Parliament or monarch in Britain

---

[29] See Garry Wills's brilliant demolition of the myth of three co-equal branches in *A Necessary Evil* (New York: Simon & Schuster, 1999), chap. 5. See also Spitzer, *President and Congress*, 13–16.

[30] Harold Hongju Koh, *The National Security Constitution* (New Haven, CT: Yale University Press, 1990), 75–76.

[31] Lowi, *The Personal President*, 35.

[32] Francis D. Wormuth and Edwin B. Firmage, *To Chain the Dog of War: The War Power of Congress in History and Law* (Urbana, IL: University of Illinois Press, 1989), 109.

or other final authority. When George Washington was commissioned to head America's revolutionary forces in 1775, he was named "General and Commander in Chief, of the Army of the United Colonies." Thereafter, he was subject to strict and specific instructions by Congress. Colonial governors also typically bore the CIC title, to function under the authority of their state legislatures.[33] Even after the adoption of the modern Constitution, the title was not limited only to the president. Major General Anthony Wayne, for example, who headed military forces in the Northwest Territory in the 1790s, was called "commander-in-chief."[34]

The records of the Constitutional Convention include no debate over the CIC clause (a fact usually taken to infer that little controversy surrounded its inclusion), but several of the convention delegates referenced the power in state ratification debates or at other times. Those comments generally conformed to the fullest explanation of the power, expressed by Alexander Hamilton in *Federalist Paper 69*:

> The President is to be commander-in-chief of the army and navy of the United States. In this respect his authority would be nominally the same with that of the king of Great Britain, but in substance much inferior to it. It would amount to nothing more than the supreme command and direction of the military and naval forces, as first general and admiral of the Confederacy; while that of the British king extend to the *declaring* of war and to the *raising* and *regulating* of fleets and armies – all of which, by the Constitution under consideration, would appertain to the legislature.[35]

This familiar quote underscores three key points: first, it acknowledges the title's British ancestry; second, it describes the CIC power in tactical terms (i.e., the direction of the use of forces); and, third, it states emphatically (the words were emphasized in the original text) that the political and organizational decisions behind war making lie with Congress. As another constitutional writer noted, "In contrast to the English system, the Framers did not want the wealth and blood of the Nation committed by the decision of a single individual."[36] James Madison echoed a

---

[33] David Gray Adler, "George Bush as Commander in Chief," *Presidential Studies Quarterly* 36(September 2006): 527.
[34] In fact, the title commander-in-chief appears on Wayne's gravestone. Wormuth and Firmage, *To Chain the Dog of War*, 109.
[35] Hamilton, Madison, and Jay, *The Federalist Papers*, 417–18.
[36] Johnny H. Killian, ed., *The Constitution of the United States of America* (Washington, DC: U.S. Government Printing Office, 1987), 335.

similar point of view: "Those who are to conduct a war cannot in the nature of things, be proper or safe judges, whether a war ought to be commenced, continued, or concluded."[37] As a constitutional commentator writing in the 1920s concluded, "It is improbable that a single member of the Convention would have signed his name to the Constitution if he had supposed that that instrument might be construed as authorizing the President to initiate a foreign war, either general or partial, without the express authorization of Congress."[38]

The CIC power, therefore, did not represent the endpoint in the military chain of command. The final and highest civil authority for the CIC was Congress. That is why the fulsome constitutional powers to declare war; issue letters of marque and reprisal; raise, regulate, and finance the military; regulate international commerce; punish crimes on the high seas; settle "offenses against the law of nations;" make all laws necessary and proper to carry out the preceding powers; "and all other Powers vested by this Constitution in the Government of the United States, or in any Department or Officer thereof" were all vested in the national legislature in Article I. The very text of Article II, sec. 2, confirms Congress's final role: "The President shall be Commander in Chief of the Army and Navy of the United States, and of the Militia of the several states," it begins, "when called into the actual Service of the United States." As Louis Fisher has observed, "Congress, not the President, does the calling."[39] And congressional authority extended to imperfect or limited wars, as well as perfect or general wars.[40] In addition, Congress often limited or directed the actual movement of troops, as it did in instances from the 1790s to the 1970s.[41] Presidents were understood to have the unilateral ability to use military force only to repel sudden attacks, although this soon extended to the

[37] Gaillard Hunt, ed., *The Writings of James Madison*, 9 vols. (New York: G.P. Putnam's Sons, 1900–1910) 6: 248.

[38] Albert H. Putney, "Executive Assumption of the War Making Power," *National University Law Review* 7(May 1927): 5–6.

[39] Louis Fisher, *Presidential War Power* (Lawrence, KS: University Press of Kansas, 2004), 12.

[40] Wormuth and Firmage, *To Chain the Dog of War*, 60–63. As Edward Keynes noted in his detailed study of imperfect and undeclared wars, "the Framers recognized congressional power to determine the use of limited force against other nations to redress grievances . . . the Framers intended to vest limited as well as general war-making power in Congress rather than the President." *Undeclared War: Twilight Zone of Constitutional Power* (University Park, PA: Pennsylvania State University Press, 1982), 37.

[41] Wormuth and Firmage, *To Chain the Dog of War*, 114–16.

"hot pursuit" of criminals, pirates, and others, even across international boundaries.[42]

Two early Supreme Court cases from 1800 and 1801 concluded that Congress could effect its control over war decisions either by formal declaration or statute. As Chief Justice John Marshall wrote in *Talbot v. Seeman*, "the whole powers of war being, by the constitution of the United States, vested in congress, the acts of that body can alone be resorted to as our guides."[43] In 1804, the Court ruled in *Little v. Barreme* that Congress-made law superseded a contrary presidential order pertaining to the military conduct of American naval vessels.[44] These rulings conform to political scientist Peter Irons's view that "the president's title and role as commander in chief gave him no powers that Congress could not define or limit."[45]

On the other hand, presidents often rankled at Congress's intrusions and found ways to use American military force despite the absence of formal congressional approval and eventually claimed ever greater authority based, they said, on the CIC power.[46] When Congress issued specific military directions to the president, they were increasingly challenged as an encroachment on the CIC power, on both the practical grounds of avoiding cumbersome congressional micro-management of military matters and the constitutional basis that it would emasculate the CIC power. As President William H. Taft said after his presidency, " . . . in the carrying on of war as Commander-in-Chief, it is he who is to determine the movements of the army and of the navy. Congress could not take away from him that discretion and place it beyond his control. . . . "[47]

Exceptions notwithstanding, presidents in the nineteenth century generally adhered to the Congress-dominant model concerning military actions. The tipping point for the reinterpretation of the CIC power came at the outset of the twentieth century,[48] and especially since 1950,

---

[42] Max Farrand, *The Records of the Federal Convention of 1787*, 4 vols. (New Haven, CT: Yale University Press, 1966), II, 318; Spitzer, *President and Congress*, 152.

[43] *Talbot v. Seeman*, 5 U.S. 1, at 28 (1801). See also *Bas v. Tingy*, 4 U.S. 37 (1800).

[44] *Little v. Barreme*, 6 U.S. 170 (1804).

[45] Peter Irons, *War Powers* (New York: Henry Holt, 2005), 25.

[46] Louis Henkin, *Constitutionalism, Democracy, and Foreign Affairs* (New York: Columbia University Press, 1990), 25.

[47] William Howard Taft, *The President and His Powers* (New York: Columbia University Press, 1916), 129.

[48] Fisher, *Presidential War Power*, chaps. 2 and 3. Presidents in recent decades have asserted that the reference to "The executive power" in Article II also bestowed a

when presidents' ever-more aggressive applications of military force were increasingly accompanied by more expansive assertions of constitutional power.[49]

It is one thing to say that presidents gradually expanded their interpretation and use of military powers as CIC over the decades and centuries; it is quite another to assert that the Constitution as written in 1787 already gave presidents incomparably vast military powers, and that these vast powers far exceed the actual powers exercised (or even contemplated) by presidents throughout history. Yet, it is this latter assertion that lies at the core of the unitary view of the CIC power.

The Commander-in-Chief According to Yoo

To return to the George W. Bush administration, the initial reconceptualization of the CIC power was first articulated in then–Deputy Assistant Attorney General John Yoo's September 25, 2001, memorandum addressed to the Deputy Counsel to the President, Timothy Flanigan. This memorandum depicted the president's powers over war-making and the use of troops abroad in the most sweeping terms imaginable. Mostly citing court cases (discussed herein) and a sprinkling of secondary sources,

---

constitutional basis for presidential military action. Yet, as David Gray Adler convincingly shows, that power or title bore with it no unilateral military authority. In fact, such an idea was emphatically rejected by the Framers. "The Constitution and Presidential Warmaking: The Enduring Debate," *Political Science Quarterly* 103(Spring 1988): 14–15.

[49] The prodigious literature confirming this understanding includes Clinton Rossiter, *The Supreme Court and the Commander in Chief* (Ithaca, NY: Cornell University Press, 1976; first published 1951); Corwin, *The President: Office and Powers*, chap. 6; Rossiter, *The American Presidency*, 22; Louis Henkin, *Foreign Affairs and the Constitution* (Mineola, NY: Foundation Press, 1972); Charles A. Lofgren, "War-Making Under the Constitution," *Yale Law Journal* 81(March 1972): 672–702; W. Taylor Reveley, *War Powers of the President and Congress* (Charlottesville, VA: University of Virginia Press, 1981); Keynes, *Undeclared War*; Jules Lobel, "Covert War and Congressional Authority," *University of Pennsylvania Law Review* 134(June 1986); Donald L. Robinson, *"To the Best of My Ability"* (New York: W.W. Norton, 1987); Adler, "The Constitution and Presidential Warmaking"; Wormuth and Firmage, *To Chain the Dog of War*; Michael J. Glennon, *Constitutional Diplomacy* (Princeton, NJ: Princeton University Press, 1990); Koh, *The National Security Constitution*; Spitzer, *President and Congress*; Fisher, *Presidential War Power*; Louis Fisher, *Congressional Abdication on War and Spending* (College Station, TX: Texas A&M University Press, 2000). Some of these writers disagree about the legality or propriety of modern expansive executive war making but all broadly agree in their view of what the founders intended and how the power evolved.

Yoo's memorandum stakes out the position that the other branches of government may impose no limits whatsoever on actions taken by the president as CIC if the president believes such actions are warranted in defense of the nation. The memorandum concludes that legislative enactments may not place "any limits on the President's determinations as to any terrorist threat, the amount of military force to be used in response, or the method, timing, and nature of the response. These decisions, under our Constitution, are for the President alone to make."[50] Similar sweeping assertions appear in numerous subsequent memoranda authored or co-authored by Yoo and others.[51]

Three factors catapulted Yoo's writings to the forefront of administration thinking: preexisting sympathies to grand presidential power claims among top Bush administration figures, including William Haynes, David Addington, Timothy Flanigan, and Vice President Cheney; Yoo's "academic background and interests,"[52] stemming from his professional university affiliation and law journal writing on presidential power and foreign affairs; and the shocking nature of the 9/11 attacks. The impact of Yoo's writing was such that Yoo was allowed to bypass the normal clearance process to which opinions from the Office of Legal Counsel would otherwise normally be subject.[53] According to later news accounts, Attorney General John Ashcroft was not consulted in the making of these early, key decisions and "was enraged to discover that Yoo, his subordinate, exercised such influence."[54] This memorandum provided the underpinning of subsequent statements and memoranda asserting newly ambitious executive powers, including those found in the August 2002 and April 2003 documents referenced previously.

Because these latter documents represented more mature and fully vetted administration policy statements, the primary focus here is on them. And, because both the August 2002 and April 2003 documents make the

[50] Yoo, "The President's Constitutional Authority to Conduct Military Operations Against Terrorists and Nations Supporting Them."

[51] See Louis Fisher, "Lost Constitutional Moorings: Recovering the War Power," *Indiana Law Journal* 81(Fall 2006): 1240–44.

[52] Tim Golden, "A Junior Aide Had a Big Role in Terror Policy," *New York Times*, December 23, 2005, A1.

[53] Golden, "A Junior Aide Had a Big Role in Terror Policy"; Jane Mayer, "Outsourcing Torture," *The New Yorker*, February 14, 2005. Accessed at http://www.newyorker.com/printables/fact/050214fa_fact6 on October 12, 2006.

[54] Barton Gellman and Jo Becker, "The Cheney Vice Presidency: 'A Different Understanding with the President,'" *Washington Post*, June 24, 2007, A1.

same case and cite the same evidence, I confine myself to an analysis of the second, the April 2003 report.[55] Before proceeding to that analysis, however, it is worth noting that public accounts of these documents referred to them repeatedly – and specifically regarding the Yoo-inspired analysis of the CIC power – not just as administration briefs or policy documents but also as writings "justified in intellectual terms,"[56] "scholarly arguments," and "scholarly efforts," referencing Yoo's academic background and writings.[57]

From Law Journal to Law

Currently a faculty member at the University of California at Berkeley Law School, John Yoo went on leave from that institution to serve as general counsel to the U.S. Senate Judiciary Committee from 1995 to 1996 and to serve in the second Bush administration's Office of Legal Counsel from 2001 to 2003. Of particular note, however, is his authorship of an article that appeared in the *California Law Review* in 1996,[58] in which he examined the historical and legal background of the war power. Yoo cited his article, plus two others of his authorship,[59] in his September 2001 memorandum about the conduct of military operations by the president.

[55] Even though the earlier document is the product of the Office of Legal Counsel, therefore suggesting greater legal import, I focus on the second document because it was produced later and involved not only the same arguments but at least some of the same people, including John Yoo. R. Jeffrey Smith and Dan Eggen, "Gonzales Helped Set the Course for Detainees," *Washington Post*, January 5, 2005, A1.

[56] Mayer, "Outsourcing Torture."

[57] Dana Priest and R. Jeffrey Smith, "Memo Offered Justification for Use of Torture," *Washington Post*, June 8, 2004, A1; Golden, "A Junior Aide Had a Big Role in Terror Policy"; "Yoo Presidency, The"; Daniel Klaidman, Stuart Taylor, Jr., and Evan Thomas, "Palace Revolt," *Newsweek*, February 6, 2006, 38; Rosen, "Power of One." Many in the academic community were harshly critical of the scholarly probity of Yoo's writing: Adam Liptak, "Legal Scholars Criticize Torture Memos," *New York Times*, June 25, 2004, A14; Liptak, "How Far Can a Government Lawyer Go?" *New York Times*, June 27, 2004, 4–3.

[58] John C. Yoo, "The Continuation of Politics by Other Means: The Original Understanding of War Powers," *California Law Review* 84(March 1996): 170–305. Yoo's arguments from his 1996 article also appear in a subsequent article (with an unintentionally ironic subtitle): "CLIO at War: The Misuse of History in the War Powers Debate," *University of Colorado Law Review* 70(Fall 1999): 1169–1222.

[59] John C. Yoo, "Kosovo, War Powers, and the Multilateral Future," *University of Pennsylvania Law Review* 148(May 2000): 1673–1731; Yoo, "UN Wars, US War Powers," *Chicago Journal of International Law* 1(Fall 2000): 355–73.

Yet, the 1996 article was the linchpin of his policy writing in the Bush administration and, therefore, of what became Bush administration policy.

In this article, Yoo made several startling arguments that also emerge in the Bush administration documents discussed herein. Alternately rejecting[60] and misconstruing[61] the vast majority of scholarship on the subject, Yoo asserted that the constitutional war powers were designed to "encourage presidential initiative in war," meaning that presidents were to have the leading role in initiating war; that Congress's role in war making was not based on its power to declare war but instead on its funding and impeachment powers; and that "[t]he courts were to have no role at all" in war-related matters.[62]

Yoo's article is significant for three reasons. First, it stakes out a new and unprecedentedly aggressive view of the CIC power – a view that goes beyond past writings that argue for a strong executive.[63] Second,

---

[60] In his 1996 law review article, Yoo belittles both the "uniformity" and "harshness" of scholarship on contemporary views of the constitutional war power as exercised by the president (thereby conceding that his views contradict standard understanding), dismissing it by saying that these traits belong "only to the most recent [i.e., from the Vietnam era forward] works on war powers." "The Continuation of Politics by Other Means," 171.

[61] In his September 2001 memorandum, Yoo places his views in the mainstream, asserting, incorrectly, that "Some commentators have read the constitutional text differently [from Yoo]." In a footnote, Yoo cites sources that he claims support his view that "the President has a constitutional authority to initiate military hostilities without prior congressional authorization." Aside from citing six contemporary law journal articles (including one by him), he cites Corwin's seminal book *The President: Office and Powers*. Yet, Corwin's view on the CIC power is the opposite of that attributed to him by Yoo. Far from coming from the Constitution, Corwin's analysis demonstrates how ambitious presidential CIC power claims have grown and evolved over time. Corwin concludes his chapter with the verdict that "the President's power as Commander-in-Chief has been transformed from a simple power of military command to a vast reservoir of indeterminate powers in time of emergency. . . ." (261). Further, Corwin viewed these developments with alarm. See, for example, Corwin's article, "Of Presidential Prerogative," reprinted in Kenneth D. Crews, ed., *Corwin's Constitution: Essays and Insights of Edward S. Corwin* (Westport, CT: Greenwood Press, 1986), 189–210.

[62] Yoo, "The Continuation of Politics," 170.

[63] Among the most aggressive statements of the modern strong presidency argument are Gordon S. Jones and John A. Marini, eds., *The Imperial Congress* (New York: Pharos Books, 1988); Crovitz and Rabkin, *The Fettered Presidency*; and Terry Eastland, *Energy in the Executive* (New York: Free Press, 1992). None of these sources offers arguments about the CIC power on the scale of Yoo. The broader contours of the debate over competing views of presidential power are analyzed in Spitzer, *President and Congress*, chap. 7; Tatalovich and Engeman, *The Presidency and Political Science*.

consistent with the conservative fixation on original intent,[64] it seeks to ground in the Constitution itself, subsequent case law, and history the view that the presidential CIC power is beyond the reach of the other branches of government (in the process all but abandoning the separation of powers paradigm), instead of arguing for a strong executive based on historical evolution, political preference, or policy necessity (although Yoo does cite the actions of past presidents). Third, it provided the key intellectual underpinning for the Bush administration memoranda and policy, discussed herein.[65] The connection between Yoo's 1996 article and Bush administration policy was made succinctly by Yoo himself in a 2005 interview, when he stated flatly that Congress did not have the power to "tie the President's hands in regard to torture as an interrogation technique. It's the core of the Commander-in-Chief function. They can't prevent the President from ordering torture."[66]

In two articles, Louis Fisher examines and thoroughly refutes Yoo's primary arguments.[67] Fisher notes that Yoo fails to distinguish between defensive military actions ordered by the president and the initiation of offensive military operations; distorts the meaning of the all-important power of Congress to declare war; misjudges the courts' power to adjudicate war-related disputes; ignores or misrepresents the numerous instances when Congress has granted the executive authorization by statute to conduct military operations; wrongly argues that the Constitution's founders adopted the British government's model of war powers because the founders actually rejected that model; and asserts, bizarrely,

---

[64] Original intent is the political and constitutional mantra of conservative constitutionalism, from Robert Bork and the Federalist Society to George W. Bush. Fisher, "Lost Constitutional Moorings," 1234. For an excellent discussion of the fixation with and limitations of the original intent or "originalism" approach, see Daniel A. Farber and Suzanna Sherry, *Desperately Seeking Certainty: The Misguided Quest for Constitutional Foundations* (Chicago: University of Chicago Press, 2002), chap. 2.

[65] Neither Yoo's article nor any other secondary source is cited in the 2003 Report, but his arguments and evidence are distinctive, they are repeated in the Report's arguments, and numerous press accounts attribute these ideas to him; e.g., Margulies, *Guantánamo and the Abuse of Presidential Power*, 128.

[66] Mayer, "Outsourcing Torture." Consistent with the thesis of his 1996 article, Yoo said in the interview that Congress's only constitutional option to alter the president's actions was through impeachment.

[67] Louis Fisher, "Unchecked Presidential Wars," *University of Pennsylvania Law Review* 148(May 2000): 1637–72 (see 1658–68 for the discussion on Yoo); and Fisher, "Lost Constitutional Moorings," 1234–40.

that Congress's only means to control an executive-initiated war is through the spending power or impeachment.[68] The fact that Yoo's arguments from 1996 made their way into Bush administration policy documents is, in and of itself, no startling revelation. What is significant is the elevation of these arguments from lawyer's brief to policy, owing in no small measure to its treatment as academic scholarship. As noted previously, press references to many of the documents discussed herein, as well as references by government spokespeople, referred repeatedly to these writings as "scholarly effort[s] to define the perimeters of the law."[69] If we take Yoo's law review article and other similar writings[70] as part of the construction of a scholarly – as distinct from political – provenance for the unitary executive view of the CIC power, then it provides another constitutional subject that has acquired a scholarly aura because of law review publications. As one later account reported, Yoo "became the theorist of an insurrection against legal limits on the commander in chief."[71]

The Bush Commander-in-Chief

The section of the 2003 "Working Group Report on Detainee Interrogations" dealing with presidential power makes two expansive claims: (1) that the president's CIC power is an ultimate and final authority, meaning that decisions made by the president pursuant to this authority are subject only to his final judgment, even asserting that the CIC power could allow the president to "render specific conduct, otherwise criminal, *not unlawful*";[72] and (2) actions taken by the president as CIC are nonreviewable by and beyond the reach of the legislative and judicial branches.

---

[68] Fisher, "Unchecked Presidential Wars," 1659–71.

[69] Priest and Smith, "Memo Offered Justification."

[70] Yoo is the author of a book that expands on the arguments from his 1996 article: *The Powers of War and Peace: The Constitution and Foreign Affairs After 9/11* (Chicago: University of Chicago Press, 2005). Yoo's erroneous analysis extends to this book. For example, he discusses the debate at the Constitutional Convention concerning war powers, quoting the statements of Charles Pinckney, John Rutledge, and James Wilson, all of whom spoke against giving the war power to the president, as Yoo correctly quotes them. Yoo then ends the paragraph with a conclusion that contradicts the quotes that appear in the same paragraph: "At this point in the debate, the Framers seemed to agree that vesting the president with all the 'executive powers' of the Articles of Confederation would include the power over war and peace" (92).

[71] Gellman and Becker, "The Cheney Vice Presidency."

[72] "Working Group Report," 50. Emphasis in original.

According to news reports, the 2002 and 2003 memoranda were produced as the result of requests to use torture techniques that came from
interrogators at Guantánamo, who were frustrated at their inability to
obtain information from resistant prisoners.[73] Yet, any government sanc-
tioning of such techniques would have directly contradicted the 1994
International Convention Against Torture and the Torture Victims Protection Act passed by Congress, among other international and domestic
acts. Thus, much of the text of the government memoranda and reports,
including the two cited here, offered arguments as to why these legal
enactments would not apply to sanctioned use of torture by American
military or other personnel.[74]

The Bush Administration's 2003 "Working Group Report" (hereafter,
the "Report"), presented to Defense Secretary Donald Rumsfeld, articulated a singularly broad and sweeping view of the CIC power. The evi-
dentiary support for its executive-power claims consisted almost entirely
of court cases, although its logic and case law cites were rooted in Yoo's
2001 memorandum, which in turn arose from his 1996 law journal article.
As the subsequent discussion shows, the Report's use of cases was highly
and misleadingly selective.

The administration's power claims in this Report can be summarized
as three sets of assertions, which I present in the next section. I then offer
a detailed critique of these three in order. The primary evidence cited in
the Report (as in the earlier Office of Legal Counsel document) is built
largely on selected quotes from court cases that misrepresent the actual
expressions of the Court. Contradictory conclusions from other cases are
ignored, as is the vast secondary material that also reaches conclusions
contrary to those of the administration.

Distorting the Courts

Assertion 1

The Report asserts that the president's CIC power is for the president to
exercise (1) alone and (2) with finality, verdicts buttressed by reference
to an 1874 Supreme Court case, *Hamilton v. Dillin*.[75] According to the

[73] Bravin, "Pentagon Report."
[74] In domestic law, the key sections are 18 U.S.C., sec. 2340 and 2340A, which criminalized
the use of torture committed by Americans within or outside of America's borders.
[75] 88 U.S. 73 (1874).

Report, "As the Supreme Court has recognized . . . the President enjoys complete discretion in the exercise of his Commander-in-Chief authority including in conducting operations against hostile forces." Then, quoting from *Hamilton*, the Report says that because "both '[t]he executive power and the command of the military and naval forces is vested in the President,' the Supreme Court has unanimously stated that it is '*the President alone* who is constitutionally invested with the *entire charge of hostile operations*.'"[76] Elsewhere in the Report, it asserts that "Congress lacks authority under Article I to set the terms and conditions under which the President may exercise his authority as Commander-in-Chief to control the conduct of operations during a war."[77] To emphasize the inviolate and singular nature of the CIC power, the Report asserts "the President's constitutionally superior position [superior in relation to Congress] as Chief Executive and Commander-in-Chief in the area of military operations."[78]

Assertion 2

The Report then asserts that "criminal statutes are not read as infringing on the President's ultimate authority in these areas" because the Supreme Court has established "a canon of statutory construction" that says that laws should be interpreted in a way that "avoids constitutional difficulties so long as a reasonable alternative construction is available."[79] This "avoidance canon" is especially pertinent, the Report asserts, in any instance when a statute might impinge on the constitutional powers of another branch of government. Therefore, because the CIC power is expressly granted in Article II to the president, the "avoidance canon" dictates that Congress not impinge on the president's CIC authority. And, when it comes to foreign affairs and the war power, where the president's power is considered to be even greater than domestic affairs, this canon becomes even more pertinent, according to the Report. Because Congress may not interfere with the CIC power through legislative enactment, the prohibition against torture (18 U.S.C., sec. 2340A), "as well as any other potentially applicable statute must be construed as inapplicable to interrogations undertaken pursuant to his [the president's] Commander-in-Chief authority. . . . Congress may no more regulate the President's ability

[76] "Working Group Report," 20. The quoted material is from *Hamilton v. Dillin* at 87. The Report's authors added the italics in the quote.
[77] "Working Group Report," 21.
[78] *Ibid.*, 21.   [79] *Ibid.*, 20.

to detain and interrogate enemy combatants than it may regulate his ability to direct troop movements on the battlefield."[80] Similarly, subordinates within the executive branch who engaged in such interrogations pursuant to the president's authority would also be exempt from prosecution arising from Congress-made law.

Assertion 3

The courts have concluded, according to the Report, that presidential decisions under the CIC power are also beyond the reach of the courts themselves. Citing and quoting the *Prize Cases*[81] from 1863, the Report says that President Lincoln's response to the Southern rebellion "was a question 'to be *decided by him*' and which the Court could not question, but must leave to 'the political department of the Government to which this power was entrusted.'"[82] The Report also cites as corroboration the courts' traditional reluctance to interfere with executive decisions in military and national security matters.

What *Hamilton* Says

The Report's heavy reliance on *Hamilton v. Dillin* obliges that it receive detailed attention here. A full reading of the case demonstrates that the Report's selective quotes from *Hamilton* are taken from it in a way that distorts and misrepresents the Court's sentiment; moreover, a full reading of the case actually contradicts the Report's assertions.

Hamilton is an obscure case[83] arising from the Civil War. Congress had granted President Lincoln the discretionary power to allow limited commerce with the Southern states during Civil War hostilities. Hamilton sued to recover fees he paid to ship cotton to the Union from Tennessee under this agreement, arguing that the fees imposed by the government were improperly levied. The Supreme Court disagreed, concluding that the fees were properly levied as part of the government's war power.

The Report argues, as summarized in Assertion 1 herein, that *Hamilton* confers sole discretion on the president, and the president alone, in all

---

[80] *Ibid.*, 21. [81] 67 U.S. 635 (1863).

[82] "Working Group Report," 24.

[83] *Hamilton* is not cited or mentioned in the most extensive and detailed book on cases related to presidential power, Peter M. Shane and Harold H. Bruff, *Separation of Powers Law* (Durham, NC: Carolina Academic Press, 1996).

matters relating to the conduct of military hostilities, exclusive of any control by Congress. Yet, the phrases quoted from *Hamilton* by the Report misrepresent the sentiment of the Court. Following is the full text (the two italicized phrases are those quoted in the Report):

> By the Constitution of the United States the power to declare war is con-fided to Congress. *The executive power and the command of the military and naval forces is vested in the President.* Whether, in the absence of Congressional action, the power of permitting partial intercourse with a public enemy may or may not be exercised by *the President alone, who is constitutionally invested with the entire charge of hostile operations*, it is not now necessary to decide, although it would seem that little doubt could be raised on the subject. In the case of *Cross v. Harrison*, it was held that the President, as commander-in-chief, had power to form a temporary civil government for California as a conquered country, and to impose duties on imports and tonnage for the support of the government and for aiding to sustain the burdens of the war, which were held valid until Congress saw fit to supersede them. . . . But without pursuing this inquiry, and whatever view may be taken as to the precise boundary between the legislative and executive powers in reference to the question under consideration, there is no doubt that a concurrence of both afford ample foundation for any regulations on the subject.[84]

Without doubt, the Court recognizes the broad power of the president as CIC. The question is whether the Report's view goes beyond this to assert that the CIC power is final and beyond any control or regulation by Congress, once Congress has exercised its power to declare war or the equivalent.[85] Yes, the president is "invested with the entire charge of hostile operations," but the full text makes clear that Congress is by no means excluded from this process under the *Hamilton* decision.

First, the Court considers the legality of presidential action in light of the fact that it occurred "in the absence of congressional action," the obvious inference being that the imprimatur of supportive congressional action would have tipped the scales in favor of the disputed executive actions, just as action by Congress barring the president from the acts in

[84] *Hamilton v. Dillin*, at 87–88.
[85] No actual declaration of war was enacted for the Civil War, given the government's assumption that the conflict was a domestic insurrection, not a conflict with a sep-arate sovereign entity. Congress did, however, enact various legislative measures to, in effect, authorize federal action against the South. Fisher, *Presidential War Power*, 47–51.

WHAT *HAMILTON* SAYS 113

question would have cut the legs out from under the president. This statement by itself is the Court's express allegiance to Congress's rightful and
decisive power over the executive actions in dispute. Second, the illustra-
tive example cited by the Court of *Cross v. Harrison* is one of comparable
presidential discretion, but subject to congressional intercession ("until
Congress saw fit to supersede them"), should it choose to do so. Again,
the Court is acknowledging here that presidential CIC decisions could
indeed be subject to subsequent congressional control. Third, the Court
concludes the paragraph by saying that, regardless of these particulars,
the circumstances in *Hamilton* are best understood in light of decisions
of both Congress and the president, thus recognizing shared decision
making. The Court is emphatically not saying in *Hamilton*, as the Report
would have it, that the CIC power is unilateral and untouchable by the
legislature. Although Congress may grant the president, whether in law
or in fact, wide latitude to prosecute a war or other military conflict that
Congress has authorized or begun, Congress is hardly barred from subsequent legislative or other regulatory involvement, whether to constrain,
modify, or expand the president's actions as CIC. And, as the courts have
noted on many other occasions, the CIC's actions stand on firmest footing
when buttressed by legislative authorization.[86]

Even more important, when the *Hamilton* case is examined as a whole,
it is clear that the Court embraces a very different model of the CIC power
from that espoused by the Report. It is, first, a conventional shared-power
view, as seen, for example, in the Court's repeated references to "the
war power of the United States government."[87] Second, even though
Hamilton's suit was aimed at the Treasury Department, which levied
and collected the disputed fees, the Court noted that Treasury's actions,
although a consequence of President Lincoln's decisions, were ultimately
the result of several prior acts of Congress. In fact, the Court began
its analysis with this: "Our first inquiry, therefore, will be, whether the
action of the executive was authorized, or, if not originally authorized,
was confirmed by Congress."[88] That is, the Court's first and most important question to resolve the matter before it (i.e., the legitimacy of the fees

---

[86] The most well-known, although hardly only, statement of this principle is Justice Robert
Jackson's famous concurring opinion in *Youngstown Sheet & Tube v. Sawyer*, 343 U.S.
579 (1952).
[87] For example, *Hamilton v. Dillin*, at 87, 97.
[88] *Hamilton v. Dillin*, at 88.

imposed by the executive branch) was whether Congress had authorized them either before or after the fact.[89]

This is important because Congress's legislative enactments of 1861, 1863, and 1864 authorized the president to declare by proclamation a specific set of actions regarding which commercial trade could and could not occur between Southern and Northern states. It therefore represented the very kind of action that the Report claims was barred by *Hamilton*: that is, the exercise of congressional authority over specific aspects of "hostile operations" against the South. If the president's "entire charge of hostile operations" were beyond Congress's control, then President Lincoln would not have needed approval from Congress for the actions, once Congress had recognized the existence of the state of hostilities between the North and the South. Thus, both the facts and the conclusion of the *Hamilton* case contradict the Report's interpretation.

Finally, the *Hamilton* Court rests its decision in support of the government's actions on the "concurrence of both" legislative and executive branches. This is surely the antithesis of the Report's unsubstantiated proposition that the CIC power is not only separate from but also somehow superior to or beyond the reach of legislative powers.

I turn now to other evidence cited by the Report in order to examine the veracity of the three sets of assertions that underlie the Bush administration's document. As was true of *Hamilton*, the Report misrepresents the conclusions of other Court cases, and omits other key evidence.

Other Cases

The Report also cites a few other cases in support of its view of the CIC power. It quotes the *Department of Navy v. Egan*, a 1988 case, as saying "unless Congress specifically has provided otherwise, courts traditionally have been reluctant to intrude upon the authority of the Executive in military and national security affairs."[90] Yet, this cite undercuts the

---

[89] In the early months of the Civil War, Lincoln acted unilaterally, without congressional authority, to meet the military crisis posed by the secession of the Southern states. Once Congress convened in July 1861, he sought and received retroactive legislative authority for the actions he had taken, a fact that the *Prize* Court noted with approval as important to upholding Lincoln's actions.

[90] "Working Group Report," 20; quoted from *Department of Navy v. Egan*, 484 U.S. 518, 530 (1988).

Report's premise because it expressly notes the Court's approving nod to the existence of congressional authority to intrude (even though such intrusion might be "reluctant" on the part of Congress). Recognizing this, the Report then casts aspersions on the prospect of congressional interference by referring to "the President's constitutionally superior position as Chief Executive and Commander-in-Chief in the area of military operations," citing *Department of Navy* where it, in turn, cites a 1981 case, *Haig v. Agee*, which the Report cites this way: "deference to Executive Branch is 'especially' appropriate 'in the area of national security.'"[91] This reference to deference to the executive as being especially appropriate is a far cry from an expression or endorsement by the Court of presidential "superiority" as either chief executive or CIC. Moreover, an examination of *Haig* reveals an approving discussion by the Court of foreign policy powers shared by "the political branches," executive and legislative – again, at odds with the Report's unilateralist view.[92] Finally, the *Haig* case dealt with the revocation of a citizen's passport – a diplomatic matter that, as *Haig* noted,[93] Congress had previously delegated to the executive.

The Report's second assertion, as described previously, posits a judicial "canon of statutory construction" that seeks to avoid circumstances in which one branch of government might impinge on another's constitutional powers. Because the courts often note that executive power in foreign affairs is entitled to special deference (while also noting Congress's right to regulate through legislation), Congress may not apply criminal statutes to actions implemented in connection with the President's CIC power, argues the Report.

Yet, early in the country's history, the courts said otherwise. A federal circuit court in 1806 upheld the criminal prosecution of Colonel William Smith for military actions that he claimed were "begun, prepared, and set on foot with the knowledge and approbation of the executive department of our government." Rejecting Smith's claim that the president could authorize actions in contradiction to congressional enactments, Supreme Court Justice William Paterson, riding circuit in the New York federal

---

[91] "Working Group Report," 21; *Haig v. Agee*, 453 U.S. 280, 291 (1981). The quote-within-a-quote wording is from *Haig*.

[92] *Haig* at 291–292 cites *Chicago & Southern Air Lines v. Waterman S.S. Corp*, 333 U.S. 103 (1948); *Harisiades v. Shaughnessy*, 342 U.S. 580 (1952); and *Zemel v. Rusk*, 381 U.S. 1 (1965).

[93] *Haig* at 293–94.

court, ruled that "The president of the United States cannot control the statute, nor dispense with its execution, and still less can he authorize a person to do what the law forbids." Assuming the president had known about the actions, "it would not justify the defendant in a court of law, nor discharge him from the binding force of the act of congress." Despite the fact that the decision did not come from the full Supreme Court, it is notable because Justice Paterson had been a delegate to the Constitutional Convention of 1787 and had participated in the drafting of the war-powers clause.[94]

Congress has long deferred to executive judgments in foreign and military policy, and that deference increased from the nineteenth to the twentieth centuries, as Congress yielded ever more discretion to the executive. None of this history means, however, that Congress may not regulate executive-branch conduct, including war-related decisions.[95] Congress's foundational constitutional powers to declare war and to organize, regulate, and finance the military provide Congress with every ability to apply criminal statutes to executive-branch conduct in military or other matters. Indeed, Congress created the modern Uniform Code of Military Justice in 1950, the system of criminal law separate from the civilian criminal justice system that defines and punishes criminal activity within the military establishment, including allegations of torture.[96] And, throughout American history, Congress has regulated through legislation numerous aspects of executive authority during wartime, including activities carried out by presidents acting through CIC power.[97] In 1942, the Supreme Court observed this about Congress's ability to apply the legislative power to executive actions, even as CIC:

> The Constitution thus invests the President as Commander in Chief with the power to wage war which Congress has declared, and to carry into effect

---

[94] *U.S. v. Smith*, 27 Fed. Cas. 1192, 1229 (C.C.N.Y. 1806). Quoted in Irons, *War Powers*, 40–41. See also Fisher, *Congressional Abdication*, 19–20.

[95] See, for example, Rossiter, *The Supreme Court and the Commander in Chief*, 89–92.

[96] The Uniform Code of Military Justice of 1950, 64 Stat. 107. Prior congressional enactments regarding military justice date to the Continental Congress, and congressional enactments beginning in 1789, with significant enactments in 1863 and 1916. See Louis Fisher, *Military Tribunals and Presidential Power: American Revolution to the War on Terrorism* (Lawrence, KS: University Press of Kansas, 2005).

[97] For a list of congressional legislation pertinent to presidential CIC actions in wartime, see Corwin, *The President*, chap. 6; Killian, *The Constitution of the United States of America*, 349–51.

all laws passed by Congress for the conduct of war and for the government and regulation of the Armed Forces, and all laws defining and punishing offences against the law of nations, including those which pertain to the conduct of war.[98]

More recently, Congress has imposed specific statutory restrictions to constrain military actions and decisions taken or contemplated by the president as CIC in Vietnam, Angola, Nicaragua, Honduras, and Costa Rica.[99] Although Congress might be ill-advised to micro-manage operational or battlefield decisions, it does not somehow surrender its authority once hostilities have begun.

In fact, political scientist Clinton Rossiter summarized Court decisions pertaining to the CIC power as it relates to congressional authority in a very different way. Writing more than a half-century ago, Rossiter said, "the Court has made it a practice never to approve a challenged presidential or military order solely on the authority of the commander-in-chief clause if it can find a more specific and less controversial basis." The courts "will do everything in their power to avoid considering an unusual action in terms of the President's power alone, and will seize with manifest relief on any evidence of congressional approval."[100] This was as true in 1951, the year Rossiter's book was published, as it was in 2004, as the following discussion of that year's *Hamdi* case shows.

The Report's third assertion, as described previously, is that presidential decisions taken as CIC are beyond the reach of the courts, citing the *Prize Cases*, saying that Lincoln's response to the Southern rebellion "was a question 'to be *decided by him*' and which the Court could not question, but must leave to 'the political department of the Government to which this power was entrusted [italics added in Report].'"[101] Is the *Prize* court actually saying that the courts may play no role in matters regarding the president's exercise of the CIC power?

Following is the full paragraph from the 1863 case, with the phrases quoted by the Report in italics:

Whether the President in fulfilling his duties, as Commander-in-chief, in suppressing an insurrection, has met with such armed hostile resistance,

---

[98] *Ex parte Quirin*, 317 U.S. 1, at 26 (1942).
[99] Louis Fisher, "Congressional Checks on Military Initiatives," *Political Science Quarterly* 109(Winter 1994–95): 756–58.
[100] Rossiter, *The Supreme Court and the Commander in Chief*, 6.
[101] "Working Group Report," 24.

and a civil war of such alarming proportions as will compel him to accord to them the character of belligerents, is a question *to be decided by him*, and this Court must be governed by the decisions and acts of *the political department of the Government to which this power was entrusted.* 'He must determine what degree of force the crisis demands.' The proclamation of blockade is itself official and conclusive evidence to the Court that a state of war existed which demanded and authorized a recourse to such a measure, under the circumstances peculiar to the case.[102]

The *Prize Cases* arose because of a naval blockade thrown up around Southern ports after the outbreak of the Civil War, at the direction of President Lincoln, but without congressional authority (Congress later gave its authorization). The owners of ships seized by Union vessels sued for their return, arguing that the seizures resulted from orders that Lincoln did not have the power to give. The Court upheld the seizures, saying that the president was obligated to meet the emergency as it confronted the country. In the just-quoted excerpt, the Court accepts Lincoln's argument that military action was necessary. A court is a court, not a phantom CIC. But the Court is not saying that CIC decisions are beyond its reach. Were that so, it should and would not have agreed to hear the case or, if to hear it, to say that Lincoln's actions as CIC could not be reviewed by the Court on their merits. And, the circumstances giving rise to the *Prize Cases* were those when, in the absence of congressional approval, the CIC power is greatest: responding to an attack on the United States.[103]

More important, the Court has ruled on the merits of the CIC power in other cases. In *Little v. Barreme* (1804) in particular, the Court invalidated a presidential proclamation in time of war because it contradicted a contrary congressional statute.[104] Other cases where the Supreme Court ruled on the merits of the CIC power include *Ex Parte Quirin* (1942), *Korematsu v. U.S.* (1944), and *Youngstown Sheet and Tube v. Sawyer* (1952).[105]

---

[102] *Prize Cases*, 67 U.S. 635, 670 (1863).

[103] Oddly, the "Working Group Report" does not use this argument of CIC powers as greatest when the country is subject to a sudden attack to good effect.

[104] 6 U.S. 170 (1804).

[105] Rossiter's entire 1951 book is an exegesis on areas of law where the Supreme Court has ruled on these aspects of the CIC power: the president's powers of martial rule, defensive war, courts-martial and military commissions, and authority over conquered territory. Rossiter also examines Court rulings regarding Congress's war powers and the Courts' lack of power to declare peace. *The Supreme Court and the Commander in Chief*. Rossiter also describes how "the Supreme Court, in deciding several hundred cases involving the scope of the national war powers, has interpreted the President's

Most of these cases are not cited in the Report, a fact that yielded fierce criticisms from the legal community when the Report was made public. Various legal writers called the research in the Report "extreme, one-sided and poorly supported by the legal authority relied on," "embarrassingly weak, just short of reckless." Noting the failure to mention the keystone *Youngstown* case, another commentator concluded that "[i]t is not legitimate to produce a legal opinion that fails even to cite the most relevant landmark Supreme Court precedent."[106]

In the recent case of *Hamdi v. Rumsfeld* (2004), the Court squarely confronted and rejected the Bush administration's contentions that decisions made by and under the CIC power were unreviewable by the courts and beyond the reach of Congress. Although the Report was written a year before *Hamdi*, its arguments were addressed by the Court in its decision. Regarding the role of Congress, the Bush administration argued before the Court that no authorization from Congress was required as a basis for the president's actions because his Article II powers were sufficient. Yet, the administration evidently lacked confidence in this view because it also argued that congressional enactments supported its actions. While the Court said that it chose not to rule on whether executive authority alone was sufficient to justify the president's actions, it did choose to accept the administration's "alternative position," which was predicated on interbranch authority:

> The Government maintains that no explicit congressional authorization is required, because the Executive possesses plenary authority to detain pursuant to Article II of the Constitution. We do not reach the question whether Article II provides such authority, however, because we agree with the Government's alternative position, that Congress has in fact authorized Hamdi's detention, through the AUMF [Authorization for Use of Military Force, enacted immediately after the 9/11 attacks].[107]

status and authority as commander in chief." *The Supreme Court and the Commander in Chief*, v. Yet, Rossiter also notes that Court involvement in such matters has been minimal and that for the most part, war-related matters have been determined by the president, Congress, and the people (126–132).

[106] Liptak, "Legal Scholars Criticize Torture Memos." Yale Law School Dean Harold Koh (who worked in the Clinton administration) called the torture memorandum "perhaps the most clearly erroneous legal opinion I have ever read." Quoted in Joseph Margulies, *Guantánamo and the Abuse of Presidential Power* (New York: Simon and Schuster, 2006), 91.

[107] *Hamdi v. Rumsfeld*, 542 U.S. 507 (2004), at 516–17.

On the question of whether the courts had a right to intervene, *Hamdi* was more emphatic:

> While we accord the greatest respect and consideration to the judgments of military authorities in matters relating to the actual prosecution of a war, and recognize that the scope of that discretion necessarily is wide, it does not infringe on the core role of the military for the courts to exercise their own time-honored and constitutionally mandated roles of reviewing and resolving claims like those presented here.[108]

The Court then expressed displeasure with an executive-only justification for military action, evincing instead a clear preference for a shared-powers view for the exercise of war-related authority, consistent with the view found in *Hamilton*, the *Prize Cases*, and twentieth-century cases:

> [W]e necessarily reject the Government's assertion that separation of powers principles mandate a heavily circumscribed role for the courts in such circumstances. Indeed, the position that the courts must forgo any examination of the individual case and focus exclusively on the legality of the broader detention scheme cannot be mandated by any reasonable view of separation of powers, as this approach serves only to *condense* power into a single branch of government. We have long since made clear that a state of war is not a blank check for the President when it comes to the rights of the Nation's citizens. *Youngstown Sheet & Tube*, 343 U.S., at 587, 96 L. Ed. 1153, 72 S. Ct. 863. Whatever power the United States Constitution envisions for the Executive in its exchanges with other nations or with enemy organizations in times of conflict, it most assuredly envisions a role for all three branches when individual liberties are at stake.[109]

In 2006, the Supreme Court again issued a sharp rebuke to Bush administration assertions of unilateral authority in *Hamdan v. Rumsfeld*.[110] In a 5–3 vote, the Court rejected the Bush administration's plan to try detainees at Guantánamo base by military commission on the grounds that the administration had no statutory authority to take such action (it subsequently obtained congressional approval later that year), and that it violated the Uniform Code of Military Justice. It also said that the commissions violated international law, saying that the government had to abide by

---

[108] *Hamdi*, 535.

[109] *Hamdi*, 535–36. The Court goes on to say that allowing the executive the right to deny a citizen the right of the writ of habeas corpus "would turn our system of checks and balances on its head"; only Congress could suspend the writ for a citizen detained as an enemy combatant (at 536).

[110] *Hamdan v. Rumsfeld*, 165 L.Ed. 2d 723 (2006).

Common Article 3 of the Geneva Conventions (which the United States signed in 1949) pertaining to the treatment of the detainees. And, the Court rejected the idea that it lacked jurisdiction to decide the case.[111]

Although *Hamdi* and *Hamdan* were significant rebukes to Bush administration positions, it would be a mistake to view these cases, or past Court rulings, as a defeat for strong executive authority in foreign policy or military matters. The repeated, almost slavish devotion to broad executive authority in foreign affairs found almost uniformly in Court cases dealing with such matters grants the executive branch enormous leeway – far more than exists in domestic affairs.[112] Nevertheless, extant Court rulings on the subject reject the extremist view of unitary executive control advanced by the Bush administration in the Report.[113]

A Political Document or a Legal One?

Leaving aside the numerous problems with the research, arguments, and conclusions found in the "Working Group Report," the document could be minimized, or perhaps even dismissed, for a number of seemingly plausible reasons. First, the document was the product of an internal, executive branch review intended to be kept confidential for a decade, suggesting a deliberate preference to keep the views expressed therein out of the public (and, by inference, the legal) debate. Second, the Report can be viewed as lawyers' mental gymnastics – an on-paper vetting of

---

[111] Linda Greenhouse, "Justices, 5–3, Broadly Reject Bush Plan to Try Detainees," *New York Times*, June 30, 2006, A1.

[112] The Court's repetitively expressed deference to the executive in foreign policy matters is found not only in foreign policy cases but in those dealing with domestic policy as well. See Michael A. Genovese and Robert J. Spitzer, *The Presidency and the Constitution: Cases and Controversies* (New York: Palgrave/Macmillan, 2005).

[113] Even on the current Supreme Court, there is support for the Bush administration view of executive power. As noted, Justice Alito helped construct this view when he worked in the Reagan White House in the 1980s. In his dissent in the *Hamdi* case, Justice Clarence Thomas embraced the Bush administration's arguments, in that he agreed that the Court did not have the right to adjudicate, and in his citation of the unitary theory: "This detention falls squarely within the Federal Government's war powers, and we lack the expertise and capacity to second-guess that decision" (579); "The Founders intended that the President have primary responsibility – along with the necessary power – to protect the national security and to conduct the Nation's foreign relations. They did so principally because the structural advantages of a unitary Executive are essential in these domains" (580). Chief Justice John Roberts may also have similar sympathies, based on his prior record as an appellate court judge.

arguments and ideas to defend a policy position for the sake of examining the boundaries of an idea. The existence of the Report in and of itself does not necessarily mean that it was, or would have become, Bush administration policy. This was, in fact, the public explanation for this and other memoranda made public in 2004 that justified the American use of torture. According to White House Counsel Alberto Gonzales, this and other memoranda were "unnecessary, over-broad discussions" that were "not relied upon" by the administration. "In reality, they do not reflect the policies that the administration ultimately adopted."[114]

Yet, the reasons in support of taking this and other similar documents seriously are considerable. First, the fact that the Report is a lawyer's brief on behalf of the unitary executive position and not a balanced scholarly examination does not render it irrelevant to policy-making – quite the contrary. If anything, the Report's one-sidedness reveals an administration that had already decided the direction in which it wished to proceed and had gone in search of a post hoc legal justification to legitimize conclusions already drawn. Later news reports confirmed this verdict when it was reported that these key policies were formulated by three top administration lawyers: "Addington, Flanigan and Gonzales were really a triumvirate," according to former White House associate counsel Bradford A. Berenson. With Vice President Cheney pulling the strings, these decision makers bypassed the Secretary of State, the national security advisor, the Justice Department, the intelligence agencies, and the other offices and officials who would normally have played a major decision-making role in such matters.[115] As former Bush administration advisor Philip Zelikow concluded, the legal opinions of this handful of lawyers "became policy guides."[116] For this reason alone, the shroud of academic legitimacy attached to John Yoo's work on this subject insofar as it was dubbed "scholarly" becomes critical in elevating it above the merely "political."

Second, the administration's quoted repudiation of these positions does not actually disavow the views expressed, and actions speak louder than words. When the administration reversed itself in December 2004 and

[114] Quoted in Dana Milbank, "The Administration vs. the Administration," *Washington Post*, June 29, 2004, A21.

[115] Gellman and Becker, "The Cheney Vice Presidency."

[116] Philip Zelikow, "Legal Policy for a Twilight War," Annual Lecture, *Houston Journal of International Law*, April 26, 2007, accessed at http://www.hnn.us/articles/39494.html on May 30, 2007.

publicly disavowed its previous permissive arguments on behalf of torture, it remained silent on its prior views related to CIC powers. According to one account, the administration's policy revision "pointedly *does not* retreat from the position in the Bybee/Yoo memo that the commander in chief has the inherent power to overrule Congress and order the use of torture."[117] Further, during his confirmation hearings before the U.S. Senate in January 2005, attorney general nominee Gonzales said, when asked if he believed that the president had the power to ignore a congressional ban on torture if he felt it to be unconstitutional, "I guess I would have to say that hypothetically that authority may exist."[118] And, speaking to a gathering of legal scholars in 2006 (and three months after the *Hamdan* case ruling), Gonzales said that "A proper sense of judicial humility requires judges to keep in mind the institutional limitations of the judiciary and the duties expressly assigned by the Constitution to the more politically accountable branches." Removing all doubt about his reference, he continued: "The Constitution, for example, clearly makes the President the Commander in Chief of the armed forces. . . . The Supreme Court has long recognized, moreover, the executive's pre-eminent role in foreign affairs. The Constitution, by contrast, provides the courts with relatively few tools to superintend military and foreign policy decisions, especially during war time. Judges must resist the temptation to supplement those tools based on their own personal views. . . ."[119] Gonzales's comments were widely interpreted to be a warning to the courts regarding the then-brewing controversy over the handling of detainees and likely subsequent litigation expected in the aftermath of legislation enacted to give the administration the power to create military tribunals.[120]

Third, the positions set out in the Report are consistent with the Bush administration's "expansive view of presidential power," seen particularly

[117] Margulies, *Guantánamo and the Abuse of Presidential Power*, 108.
[118] Daniel Levin, Acting Assistant Attorney General, Office of Legal Counsel, U.S. Department of Justice, "Memorandum for James B. Comey, Deputy Attorney General," December 30, 2004; accessed at http://www.usdoj.gov/olc/dagmemo.pdf; Eric Lichtblau, "Gonzales Speaks Against Torture at Senate Confirmation Hearing," *New York Times*, January 7, 2005, A18.
[119] "Prepared Remarks of Attorney General Alberto R. Gonzales at the Georgetown Judiciary Conference," September 29, 2006, accessed at www.usnewswire.com on September 30, 2006.
[120] For example, see Jurist Legal News and Research, http://jurist.law.pitt.edu/paperchase, accessed on September 30, 2006. Coincidentally, retired Supreme Court Justice Sandra Day O'Connor, speaking at the same conference earlier in the week, warned against growing efforts at "judicial intimidation."

in its approach to national security matters, with White House Counsel Gonzales dubbed by the *New York Times* as Bush's "architect of widening executive authority."[121] More specifically, the Report's views found their way into administration briefs before the courts (referenced, e.g., in the quotes from the *Hamdi* case) as well as in other public and official pronouncements. For example, in testimony before the U.S. Senate Judiciary Committee in 2002, John Yoo testified on behalf of the administration that the president's chief executive power, along with his authority as CIC, "make clear that the president has the constitutional authority to introduce U.S. armed forces into hostilities when appropriate, with or without specific congressional authorization."[122] Another primary architect of presidential power expansionism, Vice President Dick Cheney, has said repeatedly that presidential power needs to be increased because of its alleged decline in recent years. According to Cheney: "I have repeatedly seen an erosion of the powers and ability of the president of the United States to do his job. . . . We are weaker today as an institution because of the unwise compromises that have been made over the last 30 to 35 years."[123] Cheney's chief architect and point man for this view, David Addington, is a well-known proponent of the "unitary executive" view (discussed previously), which considers presidential power as both too little and in need of expansion.[124] The idea that presidential power has receded in the last three decades is, as noted previously, at odds with most scholarly assessments of the institution[125] and met with widespread

---

[121] Eric Lichtblau, "Broad Influence for Justice Dept. Choice," *New York Times*, November 21, 2004, 30.

[122] John Yoo, Deputy Assistant Attorney General, Office of Legal Counsel, U.S. Department of Justice, "Applying the War Powers Resolution to the War on Terrorism," testimony before the Subcommittee on the Constitution, Committee on the Judiciary, U.S. Senate, April 17, 2002.

[123] Dana Milbank, "In Cheney's Shadow, Counsel Pushes the Conservative Cause," *Washington Post*, October 11, 2004, A21.

[124] According to the *Washington Post*, "Addington's influence – like Cheney's overall – extends throughout the government in his bid to expand executive power. He goes through every page of the federal budget in search of riders that could restrict executive authority. He meets daily with White House Counsel Alberto R. Gonzales and often raises objections to requests for information from Congress or the public, officials say. He also routinely works to defeat proposals from the State Department, where the pervasive internationalist philosophy is at odds with Cheney's neoconservatism." Milbank, "In Cheney's Shadow."

[125] For example, Spitzer, *President and Congress*; Kenneth R. Mayer, *With the Stroke of a Pen* (Princeton, NJ: Princeton University Press, 2001); Phillip J. Cooper, *By Order*

condemnation from the legal community, human rights groups, and even military lawyers.[126] Even conservatives that might be expected to be sympathetic to the Bush administration, such as lawyer Bruce Fein, find fault with the administration's view. Speaking of Addington and others in the administration, Fein said: "They're in a time warp. If you look at the facts, presidential powers have never been higher."[127]

In a speech before the Federalist Society in November 2004 (shortly before he left office), Attorney General Ashcroft also fired a broadside directed at the courts for their decisions against Bush administration actions abroad, saying that "judicial activists" "threaten the president's constitutional responsibility to defend American lives and liberties. . . . The danger I see here," Ashcroft continued, "is that intrusive judicial oversight and second-guessing of presidential determinations in these critical areas can put at risk the very security of our nation in a time of war."[128] In the face of the Court's rebuke in *Hamdi* and other cases, Ashcroft's response was that the Court's rulings are harmful to national security. One may reasonably conclude that the aggressive advancement of presidential power is a publicly articulated and continuing Bush administration priority, including but not limited to the CIC power.

Conclusion: Reinventing the Commander-in-Chief

The strong-president/whig-president debate is nearly as old as the institution itself. From the Pacificus–Helvidius debates between Madison and Hamilton in the 1790s, to the classic statements of presidential activism and restraint by Theodore Roosevelt and William H. Taft,[129] respectively, to the present, no final single conclusion can be drawn regarding the

---

of the President (Lawrence, KS: University Press of Kansas, 2002); William G. Howell, *Power Without Persuasion* (Princeton, NJ: Princeton University Press, 2003).

[126] Liptak, "Legal Scholars Criticize Torture Memos"; Adam Liptak, "How Far Can a Government Lawyer Go?," *New York Times*, June 27, 2004, 4–3; Dana Priest and R. Jeffrey Smith, "Memo Offered Justification for Use of Torture," *Washington Post*, June 8, 2004, A1.

[127] Milbank, "In Cheney's Shadow."

[128] "Prepared Remarks of Attorney General John Ashcroft," delivered before the Federalist Society, November 12, 2004. Accessed at http://www.usdoj.gov/ag/speeches/2004/111204federalist.htm

[129] Readings on the presidency typically include these writings by Roosevelt and Taft, among others. See, for example, James P. Pfiffner and Roger H. Davidson, eds., *Understanding the Presidency* (New York: Pearson Longman, 2007).

scope and dimensions of the president's powers expressed in the brief and naggingly vague Article II. That does not mean, however, that there is no agreed-upon meaning or that it is a constitutional Rorschach inkblot upon which any politician or lawyer may impose any meaning that suits contemporary political ends. Just as the constitutionally granted presidential veto does not include a constitutional item veto, as discussed in Chapter 3 (whether it should do so is an entirely different question), neither does the constitutional CIC power bestow upon the president the power to ignore law or brush aside the idea of judicial review. These actions may be good or bad, necessary or unnecessary, beneficial or pernicious, but they are not authorized by the wording of Article II, sec. 2.

Indeed, strong arguments can and have been made that the president should exercise CIC powers more broadly, based on some combination of prerogative powers, strategic necessity, political consensus, and historical evolution of an office (and a nation) that has undergone dramatic growth and change in two hundred years. One of the most vigorous proponents of the strong presidency in recent decades, Clinton Rossiter, epitomized the combination of a realistic view of founders' intentions with unabashed preference for the modern strong presidency. "The framers of the Constitution," Rossiter observed, "to be sure, took a narrow view of the [commander-in-chief] authority they had granted."[130] Yet, he also understood and approved of presidential efforts to enlarge the CIC power: "We have placed a shocking amount of military power in the President's keeping, but where else, we may ask, could it possibly have been placed?"[131] Writing more recently about the war power, political scientist David Mervin concedes that the standard view of the CIC power as defined in the Constitution "is broadly correct." Yet, he continues, "there are grounds for questioning how far those original aims should continue to control constitutional interpretation." After all, "the framers, for all their undoubted wisdom, got some things disastrously wrong by modern standards."[132]

It is beyond dispute that both the United States and the office of the presidency are profoundly different in the twenty-first century than in the

---

[130] Rossiter, *The American Presidency*, 22.   [131] *Ibid.*, 23.

[132] David Mervin, "Demise of the War Clause," *Presidential Studies Quarterly* 30 (December 2000): 770–71. For a similar view, see Richard M. Pious, "Resolved, Presidents Have Usurped the War Power that Rightfully Belongs to Congress," and the opposing essay by Nancy Kassop, in *Debating the Presidency*, eds. Richard J. Ellis and Michael Nelson (Washington, DC: CQ Press, 2006), 92–109.

eighteenth, and that the demands of modern political reality necessitate a considerably expanded executive power. As noted at the beginning of this chapter, the modern separation of powers arrangement is not the legislative-centered system it was in the late eighteenth and early nineteenth centuries. It is also a truism that the constitutional system has survived a span of four centuries largely because it has been flexible enough to adapt to changes that no one could have anticipated in 1787.

Yet, none of these arguments for a strong executive justifies the invention of a fictionalized constitutional past. The desire to mold constitutional, originalist understandings to fit contemporary political needs is understandable but reprehensible. The first job of academic scholars is to make every effort to get it right. The abiding concerns of this book are that legal training encourages deceptive constitutional arguments and that law journals make it far too easy for writing that possesses the trappings of scholarship to get it wrong.

In the case of the Bush administration's views regarding the CIC power, they are of immediate significance not only for that administration's actions and decisions but also because they may be drawn on by future administrations to justify subsequent actions and theories not otherwise supported by past arguments or precedent. The history of the presidency is littered with examples of such precedent-based justifications.

In addition, however, the significance of these views extends in two other directions. One occurs when the policy's architects become decision makers and law school faculty. Jay Bybee, for example, a chief author of several of the internal Bush administration documents when he served as head of the Department of Justice's Office of Legal Counsel, is now a federal judge on the U.S. Court of Appeals for the Ninth Circuit, a vantage point from which he may well have the opportunity to apply the views he helped construct. And, although he did not serve in the second Bush administration, Supreme Court Justice Alito was elevated to the high court by Bush and is similarly positioned to ratify the suspect unitary theory he helped invent in the 1980s. Lawyers joining law school faculty have been and will also be well positioned to advance these arguments in the classroom and in publications.

The other direction is public debate and public policy. A one-sided lawyer's brief that morphs into the government's legal position and that, in turn, becomes policy describes a policy process built on an inadequate foundation and false pretenses. As Zelikow warned, such processes as they unfolded in the second Bush administration were "developed and implemented in a flawed manner" because of "the way law and lawyers were used to rationalize the policy and frame the debate."[133] Another recent critique of the second Bush presidency charges that "Government lawyers have become instruments by which fundamental constitutional principles are eroded." The series of memoranda discussed in this chapter, issued by Bush's lawyers, has pushed the nation's government "to a monarchical vision . . . with a correlative neutering of the Constitution's checks and balances."[134]

One might argue, of course, that the Bush administration would have proceeded much as it did with or without John Yoo's law journal writings. Yet, as this account has shown, the role of such writings was vital because they invented and legitimated a constitutional provenance for a contemporary legal construct that gave the unitary CIC a kind of status and dignity that it could not have otherwise claimed.

When former President Richard Nixon offered as a justification for his involvement in the Watergate scandal the excuse that "When the president does it, that means that it is not illegal,"[135] no one accepted that statement as a serious or valid legal (much less constitutional) defense; in fact, Nixon's pronouncement was received with little more than guffaws. Yet, the law journal writings on the CIC power have succeeded in constructing a constitutional edifice around Nixon's statement – and no one is laughing now.

---

[133] Zelikow, "Legal Policy for a Twilight War."
[134] Frederick A. O. Schwarz, Jr., and Aziz Z. Huq, *Unchecked and Unbalanced: Presidential Power in a Time of Terror* (New York: The New Press, 2007), 187.
[135] Quoted in Stanley I. Cutler, *The Wars of Watergate* (New York: Knopf, 1990), 614. The comment was from Nixon's interview by David Frost in 1977.

5 . . . . . The Second Amendment

In a notable, even startling case that received nationwide attention, the U.S. Court of Appeals for the District of Columbia Circuit ruled in 2007 that a DC law barring city residents from keeping handguns in their homes violated citizens' Second Amendment right to have guns, aside and apart from service in a militia. This 2–1 decision in *Parker v. District of Columbia*[1] was notable for two reasons: first, it contradicted four Supreme Court rulings and nearly fifty lower federal court rulings on the meaning of the Second Amendment; and second, if allowed to stand, it would be the first time in American history that a federal court had struck down a gun-control law as a violation of the Second Amendment (in late 2007, the Supreme Court agreed to hear the case as *District of Columbia v. Heller*). Woven throughout the *Parker* decision were arguments from and references to law journal articles and other cases that cited those articles, which developed and advanced the *Parker* majority's view of this amendment. If allowed to stand, this decision could have profound policy consequences for American gun laws, not only in the nation's capital but also throughout the country.[2]

A large and increasingly influential body of legal writing has argued for a new and very different interpretation of the Second Amendment's

---

[1] 478 F.3d 370 (D.D. Cir. 2007).
[2] Jeffrey Rosen, "Forced into a Gun Debate," *Time Magazine*, May 7, 2007, 33; Robert J. Spitzer, "Working Hard to Misconstrue the 2nd Amendment," History News Network, March 12, 2007, accessed at http://hnn.us/articles/36395.html. The Supreme Court was scheduled to hear oral argument in the *Heller* case (No. 07-290) in March 2008, with a

fabled "right to bear arms" – different, that is, from the verdict delivered by the Constitution's founders, history, and the courts. This emerging discourse, which I refer herein to generally as the individualist view, shares three key traits. First, this new theory of the Second Amendment has emerged and proliferated almost entirely from lawyers writing in law journals; second, this emergent body of writing is exerting progressively more influence over Second Amendment interpretation, writings in the public press, and perhaps public policy; and third, this new theory of the Second Amendment is stunningly and fatally defective.

Other writing covers, in considerable detail, the substance of the arguments concerning the basis for and meaning of the Second Amendment.[3] I therefore raise them much more briefly here. Virtually any discussion of the right to bear arms presupposes a debate over gun control. But the primary purpose of this chapter is not to rehash arguments over the utility, desirability, or consequences of gun control. Perfectly respectable arguments on that subject can and have been made on both sides of the ever-contentious gun debate.[4] Instead, this chapter examines the provenance of Second Amendment writings as they have evolved in law journals, to compare this provenance with claims made about it, and to discuss the distinctive traits of this literature's development – distinctive, that is, in comparison with scholarly writing in other disciplines, yet entirely parallel with the other law journal writing discussed in this book.

This chapter first provides a brief explication of the meaning of the Second Amendment. It then examines the manner in which the debate over this amendment has been depicted in recent news accounts, and then proceeds to the two chief, emergent critiques of Second Amendment analysis: the individualist view and the so-called right of revolution. Following that, four collateral claims arising from and connected with the individualist and revolutionist perspectives are examined in the light of an assessment of the provenance of Second Amendment writings in law journals, as is the reputed role of the Fourteenth Amendment, and some political forces at play behind the scenes.

decision expected in June 2008. Linda Greenhouse, "Justices Will Decide if Handgun Kept at Home Is Individual Right," *New York Times*, November 21, 2007, A1.

[3] See Robert J. Spitzer, *The Right to Bear Arms: Rights and Liberties Under Law* (Santa Barbara, CA: ABC-CLIO, 2001).

[4] See Robert J. Spitzer, *The Politics of Gun Control* (Washington, DC: CQ Press, 2007).

The Meaning of the Second Amendment

Few parts of the Constitution are so often invoked yet so little understood as the Second Amendment. Politics aside, the meaning of the Second Amendment is relatively clear. As the text itself says, "A well regulated Militia, being necessary to the security of a free State, the right of the people to keep and bear Arms, shall not be infringed." Supreme Court Chief Justice Warren Burger wrote that the Second Amendment "must be read as though the word 'because' was the opening word,"[5] as in "[Because] a well-regulated Militia [is] necessary to the security of a free State. . . ." As debate concerning the amendment preceding and during the First Congress (when the Bill of Rights was formulated and then sent to the states for ratification) made clear, the amendment was added to allay the concerns of anti-Federalists and others who feared that state sovereignty and, more specifically, the ability of states to meet military emergencies on their own would be impinged or neglected by the new federal government. The new government had been given vast new powers under the new Constitution, particularly and alarmingly over the use of military force – and not just over a standing army but also over the militias, which under the old Articles of Confederation had been under the sole control of the states. As the new Constitution stipulated in Article I, sec. 8, Congress would now possess the power of "calling forth the Militia," as well as "organizing, arming, and disciplining the Militia, and for governing such part of them as may be employed in the Service of the United States," leaving to the states only "the Appointment of the Officers, and the Authority of Training the Militia according to the discipline prescribed by Congress." Further, the president would act as commander-in-chief of the state militias (noted in Article II, sec. 2).

In other words, the inclusion of the Second Amendment embodied the Federalist assurance that the states would be allowed to retain some control over their militias, and that they might also function as a viable military entity separate from if also supplemental to the national army (and national control of the militias) at a time when military tensions within and between the states ran high, suspicions of a national standing army persisted, and military takeovers were the norm in world affairs.[6]

---

[5] Warren Burger, "The Right to Bear Arms," *Parade*, January 14, 1990, 5.
[6] Garry Wills, *A Necessary Evil* (New York: Simon and Schuster, 1999), 119–21.

Debate concerning what became the Second Amendment during the First Congress dealt entirely with the narrow military questions of the need to maintain civilian government control over the military, the unreliability of militias as compared with professional armies, possible threats to liberties from armies as compared with militias, and whether to codify the right of conscientious objectors to opt out of military service (an early version of the amendment included such language).[7]

As four Supreme Court cases (discussed herein) and more than forty lower federal court rulings have said in their rulings, the Second Amendment pertains only to citizen service in a government-organized and -regulated militia – what is typically referred to as the collective or militia-based understanding of the amendment.[8] The reference to "the right of the people to keep and bear arms" addressed the typical militia practices of the eighteenth and early nineteenth centuries, when militia-eligible males were not only obliged but also required to obtain and bring their own arms if called into service because the national and state governments generally lacked the resources to properly arm the militia.[9]

Militias played a vital if inconsistent role in America's war of independence and in meeting various small-scale military emergencies after the revolutionary period, such as the Whiskey Rebellion in 1794, but the abysmal performance of civilian (also referred to as unorganized or general) militias in the War of 1812 essentially ended the government's use of such forces to meet military emergencies. Military historians Allan Millett and Peter Maslowski noted that "After the War of 1812 military planners realized that no matter how often politicians glorified

---

[7] Helen E. Veit, Kenneth R. Bowling, and Charlene Bangs Bickford, eds., *Creating the Bill of Rights* (Baltimore: Johns Hopkins University Press, 1991), 182–84, 198–99.

[8] In his important new book, historian Saul Cornell argues that the debate between the collective and individualist views of the Second Amendment is misplaced, asserting instead that the amendment was, in fact, a "civic right," referring to the obligations of citizens to the state to be armed so that they would be ready to serve in the militia. Cornell's argument is persuasive, but it is consistent with the militia-based meaning of the amendment discussed herein. *A Well-Regulated Militia: The Founding Fathers and the Origins of Gun Control in America* (New York: Oxford University Press, 2006).

[9] The Uniform Militia Act of 1792 (1 Stat. 271) defined the nation's militia as "every free and able-bodied white male citizen of the respective states" between the ages of eighteen and forty-five, and legally obligated them to provide their own weapons, ammunition, and related accoutrements. All the states enacted similar laws, but none of them included any mechanism for enforcement; as a result, the laws were generally ignored. See Spitzer, *The Right to Bear Arms*, 28–30, 159–65.

citizen-soldiers . . . reliance on the common militia to reinforce the regular Army was chimerical."[10] As political scientist Stephen Skowronek observed, "By the 1840s the militia system envisioned in the early days of the republic was a dead letter. Universal military training fell victim to a general lack of interest and administrative incompetence at both the federal and state levels."[11] Legal writers Keith A. Ehrman and Dennis A. Henigan concluded that the "history of the state militias between 1800 and the 1870s is one of total abandonment, disorganization, and degeneration."[12] Instead, the government came to rely on professional military forces that were expanded in times of emergency by the military draft. The select or volunteer militias used in the Civil War (and which also date to colonial times) survived and were institutionalized and brought under federal military authority as the National Guard in the Dick Act of 1903 and the National Defense Act of 1916.[13] Further, even if the Second Amendment did pertain to personal weapons ownership or use outside of militia service, the courts have refused to incorporate it via the Fourteenth Amendment, unlike most of the rest of the Bill of Rights, thereby limiting its relevance to federal action. In any case, the Second Amendment provides no protection for personal weapons use, including hunting, sporting, collecting, or even personal self-protection (this latter is covered under criminal law and the common law tradition).

---

[10] Allan R. Millett and Peter Maslowski, *For the Common Defense: A Military History of the United States* (New York: Free Press, 1984), 129. The authors quote Representative Jabez Upham, who observed in 1808 during debate in the House of Representatives that reliance on citizen militias "will do very well on paper; it sounds well in the war speeches on this floor. To talk about every soldier being a citizen, and every citizen being a soldier, and to declaim that the militia of our country is the bulwark of our liberty is very captivating. All this will figure to advantage in history. But it will not do at all in practice" (129).

[11] Stephen Skowronek, *Building a New American State* (New York: Cambridge University Press, 1982), 315, note 17. See also James M. McPherson, *Battle Cry of Freedom* (New York: Oxford University Press, 1988), 317; William Riker, *Soldiers of the States: The Role of the National Guard in American Democracy* (Washington, DC: Public Affairs Press, 1957), chap. 3.

[12] Keith A. Ehrman and Dennis A. Henigan. "The Second Amendment in the Twentieth Century: Have You Seen Your Militia Lately?," *University of Dayton Law Review* 15(Fall 1989): 36.

[13] 32 Stat. 775–80 (1903); 39 Stat. 166 (1916). See also Millett and Maslowski, *For the Common Defense*, 247–49; Riker, *Soldiers of the States*; and Jerry Cooper, *The Rise of the National Guard* (Lincoln, NE: University of Nebraska Press, 1997).

Despite the definitive nature of constitutional reading, historical lessons, and court rulings, some legal writers, publishing in law journals, have sought to spin out other interpretations of the Second Amendment. These writers have succeeded in finding legitimacy for a variety of erroneous and even nonsensical arguments concerning the meaning of the Second Amendment through such publications. Arguments advanced in these publications have, in turn, seeped into the public press, a phenomenon also observed in the debate over the inherent item veto. When this happens, it may easily magnify what might otherwise be a minor distortion.

To take one example, an article in the *Wall Street Journal* reported in 1999 that one of the key factors leading to new academic interest in the Second Amendment was "a recently unearthed series of clues to the Framers' intentions." The article cited two examples of these so-called new "clues." One was an allegedly recently discovered "early draft" of the Second Amendment authored by James Madison in which "he made 'The right of the people' the first clause [of the Second Amendment]. . . ." The second was a letter written by Thomas Jefferson to an English scholar, John Cartwright, in which "Jefferson wrote that 'the constitutions of most of our states assert, that all power is inherent in the people; . . . that it is their right and duty to be at all times armed.'" (No citations or attributions were provided in the article as to who made these "discoveries" or who claimed that they were new or significant; however, five legal writers were prominently mentioned in the article, four of whom have authored law journal articles promoting the individualist view.)[14] Despite the article's claim to the contrary, neither of these quotes is "recently unearthed," nor are they "clues" to the meaning of the Second Amendment.

The first of these quotes has been known to scholars of the Constitution for decades because it was part of Madison's original Bill of Rights resolution, offered in the House of Representatives on June 7, 1789, and has been a part of publicly available congressional records from that day to this. It has also been cited in past writings on the Second Amendment

---

[14] Collin Levey, "Liberals Have Second Thoughts on the Second Amendment," *Wall Street Journal*, November 22, 1999, 23. The five law professors cited in the article who have written on the Second Amendment supporting the individualist interpretation (in Tribe's case, the positive comments appear in his constitutional law case book) and/or voiced support for it are Sanford Levinson, Akhil Amar, Daniel Polsby, Lawrence Tribe, and William Van Alstyne.

and the Bill of Rights.[15] It is thus no new discovery nor does it alter what is already known about the Second Amendment.

The Jefferson letter to Cartwright was reprinted in *The Writings of Thomas Jefferson*, published in 1904. Leaving aside the facts that Jefferson did not attend the Constitutional Convention of 1787, was not a member of the First Congress, and penned the letter in question in 1824, the full quotation from which the previous brief excerpt was drawn makes clear what Jefferson was writing about:

> The constitutions of most of our States assert, that all power is inherent in the people; that they may exercise it by themselves, in all cases to which they think themselves competent (as in electing functionaries executive and legislative, and deciding by a jury of themselves, in all judiciary cases in which any fact is involved), or they may act by representatives, freely and equally chosen; that it is their right and duty to be at all times armed; that they are entitled to freedom of person, freedom of religion, freedom of property, and freedom of the press.[16]

Jefferson was referring to state constitutions and offering a "seat-of-the-pants" listing of Bill of Rights freedoms, therefore including the reference to being armed as a right and duty (federal and state laws then required men of militia age to be so armed for militia service). Nothing Jefferson said in this letter amounts to a new contribution to the understanding of the Second Amendment, nor does it contradict existing meaning. Yet, a reader of the *Wall Street Journal* might reasonably conclude that these so-called new "clues" to the Second Amendment are both when, in fact, they are neither. Fortunately, one does not need to channel the spirits of

---

[15] Recent cites of this early version of Madison include in Spitzer, *The Politics of Gun Control*, 34 (1995 edition), which in turn appeared in Veit, Bowling, and Bickford, *Creating the Bill of Rights*, 12. Here is Madison's text from June 8, 1789: "The right of the people to keep and bear arms shall not be infringed; a well armed, and well regulated militia being the best security of a free country; but no person religiously scrupulous of bearing arms, shall be compelled to render military service in person." It is obvious from the full text that the reference to the bearing of arms is directly linked to militia service, national security, and the vexing problem of providing exemptions for such service for those with religious objections. The reference to religious exemption was dropped from the final text of the Second Amendment because of the concern that too many militia-eligible men would be encouraged to use it as a loophole to avoid military service, thereby depleting the military ranks. See Veit, Bowling, and Bickford, *Creating the Bill of Rights*, 182–84.

[16] Andrew A. Lipscomb, ed., *The Writings of Thomas Jefferson* (Washington, DC: The Thomas Jefferson Memorial Association, 1904), XVI, 45.

the Constitution's founders in order to discern the meaning of the Second Amendment because the courts have also ruled on the meaning of this amendment.

Supreme Court Rulings

The Second Amendment has generated relatively little constitutional law compared with other parts of the Bill of Rights. In a few instances, however, the Supreme Court has ruled directly on the meaning of this amendment.

In the first case, *U.S. v. Cruikshank*,[17] Cruikshank and two other defendants were charged with thirty-two counts of depriving Blacks of their constitutional rights, including two counts claiming that the defendants had deprived Blacks of firearms possession, in violation of the Enforcement Act of 1870. Speaking for the Court in 1876, Chief Justice Waite wrote that:

> The second and tenth counts are equally defective. The right there specified is that of "bearing arms for a lawful purpose." This is not a right granted by the Constitution. Neither is it in any manner dependent upon that instrument for its existence. The Second Amendment declares that it shall not be infringed; but this, as has been seen, means no more than that it shall not be infringed by Congress. This is one of the amendments that has no other effect than to restrict the powers of the National Government. . . .[18]

The court in this case established two principles that it and lower federal courts have consistently upheld: first, that the Second Amendment poses no obstacle to at least some regulation of firearms (the court upheld a law that regulated the carrying of weapons, including firearms);[19] and second, that the Second Amendment is not "incorporated," meaning that it pertains only to federal power, not state power (this is what the court meant when it referred to the Second Amendment not being "infringed by Congress"). Admittedly, the Supreme Court did not begin to incorporate parts of the first ten amendments until 1897. But the Court has never accepted the idea of incorporating the entire Bill of Rights,[20] and it has

---

[17] 92 U.S. 542 (1876).   [18] *U.S. v. Cruikshank*, 553.

[19] Cornell, *A Well Regulated Militia*, 195.

[20] Daniel A. Farber, William N. Eskridge, Jr., and Philip Frickey, *Constitutional Law* (St. Paul, MN: West Publishing, 1993), 398.

never incorporated the Second Amendment, despite numerous opportunities to do so.[21]

Ten years after *Cruikshank*, the Court ruled in *Presser v. Illinois*[22] that an Illinois law that barred paramilitary organizations from drilling or parading in cities or towns without a license from the governor was constitutional and did not violate the Second Amendment. Herman Presser challenged the law, partly on Second Amendment grounds, after he was arrested for marching and drilling his armed fringe group, *Lehr und Wehr Verein*, through Chicago streets. In upholding the Illinois law, the Court reaffirmed that the Second Amendment did not apply to the states, citing *Cruikshank*. Speaking for a unanimous court in 1886, Justice Woods also went on to discuss the relationship between citizens, the militia, and the government in paragraphs that explain why the Second Amendment, in the Court's view, did not protect Presser's actions:

> It is undoubtedly true that all citizens capable of bearing arms constitute the reserved military force or reserved militia of the United States as well as of the States; and, in view of this prerogative . . . the States cannot, even laying the constitutional provision in question out of view, prohibit the people from keeping and bearing arms, so as to deprive the United States of their rightful resource for maintaining the public security, and disable the people from performing their duty to the General Government. But, as already stated, we think it clear that the sections under consideration do not have this effect.[23]

The Court then went on to ask whether Presser and his associates had a right to organize with others as a self-proclaimed and armed military organization, against state law. No, the Court answered, because such activity "is not an attribute of national citizenship. Military organization and military drill and parade under arms are subjects especially under the control of the government of every country. They cannot be claimed as a right independent of law."[24] In other words, militias exist only as defined and regulated by the state or federal government, which in Illinois at the time was the eight-thousand–member Illinois National Guard (as the

---

[21] Also left unincorporated up to the present day are the Third Amendment, the grand jury clause of the Fifth Amendment, the Seventh Amendment, the excessive fines and bail clause of the Eighth Amendment, and the Ninth and Tenth Amendments. Louis Fisher, *American Constitutional Law* (Durham, NC: Carolina Academic Press, 1999), 428–29.

[22] 116 U.S. 252 (1886).   [23] *Presser v. Illinois*, 265–66.

[24] *Ibid.*, 267.

Court noted in its decision). To deny the government the power to define and regulate militias would, according to the Court, "be to deny the right of the State to disperse assemblages organized for sedition and treason, and the right to suppress armed mobs bent on riot and rapine [pillaging]."[25] Thus, the *Presser* case confirmed the understanding that the right to bear arms came into play only in connection with citizen service in a militia, as formed and regulated by the government. The Court emphatically rejected the idea that citizens could create their own militias, much less that the Second Amendment protected citizens' rights to own weapons for their own private purposes.

In 1894, the Supreme Court ruled in *Miller v. Texas*[26] that a Texas law "prohibiting the carrying of dangerous weapons" did not violate the Second Amendment. Again, the Court said that the right to bear arms did not apply to the states. The Court ruled similarly in *Robertson v. Baldwin*,[27] saying that a law barring the carrying of concealed weapons did not violate the Second Amendment. In *Patsone v. Commonwealth*,[28] the Court ruled that a Pennsylvania law prohibiting unnaturalized, foreign-born persons from possessing firearms was constitutional and did not violate the Second Amendment.

The most important Supreme Court case in this sequence is *U.S. v. Miller*.[29] This 1939 case was founded on a challenge to the National Firearms Act of 1934, which regulated the interstate transport of various weapons used by gangsters of the time. Jack Miller and Frank Layton were charged with transporting an unregistered 12-gauge sawed-off shotgun (with a barrel less than 18 inches long) across state lines in violation of the 1934 act. They challenged the act's constitutionality by claiming that it was a violation of their Second Amendment rights and that it represented an improper use of the commerce power. A federal district court sided with Miller and Layton, saying that the law was indeed a violation of the amendment, although Judge Heartsill Ragon provided no explanation or justification for this conclusion in his one-sentence opinion.[30]

On appeal to the Supreme Court, the lower court ruling was reversed and the claims of the defendants were rejected. The unanimous Court ruled that the federal taxing power could be used to regulate firearms and

[25] *Ibid.*, 268.
[26] 153 U.S. 535 (1894).
[27] 165 U.S. 275 (1897).
[28] 232 U.S. 138 (1914).
[29] 307 U.S. 174 (1939).
[30] *U.S. v. Miller*, 26 F.Supp. 1002 (1939).

that firearm registration was constitutional, as was the 1934 law. Beyond this, the Court was unequivocal in saying that the Second Amendment must be interpreted by its "obvious purpose" of assuring an effective militia as described in Article I, sec. 8, of the Constitution (to which the Court referred in its decision). Speaking for the Court, Justice McReynolds wrote:

> In the absence of any evidence tending to show that possession or use of a "shotgun having a barrel of less than eighteen inches in length" at this time has some reasonable relationship to the preservation or efficiency of a well regulated militia, we cannot say that the Second Amendment guarantees the right to keep and bear such an instrument. Certainly it is not within judicial notice that this weapon is any part of the ordinary military equipment or that its use could contribute to the common defense.[31]

In the next paragraph, the Court noted that the Constitution gave to Congress the power to call forth and regulate the militia, quoting from Congress's Article I, sec. 8, powers. It then said this:

> With obvious purpose to assure the continuation and render possible the effectiveness of such forces the declaration and guarantee of the Second Amendment were made. It must be interpreted and applied with that end in view.[32]

Thus, the Court stated that citizens could only possess a Second Amendment–based constitutional right to bear arms in connection with service in a militia. In addition, it affirmed the constitutional right of the Congress, as well as the states, to regulate firearms. Most of the rest of the decision is an extended discussion of the antecedents of the Second Amendment. Justice McReynolds cited various classic writings, colonial practices, and early state laws and constitutions to demonstrate the importance of militias and citizen armies to early America as the explanation for the presence and meaning of the Second Amendment.

Critics of this case have, on occasion, taken the wording quoted herein to mean that the Court would protect under the Second Amendment the private ownership of guns that *do* bear some connection with national defense. Such an interpretation is mistaken for two reasons. First, the court is saying that possession of a weapon like a sawed-off shotgun could only be allowed by the Court under existing law if that possession were

---

[31] *U.S. v. Miller*, 178. [32] *U.S. v. Miller*, 178.

connected with militia service. Because the two men charged with violating the 1934 law obviously did not have the gun while serving in the military, the government was justified in prosecuting them without running afoul of the Second Amendment. And, as the *Presser* case established, citizens may not create their own militias; militia service can only occur through government-organized and -regulated militias (the Court cited *Presser* in the *Miller* case).

Second, to protect the ownership of weapons based on their military utility alone (ignoring the question of whether individuals who owned firearms were doing so as part of their militia service) would justify the private ownership of a vast array of militarily useful weapons manageable by an individual – assault weapons and bazookas to howitzers and tactical nuclear weapons – all of which are "weapons" subject to government restrictions. No serious argument can be made that the Second Amendment or the *Miller* decision protects the right of citizens to possess such weapons when they are not in actual military service.[33] Remembering that the Court's judgment in this case arose from the challenge to the National Firearms Act (the source from which it drew and quoted the definition of a sawed-off shotgun, a weapon regulated by the law because its only civilian use was greater human destruction by criminals), its remedy lay in the failure of Miller and Layton to claim any credible connection to Second Amendment–based militia activities.

The Second Amendment has received brief mention in two other more recent Supreme Court cases. In *Adams v. Williams*,[34] Justice Douglas and Justice Marshall commented in a dissenting opinion of a case dealing with a search and seizure of a suspect that the Second Amendment posed no obstacle whatsoever to extremely strict gun regulations, even including the banning of weapons possession entirely. The Douglas–Marshall comments here were dicta, however.

In *Lewis v. U.S.*,[35] the Court upheld the constitutionality of a 1968 law that barred felons from owning guns, saying that the law did not violate the Second Amendment, citing *U.S. v. Miller*. In a challenge to the Gun Control Act of 1968, the Court said that gun regulations were

---

[33] Robert Hardaway, Elizabeth Gormley, and Bryan Taylor, "The Inconvenient Militia Clause of the Second Amendment: Why the Supreme Court Declines to Resolve the Debate Over the Right to Bear Arms," *St. John's Journal of Legal Commentary* 16(Winter 2002): 41–164.
[34] 407 U.S. 143 (1972).　　　　[35] 445 U.S. 55 (1980).

allowable as long as there was some "rational basis" for them, meaning that the regulations merely had to serve some legitimate purpose, which, the Court said, the 1968 law served. This standard is significant because it is one that is easily met, especially as compared with the higher standard the Court has set for laws that might conflict with other Bill of Rights freedoms, such as free speech or free press. In a footnote in the 1980 case, Justice Blackmun wrote that "These legislative restrictions on the use of firearms are neither based upon constitutionally suspect criteria, nor do they trench upon any constitutionally protected liberties. See United States v Miller . . . (the Second Amendment guarantees no right to keep and bear a firearm that does not have 'some reasonable relationship to the preservation or efficiency of a well regulated militia'). . . ."[36] Thus, the *Lewis* case made clear that the Second Amendment was not accorded the same importance as other parts of the Bill of Rights and that the Court viewed the Second Amendment in the collective/militia sense articulated in *Miller*.

None of this means that gun ownership is somehow illegal or unrecognized by the law. As the Supreme Court noted in *Staples v. U.S.*, "there is a long tradition of widespread lawful gun ownership by private individuals in this country."[37] On the other hand, this does not mean, nor did the Court say, that private firearms ownership is protected by the Second Amendment. All of the Court cases make clear that the Second Amendment comes into play only in connection with citizen service in a government-organized and -regulated militia. None of these cases endorses, protects, or implies any Second Amendment–based individual right of citizens to own firearms for their own uses or purposes.

Other Court Rulings

These Supreme Court cases represent an unbroken line to current Court thinking.[38] Lower federal courts have followed the Supreme Court's

---

[36] *Lewis v. U.S.*, 65.   [37] 511 U.S. 600, 608 (1994).

[38] The 2001 case of *U.S. v. Emerson* (270 F.3d 203; 5th Cir.) stated in its opinion that it believed the individualist view of the Second Amendment to be correct. This was the first federal court to ever accept that interpretation; however, it rejected the defendant's argument that the Second Amendment protected his right to own a gun and ordered that he be tried in a Texas court for carrying and brandishing a pistol while subject to a restraining order issued by a Texas state court that put him in violation of a federal law making such possession a crime. The Supreme Court refused to hear

reasoning on the meaning of the Second Amendment in numerous cases. Challenges to gun regulations and related efforts to win a broader interpretation of the Second Amendment (including efforts to incorporate the Second Amendment) have been uniformly turned aside. In more than forty cases since *U.S. v. Miller,* federal courts of appeal "have analyzed the Second Amendment purely in terms of protecting state militias, rather than individual rights."[39] The Supreme Court has denied certiorari

Emerson's appeal (*Emerson v. U.S.*, 536 U.S. 907; 2002) and, in 2002, he was convicted in the Texas court of unlawful firearms possession. Thus, the individualist view had no bearing on the outcome of the case. See Robert J. Spitzer, "The Second Amendment 'Right to Bear Arms' and *United States v. Emerson,*" *St. John's Law Review* 77(Winter 2003): 1–27. In 2007, however, the DC Circuit court struck down the District of Columbia's strict handgun ban on Second Amendment grounds in the case of *Parker v. District of Columbia* (478 F.3d 370; D.C. Cir.). In doing so, it not only accepted the individualist view but also used this interpretation to strike down the DC law. If this decision is allowed to stand, or is accepted on appeal to the Supreme Court and is in turn upheld, then the Supreme Court's "unbroken line" of reasoning on the meaning of the Second Amendment will have been broken. See Robert J. Spitzer, "Working Hard to Misconstrue the 2nd Amendment," History News Network, March 12, 2007, accessed at http://hnn.us/articles/36395.html.

[39] *U.S. v. Nelson,* 859 F.2d 1318, 1320 (8th Cir. 1988). The other federal court of appeals cases include *Cases v. U.S.,* 131 F.2d 916, 922–23 (1st Cir. 1942), cert. denied sub nom; *Velazquez v. U.S.,* 319 U.S. 770 (1943); *U.S. v. Tot,* 131 F.2d 261, 266 (3d Cir. 1942), reversed on other grounds, 319 U.S. 463 (1943); *U.S. v. Johnson,* 441 F.2d 1134, 1136 (5th Cir. 1971); *U.S. v. McCutcheon,* 446 F.2d 133, 135–36 (7th Cir. 1971); *Stevens v. U.S.,* 440 F.2d 144, 149 (6th Cir. 1971); *U.S. v. Decker,* 446 F.2d 164 (8th Cir. 1971); *U.S. v. Synnes,* 438 F.2d 764 (8th Cir. 1971), vacated on other grounds, 404 U.S. 1009 (1972); *Cody v. U.S.,* 460 F.2d 34, 36–37 (8th Cir. 1972), cert. denied, 409 U.S. 1010 (1972); *Eckert v. City of Philadelphia,* 477 F.2d 610 (3d Cir. 1973), cert. denied 414 U.S. 839 (1973); *U.S. v. Day,* 476 F.2d 562, 568 (6th Cir. 1973); *U.S. v. Johnson,* 497 F.2d 548, 550 (4th Cir. 1974); *U.S. v. Swinton,* 521 F.2d 1255 (10th Cir. 1975), cert. denied, 424 U.S. 918 (1976); *U.S. v. Warin,* 530 F.2d 103, 106 (6th Cir. 1976), cert. denied, 426 U.S. 948 (1976); *U.S. v. Graves,* 554 F.2d 65, 66–67 (3d Cir. 1977); *U.S. v. Oakes,* 564 F.2d 384, 387 (10th Cir. 1977), cert. denied, 435 U.S. 926 (1978); *Quilici v. Village of Morton Grove,* 695 F.2d 261, 270 (7th Cir. 1982), cert. denied, 464 U.S. 863 (1983); *Thomas v. Members of City Council of Portland,* 730 F.2d 41 (1st Cir. 1984); *U.S. v. Toner,* 728 F.2d 115 (2d Cir. 1984); *Farmer v. Higgins,* 907 F.2d 1041 (11th Cir. 1990), cert. denied, 498 U.S. 1047 (1991); *U.S. v. Hale,* 978 F.2d 1016, 1019 (8th Cir. 1992), cert. denied, 507 U.S. 997 (1993); *Fresno Rifle & Pistol Club v. Van de Camp,* 965 F.2d 723 (9th Cir. 1992); *U.S. v. Friel,* 1 F.3d 1231 (1st Cir. 1993); *Love v. Pepersack,* 47 F.3d 120, 124 (4th Cir. 1995), cert. denied 516 U.S. 813(1995); *U.S. v. Farrell,* 69 F.3d 891 (8th Cir. 1995); *Hickman v. Block,* 81 F.3d 98, 102 (9th Cir. 1996), cert. denied, 519 U.S. 912 (1996); *U.S. v. Rybar,* 103 F.3d 273 (3rd Cir. 1996), cert. denied, 522 U.S. 807 (1997); *U.S. v. Wright,* 117 F.3d 1265, 1273 (11th Cir. 1997), cert. denied, 522 U.S. 1007 (1997); *Peoples Rights Organization, Inc. v. City of Columbus,* 152 F.3d 522, 539 (6th Cir. 1998); *Gillespie v. City of Indianapolis,* 185 F.3d 693, 710 (7th Cir. 1999), cert. denied, 528 U.S. 1116 (2000); *U.S. v. Napier,* 233 F.3d 394 (6th Cir. 2000); *U.S.*

in nearly half of these cases, thus letting the lower court rulings stand.[40] The inescapable conclusion is that the Supreme Court has considered the matter settled and has no interest in crowding its docket with cases that merely repeat what has already been decided.[41] These rulings from the federal courts are consistent with the little-known fact that no federal court has ever struck down a law regulating private firearms ownership based on the Second Amendment.[42]

Several observations about the Second Amendment arise from this discussion. First, the amendment reflected a concern vital to the country's

v. *Metcalf*, 221 F.3d 1336 (6th Cir. 2000); *U.S. v. Finitz*, 234 F.3d 1278 (9th Cir. 2000), cert. denied, 531 U.S. 1100 (2001); *U.S. v. Hancock*, 231 F.3d 557 (9th Cir. 2000), cert. denied, 532 U.S. 989 (2001); *U.S. v. Baer*, 235 F.2d 561 (10th Cir. 2000); *U.S. v. Lewis*, 236 F.3d 948 (8th Cir. 2001); *U.S. v. Haney*, 264 F.3d 1161 (10th Cir. 2001); *U.S. v. Henry*, 288 F.3d 657 (5th Cir. 2002); *U.S. v. Bayles*, 310 F.3d 1302, 1307 (10th Cir. 2002); *Silveira v. Lockyer*, 312 F.3d 1052 (9th Cir. 2002), cert. denied 540 U.S. 1046 (2003); *Nordyke v. King*, 319 F.3d 1185 (9th Cir. 2003), cert. denied 543 U.S. 820 (2004); *U.S. v. Parker*, 362 F.3d 1279 (10th Cir. 2004), cert. denied 543 U.S. 874 (2004); *Bach v. Pataki*, 408 F.3d 75 (2nd Cir., 2005), cert. denied 126 S.Ct. 1341 (2006) . In a case appealed to the Supreme Court from New Jersey in 1969, *Burton v. Sills* (394 U.S. 812), a challenge to a gun law alleging a violation of the Second Amendment was "dismissed for want of a substantial federal question."

[40] In the most famous of these federal appeals court cases, the Supreme Court declined to hear an appeal of two lower federal court rulings upholding the constitutionality of a strict gun-control law passed in Morton Grove, Illinois, in 1981. The ordinance banned the ownership of working handguns, except for peace officers, prison officials, members of the armed forces and National Guard, and security guards, as long as such possession was in accordance with their official duties. The ordinance also exempted licensed gun collectors and antique firearms. Residents who owned handguns could actually continue to own them, but they were required to keep them at a local gun club instead of in the home. In *Quilici v. Village of Morton Grove* (695 F.2d 261; 7th Cir. 1982; cert. denied 464 U.S. 863; 1983), the court of appeals brushed aside arguments of those opposed to the law, including the claim that the law violated Second Amendment rights, and confirmed that possession of handguns by individuals is not part of the right to keep and bear arms; that this right pertains only to militia service; that the local law was a reasonable exercise of police power; and that the Second Amendment does not apply to the states. Stating the matter succinctly, the federal appeals court concluded: "Construing this language [the Second Amendment] according to its plain meaning, it seems clear that the right to bear arms is inextricably connected to the preservation of a militia."

[41] As Peter Linzer's study of Supreme Court certiorari denials reveals, satisfaction with lower court rulings is at least one important reason for denials. "The Meaning of Certiorari Denials," *Columbia Law Review* 79(November 1979): 1227–1305.

[42] Erwin Griswold, "Phantom Second Amendment 'Rights,'" *Washington Post*, November 4, 1990, C7. The same is true in the states, including dozens of state court rulings, with the exception of a nineteenth-century case from a Georgia state court, *Nunn v. State* (1 Kelly 243; 1846), when the court did void part of a state gun law partly on Second Amendment grounds.

144 · THE SECOND AMENDMENT

founders pertaining to the type of military force that would defend the country from manifold threats within and outside of the country, the desire to protect state power and sovereignty as distinct from that of the federal government, and the expectation that eligible militiamen would have to bring their own weapons, given the uncertainty about whether the government could or would supply adequate arms.

Second, like some other elements of the Constitution, such as the Third Amendment prohibition against the quartering of troops in peoples' homes during peacetime, the concerns that gave rise to the Second Amendment evaporated as reality changed – that is, as the country turned away from unorganized or general citizen militias and toward a professional army whose ranks were expanded in times of need by the military draft, the Second Amendment was rendered obsolete. The surviving element of the old militia system, the organized or volunteer militia, was brought mostly under federal government control through a series of federal laws enacted in the early twentieth century. Therefore, government control of what remained of the old militia system shifted mostly to the national government. Whereas this arrangement was a departure from the militia system contemplated by the Constitution's founders and the authors of the Bill of Rights, it reflected the nation's shifting military priorities and was ruled constitutional in the Supreme Court cases of *Maryland v. U.S.*[43] and *Perpich v. Department of Defense.*[44]

Third, recognizing these new military and political realities, the Court has not incorporated the Second Amendment as it has most of the rest of the Bill of Rights. The consensus of constitutional-law scholars is that the incorporation process is at an end (since the last incorporation decision in 1969), with the possible exception of the fines and bail clause of the Eighth Amendment.[45] Thus, even if the Second Amendment did protect an individual right to bear arms outside of service in a militia, it would still not apply to the states because it has not been incorporated and, therefore, would not be a right citizens could claim in their daily lives. Conversely, even if the Court reversed itself and incorporated the Second Amendment, it would apply only to the old concept of universal militia service, a practice abandoned before the Civil War.

---

[43] 381 U.S. 41 (1965).   [44] 496 U.S. 334 (1990).
[45] Richard C. Cortner, *The Supreme Court and the Second Bill of Rights* (Madison, WI: University of Wisconsin Press, 1981), 279.

The "Individualist" Critique

The central critique of the militia-based view of the Second Amendment
is that this amendment conferred an "individual" right to bear arms, aside
or apart from any government-based militia activity. That is, some argue
that the ownership of firearms is a constitutionally based protection that
applies to all individuals, without any attachment to militias or the government, just as free speech and the right to counsel apply to all individuals.
Although many variations of the individualist critique have been spun out,
the core argument is usually supported by plucking key phrases from court
cases or from colonial or federal debate that refer to a right of Americans
to own and carry guns.

This line of analysis has three problems. First, as a matter of constitutional law, the issue of the bearing of arms as it pertained to the Constitution and the Bill of Rights always came back to service in a government-
organized and -regulated military unit[46] and the balance of power between
the states and the federal government, as reflected in the two most important historical sources: the records of the constitutional convention and
those of the First Congress when the Bill of Rights was formulated. Gun
ownership was undeniably an important component of colonial and early
federal life, but practical necessity did and does not equal constitutional
protection.[47] Moreover, as a practical matter, gun ownership was relatively

---

[46] See *Presser v. Illinois*, 116 U.S. 252 (1886) at 265–66.

[47] Much of this line of analysis relies on supporting quotes accidentally or willfully pulled
out of context that, when examined in context, support the Court view. To pick an
example, Stephen P. Halbrook quotes Patrick Henry's words during the Virginia ratifying
convention as saying, "The great object is, that every man be armed. . . . Every one who
is able may have a gun." "To Keep and Bear Their Private Arms: The Adoption of the
Second Amendment, 1787–1791," *Northern Kentucky Law Review* 10(1982): 25. This
quote would seem to support the view that at least some early leaders advocated general
popular armament aside from militia purposes. Yet, here is the full quote from the
original debates: "May we not discipline and arm them [the states], as well as Congress,
if the power be concurrent? So that our militia shall have two sets of arms, double sets
of regimentals, &c.; and thus, at a very great cost, we shall be doubly armed. *The great
object is, that every man be armed.* But can the people afford to pay for double sets of
arms, &c.? *Every one who is able may have a gun.* But we have learned, by experience,
that, necessary as it is to have arms, and though our Assembly has, by a succession of laws
for many years, endeavored to have the militia completely armed, it is still far from being
the case." Jonathan Elliot, *Debates in the Several State Conventions on the Adoption of
the Federal Constitution*, 4 vols. (Washington, DC: Clerk's Office of the District Court,
1836: III, 386; emphasis added). It is perfectly obvious that Henry's comments are in
the context of a discussion of the militia and the power balance between the states and

rare among the general population from the colonial period up until the Civil War, owing in large measure to the facts that guns were difficult and expensive to produce and operate, were made of materials (mostly iron) that rusted and degraded even with regular maintenance, and were unreliable even when in working condition.[48] Even though state and federal laws required men of militia age to keep and maintain firearms, these laws were simply not followed or enforced, in part at least because of the practical problems of early gun ownership that are little appreciated today.[49]

Second, the definition of the citizen militias at the center of this debate has always been limited to men roughly between the ages of eighteen and forty-five.[50] That is, it has always excluded a majority of the country's adult citizens – men older than forty-five, the infirm of all ages, and women (who, of course, did not enjoy comparable political rights to men until the twentieth century). Even among those males who were eligible to serve, actual service in the militias was significantly less than universal. As historian John Shy notes, the composition and organization of American militias fluctuated according to military necessity of place and time,[51] underscoring the fact that militias' raison d'etre was collective defense or internal security,[52] not individual protection (although understanding that individuals might and surely did obtain protection through militia action) or other private purposes. Moreover, those who actually served "were not the men who bore a military obligation as part of their freedom."[53] That is, freedmen and property owners could and would opt out of militia

Congress. Numerous other such examples as this can be found; space limits constrain the presentation of additional illustrations. Garry Wills's conclusion about this literature is less charitable. Speaking about the individualist writers, he says that "it is the quality of their arguments that makes them hard to take seriously." "To Keep and Bear Arms," *The New York Review of Books*, 21 September 1995, 62.

[48] Alexander DeConde, *Gun Violence in America* (Boston: Northeastern University Press, 2001), 17–25.

[49] Spitzer, *The Politics of Gun Control*, 26–28.

[50] See 10 U.S.C. 311 (1983).

[51] John Shy, *A People Numerous and Armed* (Ann Arbor, MI: University of Michigan Press, 1990), 31.

[52] Shy cites as a telling example of the problem of internal security the fact that militias in the South increasingly were used as "an agency to control slaves, and less [as] an effective means of defense." *A People Numerous and Armed*, 37. Carl T. Bogus argues persuasively that the Second Amendment was supported by the Southern states precisely because they were seeking a guarantee to continue to use militias for this purpose. "The Hidden History of the Second Amendment," *U.C. Davis Law Review* 31(Winter 1998): 375–86.

[53] Shy, *A People Numerous and Armed*, 37–38.

service,[54] whereas vagrants, vagabonds, and the unemployed more often filled the ranks. Even African Americans served in early militias, as in the case of the Yamasee War waged in South Carolina from 1715 to 1716, when a militia force of six hundred White men and four hundred Black men defeated Native Americans. By the 1730s, escalating fears of slave revolts ended the practice.[55] Therefore, "universal" citizen militia service and the right to bear arms is not and never has been a right enjoyed by all citizens, unlike other Bill of Rights protections such as free speech, religious freedom, or right to counsel. This also puts to rest the idea that the phrase "the people" in the Second Amendment somehow means all of the people.[56]

Third, the matter of personal or individual self-defense, whether from wild animals or modern-day predators, does not fall within nor is it

---

[54] Saul Cornell, "Commonplace or Anachronism: The Standard Model, the Second Amendment, and the Problem of History in Contemporary Constitutional Theory," *Constitutional Commentary* 16(Summer 1999): 235.

[55] Shy, *A People Numerous and Armed*, 36–38.

[56] Obviously, the Second Amendment is talking about only those people who could serve in a militia, as the Supreme Court made clear in *Presser* and the 1939 *Miller* case. This argument is raised in Robert Dowlut, "The Right to Arms: Does the Constitution or the Predilection of Judges Reign?" *Oklahoma Law Review* 36(Winter 1983): 93–94. In *Fresno Rifle & Pistol Club v. Van De Kamp*, the court of appeals rejected the idea that the phrase "the people" had the same, uniform meaning throughout the Bill of Rights (965 F.2d 723; 9th Cir. 1992).

Some law journal articles have asserted that a 1990 Supreme Court case, *U.S. v. Verdugo-Urquidez* (494 U.S. 259), ruled that the phrase "the people" in the Second Amendment meant all citizens. See, for example, William Van Alstyne, "The Second Amendment and the Personal Right to Arms." *Duke Law Journal* 43(April 1994): 1243, note 19; Gregory L. Shelton, "In Search of the Lost Amendment: Challenging Federal Firearms Regulation Through the 'State's Right' Interpretation of the Second Amendment." *Florida State University Law Review* 23(Summer 1995): 105–39; R. J. Larizza, "Paranoia, Patriotism, and the Citizen Militia Movement: Constitutional Right or Criminal Conduct?" *Mercer Law Review* 47(Winter 1996): 605. Such interpretations are false because the *Verdugo-Urquidez* case has nothing to do with interpreting the Second Amendment. In fact, the case deals with the Fourth Amendment issue of whether an illegal alien from Mexico was entitled to constitutional protection regarding searches. In the majority decision, Chief Justice Rehnquist discussed the meaning of the phrase "the people," given that the phrase appears not only in several parts of the Bill of Rights but also in the Constitution's preamble, in order to determine its applicability to a noncitizen. Rehnquist speculated that the phrase "seems to have been a term of art" (at 265) that probably pertains to people who have developed a connection with the national community. Rehnquist's speculations about whether the meaning of "the people" could be extended to a noncitizen, and his two passing mentions of the Second Amendment in that discussion, shed no light – much less legal meaning – on this amendment.

dependent on the Second Amendment. Nothing in the history, construction, or interpretation of the amendment applies or infers such a protection. That does not mean that gun ownership or the use of guns for purposes such as personal self-defense is somehow outside of the law – far from it. Legal protection for personal self-defense arises from the British common law tradition dating back hundreds of years and modern criminal law, not from constitutional law.[57]

The "Right of Revolution"

An additional challenge to the collective or militia view that extends the individualist view even further argues that the Second Amendment does or should protect the ownership of arms for everyone because of an innate "right of revolution," or as a mechanism to keep the country's rulers responsive to the citizens. Although this theory, whether emphasizing revolutionary overthrow of a regime or an "insurrectionist" use of violence to change personnel within a regime, poses interesting intellectual questions about natural law and the relationship between citizens and the state, it does not find support anywhere in the text, background, or Court interpretation of the Second Amendment.

The Constitution itself makes its disdain for anything resembling a right of revolution clearly and forcefully because Congress is given the powers "To provide for calling forth the Militia to execute the Laws of the Union, suppress Insurrections and repel Invasions" in Article I, sec. 8; to suspend habeas corpus "in Cases of Rebellion or Invasion" in sec. 9; and to protect individual states "against domestic Violence" if requested to do so by a state legislature or governor in Article IV, sec. 4. Further, the Constitution defines treason in Article III, sec. 3, this way: "Treason against the United States, shall consist only in levying War against them [the United States was originally referred to in the plural], or in adhering to their Enemies. . . ." Finally, those suspected of treason may not avoid prosecution by fleeing to another state because the Constitution says in Article IV, sec. 2, that "A Person charged in any State with Treason . . . and

---

[57] Joel Samaha, *Criminal Law* (Minneapolis/St. Paul, MN: West, 1993), chap. 6; American Law Institute, *Model Penal Code and Commentaries* (Philadelphia: American Law Institute, 1985), vol. I, pt. 1, 380–81; Henry C. Black, *Black's Law Dictionary* (St. Paul, MN: West, 1991), 947.

be found in another State, shall on Demand of the executive Authority of the State from which he fled, be delivered up. . . ." In other words, the Constitution specifically and explicitly gives the government the power to forcefully suppress anything even vaguely resembling revolution. Such revolt or revolution is by constitutional definition an act of treason against the United States. The militias are thus to be used to *suppress*, not *cause*, revolution or insurrection.

These governmental powers were further detailed and expanded in the Calling Forth Act of 1792,[58] which gave the president broad powers to use state militias to enforce both state and federal laws in instances where the law is ignored or in cases of open insurrection. This act was passed by the Second Congress shortly after the passage of the Bill of Rights. In current law, these powers are further elaborated in the *U.S. Code* sections on "Insurrection."[59] As legal scholar Roscoe Pound noted, a "legal right of the citizen to wage war on the government is something that cannot be admitted. . . . In the urban industrial society of today a general right to bear efficient arms so as to be enabled to resist oppression by the government would mean that gangs could exercise an extra-legal rule which would defeat the whole Bill of Rights."[60] Legal writer Donald Beschle observed: "History and logic do not permit one to take the right of armed revolution as a serious proposition of positive constitutional law. Only the legal revolutions provided by the political process are recognized by the Constitution."[61] Historian Saul Cornell elaborates on the relationship between the American Revolution and subsequent American governance by noting that "Americans did accept a right of revolution. Such a right, however, was not a constitutional check, but a natural right that one could not exercise under a functional constitutional government."[62]

Any so-called right of insurrection or revolution is carried out against and outside of the government, which means against that government's Constitution as well, including the Bill of Rights and the Second Amendment. One cannot carry out a right of revolution against the government

---

[58] 1 U.S. Stat. 264.   [59] 10 U.S.C. 331–334.

[60] Roscoe Pound, *The Development of Constitutional Guarantees of Liberty* (New Haven, CT: Yale University Press, 1957), 90–91.

[61] Donald L. Beschle, "Reconsidering the Second Amendment: Constitutional Protection for a Right of Security," *Hamline Law Review* 9(February 1986): 95.

[62] Cornell, "Commonplace or Anachronism," 238.

while at the same time claiming protections within it.[63] Even though the truth of this conclusion is self-evident, legal writers Akhil Amar and Alan Hirsch do not accept it, arguing that "the Framers did envision the militia playing precisely this double role"[64] of both suppressing revolt and fomenting it. They offer this argument without providing any sources or documentation to support the claim that the framers endorsed this insurrectionist purpose of the militias. Then, even more puzzling, they retreat from their argument that some portion of the Constitution or Bill of Rights supports armed revolt against the government by saying that the case for violent revolution made by the Declaration of Independence was changed by the Constitution, which "endorsed a new kind of revolution, a peaceful means of altering or abolishing the government" by "ballots rather than bullets...."[65] They conclude with, "It may be a mistake to think of the right to armed revolt as a 'constitutional' right...."[66] At last, they get it right.

One of the most startling qualities of the individualist law review literature is the rapidity and enthusiasm with which some teachers of law embrace the virtues of armed American insurrection.[67] Law professor Sanford Levinson, for example, states in a widely cited article on the Second Amendment published in the *Yale Law Journal* that "It is not my style to offer 'correct' or 'incorrect' interpretations of the Constitution." Yet, he then proceeds to do just that, calling into question the conventional understanding of the Second Amendment. In the process, he asserts that

[63] As Justice Robert Jackson famously noted in *Terminello v. Chicago* (337 U.S. 1, 1949; at 37): "The choice is not between order and liberty. It is between liberty with order and anarchy without either. There is danger that if the Court does not temper its doctrinaire logic with a little practical wisdom, it will convert the constitutional Bill of Rights into a suicide pact."

[64] Akhil Reed Amar and Alan Hirsch, *For the People* (New York: Free Press, 1998), 174. Amar and Hirsch seek to rebut the arguments of Dennis Henigan, "Arms, Anarchy, and the Second Amendment," *Valparaiso University Law Review* 26(Fall 1991): 107–29. Amar developed his thinking on the Fourteenth Amendment and Second Amendment in two *Yale Law Journal* articles: "The Bill of Rights as a Constitution," *The Yale Law Journal* 100(March 1991): 1131–1210; "The Bill of Rights and the Fourteenth Amendment," *Yale Law Journal* 101(April 1992): 1193–1284.

[65] Amar and Hirsch, *For the People*, 175.   [66] *Ibid.*, 176.

[67] For example, Glenn Harlan Reynolds, "The Right to Keep and Bear Arms Under the Tennessee Constitution," *Tennessee Law Review* 61(Winter 1994): 669; David E. Vandercoy, "The History of the Second Amendment," *Valparaiso University Law Review* 28(Spring 1994): 1009; David C. Williams, "The Militia Movement and Second Amendment Revolution," *Cornell Law Review* 81(May 1996): 886, note 13.

the Second Amendment is an expression of republicanism that does and should take citizen participation beyond peaceful, constitutional means:

> . . . just as ordinary citizens should participate actively in governmental decisionmaking through offering their own deliberative insights, rather than be confined to casting ballots once every two or four years for those very few individuals who will actually make decisions, *so should ordinary citizens participate in the process of law enforcement and defense of liberty rather than rely on professional peacekeepers, whether we call them standing armies or police* [emphasis added].[68]

In short, Levinson offers as a bona fide constitutional argument the proposition that vigilantism and citizen violence, including armed insurrection, against the government are legal, proper, and even beneficial activities within the Second Amendment umbrella. The idea that vigilantism and armed insurrection are as constitutionally sanctioned as voting is a proposition of such absurdity that one is struck more by its boldness than by its pretensions to seriousness. Yet, it appears repeatedly in the individualist literature.[69] Levinson also asserts in this article that the Second Amendment has been largely ignored in legal publications, that the three nineteenth-century Supreme Court cases discussed earlier are of no use in interpreting the Second Amendment now because they preceded the process of Bill of Rights incorporation, and that the amendment protects the rights of citizens to use firearms for their own personal self-defense. Yet, each of these propositions is transparently false. Levinson simply ignores the more than sixty articles on the Second Amendment published in law reviews from the early 1900s until the mid-1980s.[70] The three nineteenth-century cases are not somehow invalid or irrelevant because they predate the point at which the Supreme Court began to incorporate

---

[68] Sanford Levinson, "The Embarrassing Second Amendment," *The Yale Law Journal* 99(December 1989): 642, 650–51.

[69] For example, Larizza, "Paranoia, Patriotism, and the Citizen Militia Movement," 581–636; Nelson Lund, "The Second Amendment, Political Liberty, and the Right to Self-Preservation," *Alabama Law Review* 39(Fall 1987): 103–30; Reynolds, "The Right to Keep and Bear Arms Under the Tennessee Constitution," 647–73; Van Alstyne, "The Second Amendment and the Personal Right to Arms," 1236–55. A particularly egregious example of this is David C. Williams, who says flatly that the Second Amendment "guarantees to citizens the right to own arms, so as to be ready to make a revolution." "The Militia Movement and Second Amendment Revolution," 886, note 13.

[70] For a list of these articles, indexed in standard legal periodical indices, see Robert J. Spitzer, "Lost and Found: Researching the Second Amendment," *Chicago-Kent Law Review* 76(2000): 385–401.

the Bill of Rights. As noted, the Court has incorporated the Bill of Rights selectively and has avoided including the Second Amendment, despite numerous opportunities to do so. Further, the high court cited both *Cruikshank* and *Presser* as good law as recently as 1964 in the case of *Malloy v. Hogan*.[71] And, countless personal self-defense cases have been resolved for hundreds of years by reference to criminal law, not the Second Amendment.

Finally, in none of this writing is there any actual, specific, scholarship-based consideration of what real revolution entails.[72] Groups and individuals in modern America who most closely adhere to a violence-based revolutionary ethos – the Silver Shirts, Branch Davidians, Ku Klux Klan, Los Angeles rioters, Lee Harvey Oswald, John Wilkes Booth – win no admirers from the Second Amendment writers discussed herein. As legal writer Carl Bogus aptly observes, "Timothy McVeigh understands insurrectionist theory."[73] Lawyers and others who toy with any serious notions about revolutions would be well advised to consult the voluminous scholarly literature on the subject found in political science and related fields, which details and underscores the extent to which violence (especially including but not limited to the murder of top governmental leaders), societal dislocation, and disruption of a nation's economic, social, and political fabric make revolution or armed insurrection anything but a simple, reasoned, desirable, or commensurate alternative to peaceful methods of societal change.[74] The great virtue of the American political system has precisely been its ability to effect political change through nonviolent, routinized, and orderly means. To question this profound precept is to strike at the very root of a society built on law. And the irony that some legal writers extol such a notion in law reviews is inescapable.

---

[71] 378 U.S. 1 (1964) at 5.

[72] For an extended, classic discussion of the meaning and origins of the modern concept of revolution, see Hannah Arendt, *On Revolution* (New York: Viking Press, 1963), chap. 1.

[73] Bogus, "The Hidden History of the Second Amendment," 386.

[74] A few classics in the field include Arendt, *On Revolution*; John Dunn, *Modern Revolutions* (New York: Cambridge University Press, 1972); Barrington Moore, *Social Origins of Democracy and Dictatorship* (Boston: Beacon Press, 1966); and Eric R. Wolf, *Peasant Wars of the Twentieth Century* (New York: Harper and Row, 1969). One commentator who offers meaningful and valuable analysis of the military consequences of revolutions and peasant uprisings is Colonel Charles J. Dunlap, "Revolt of the Masses: Armed Civilians and the Insurrectionary Theory of the Second Amendment," *Tennessee Law Review* 62(Spring 1995): 643–77.

Collateral Claims and the Research Record

The law journal articles that advance these arguments make a series of related, supporting claims, some of which have already been raised. They assert that (1) little to nothing of any consequential scholarly nature has been published on the Second Amendment, especially before the 1980s;[75] (2) the individualist view was or is the prevalent one in legal writings until recent critics saying otherwise came along;[76] (3) the courts have committed a kind of dereliction of duty insofar as they have been all but silent on or indifferent to explicating the meaning of the Second Amendment, to the point of neglect or willful avoidance;[77] and (4) alternately, that because three of the four Supreme Court rulings on the Second Amendment came in the nineteenth century, Court doctrine is somehow defective, irrelevant, outdated, unclear, emaciated, or "embarrassing," in particular because the three are pre-incorporation.[78] Each of these claims is false.

---

[75] Barnett and Kates, "Under Fire," 1141; Robert G. Cottrol and Raymond T. Diamond, "The Second Amendment: Toward an Afro-Americanist Reconsideration," *The Georgetown Law Journal* 80(December 1991): 311; Nicholas J. Johnson, "Beyond the Second Amendment: An Individual Right to Arms Viewed Through the Ninth Amendment," *Rutgers Law Journal* 24(Fall 1992): 72; Levinson, "The Embarrassing Second Amendment," 658; Lund, "The Second Amendment," 226; Reynolds, "The Right to Keep and Bear Arms," 647; Shelton, "In Search of the Lost Amendment," 108–10.

[76] Barnett and Kates, "Under Fire," 1141; Scott Bursor, "Toward a Functional Framework for Interpreting the Second Amendment," *Texas Law Review* 74(April 1996): 1126; Don B. Kates, "The Second Amendment and the Ideology of Self-Protection," *Constitutional Commentary* 9(Winter 1992): 361.

[77] Cottrol and Diamond, "The Second Amendment," 310; Stephen A. Halbrook, "Jurisprudence of the Second and Fourteenth Amendments," *George Mason University Law Review* 4(Spring 1981): 1; David T. Hardy, "Armed Citizens, Citizen Armies: Toward a Jurisprudence of the Second Amendment," *Harvard Journal of Law and Public Policy* 9(Summer 1986): 559; Levinson, "The Embarrassing Second Amendment," 641; Lund, "The Second Amendment," 226; Van Alstyne, "The Second Amendment and the Personal Right to Arms," 1239–40.

[78] Akhil R. Amar, "The Bill of Rights and the Fourteenth Amendment," *Yale Law Journal* 101(April 1992): 1264; Hardy, "Armed Citizens, Citizen Armies," 559–60; Don B. Kates, "Handgun Prohibition and the Original Meaning of the Second Amendment," *Michigan Law Review* 82(November 1983): 214, 218; Levinson, "The Embarrassing Second Amendment," 654; Lund, "The Second Amendment," 225; Thomas M. Moncure, "The Second Amendment Ain't About Hunting," *Howard Law Journal* 34(1991): 592; Jay R. Wagner, "Gun Control Legislation and the Intent of the Second Amendment: To What Extent Is There an Individual Right to Keep and Bear Arms?" *Villanova Law Review* 37(1992): 1410.

Several years ago, I examined nearly three hundred law journal articles dealing with gun control and the Second Amendment, published from 1912 to 1999, as cited in and culled from the *Index to Legal Periodicals*. I began my search of the *Index* from its beginning with the first volume, published in 1888, through the October 1999 index,[79] under the subject headings "weapons" and "right to bear arms." (This latter heading only appeared in the *Index* starting in Volume 31, 1991.) Of the nearly 300 cited articles that I examined, 164 articles offered significant comment or assessment concerning interpretation of the Second Amendment.[80]

A total of thirteen articles on the Second Amendment appeared in law journals from 1912 to 1959.[81] All of these articles reflected the militia

[79] I conducted my search at the Cornell University Law Library. The earliest printed edition of the *Index to Legal Periodicals* in the library was titled *An Index to Legal Periodical Literature*, by Leonard A. Jones (Boston: Charles C. Soule, 1888). It indexed articles from 158 law journals and reviews written prior to 1887. (The October 1999 issue was volume 93, #1.) I excluded from my search books as well as articles on the Second Amendment appearing in the publications of other disciplines, such as history, because my deliberate purpose is to chronicle publications on this subject within the law journal community, where virtually all of this writing has taken place. In my search, I used the *Index* cites to identify articles that likely considered Second Amendment issues and to weed out those that did not. Based on a list of likely candidates drawn from the *Index*, I then went to the bound volumes of law journals to personally examine each article to see if it did, in fact, analyze the Second Amendment and to then discern the article's point of view.

[80] Book reviews were omitted, as were articles that discussed but did not take any clear position on the meaning of the Second Amendment. The study appears in Spitzer, "Lost and Found." For a chronological list of these articles, see 385–401.

[81] My original study uncovered eleven articles published from 1912 to 1959. See Spitzer, "Lost and Found." I later discovered two additional articles, bringing the total to thirteen: "The Right to Bear Arms for Private and Public Defence," *The Central Law Journal* 1(May 28, June 4, June 11, June 18, 1874): 259–61, 273–75, 285–87, 295–96 (I treated this as a single article published in installments); S. T. Ansell, "Legal and Historical Aspects of the Militia," *Yale Law Journal* 26(April 1917): 471–80. Saul Cornell argues that the *Central Law Journal* article was published by the publication's editor and noted legal figure of the time, John Forrest Dillon. Saul Cornell, "The Early American Origins of the Modern Gun Control Debate: The Right to Bear Arms, Firearms Regulation, and the Lessons of History," *Stanford Law and Policy Review* 17(2006): 593. The other eleven articles are "The Constitutional Right to Keep and Bear Arms and Statutes Against Carrying Weapons," *American Law Review* 46(September–October 1912): 777–79; "Right to Bear Arms," *Law Notes* 16(February 1913): 207–8; Lucilius A. Emery, "The Constitutional Right to Keep and Bear Arms," *Harvard Law Review* 28(March 1915): 473–77; Daniel J. McKenna, "The Right to Keep and Bear Arms," *Marquette Law Review* 12(Fall 1928): 138–49; John Brabner-Smith, "Firearm Regulation," *Law and Contemporary Problems* 1(October 1934): 400–14; Willimina Montague, "Second

view of the Second Amendment – namely, that the Second Amendment affects citizens only in connection with citizen service in a government-organized and -regulated militia. Then, in 1960, an article published in the *William and Mary Law Review* by a William and Mary Law School student and *Review* editor, Stuart R. Hays, raised two new Second Amendment arguments that would appear often in subsequent articles. One argument asserted that the Second Amendment supported an individual or personal right to have firearms (notably for personal self-defense), separate from and in addition to citizen service in a government militia. The second novel argument was that the Second Amendment created a citizen "right of revolution" – one which, in Hays's opinion, was properly exercised by the American South during the Civil War. In Hays's words, "The Southern States. . . . were engaged in a lawful revolution. . . ."[82] Hays rested these two arguments primarily on his assertion that the English tradition defined the "right to bear arms" as incorporating both a right of revolution and a right of personal self-defense.

The Hays article incorporated an array of errors and omissions. First and foremost, his analysis of Second Amendment meaning failed to consider key primary evidence on the meaning of the Bill of Rights – namely, the debate at the First Congress, and it failed to cite the law journal articles published on the subject before 1960; Hays's article based much of its analysis on a misreading of prior British history;[83] it incorrectly cited *Dred Scott v. Sandford* (1857) as applicable to Second Amendment interpretation (the case dealt with whether a slave living in a free state was entitled to citizenship rights, but in any case was overturned by the

---

Amendment, National Firearms Act," *Southern California Law Review* 13(November 1939): 129–30; A.S.V., "Second Amendment," *St. John's Law Review* 14(November 1939): 167–69; V. Breen, et al., "Federal Revenue as Limitation on State Police Power and the Right to Bear Arms – Purpose of Legislation as Affecting its Validity," *Journal of the Bar Association of Kansas* 9(November 1940): 178–82; Frederick Bernays Weiner, "The Militia Clause of the Constitution," *Harvard Law Review* 54(December 1940): 181–220; George I. Haight, "The Right to Keep and Bear Arms," *Bill of Rights Review* 2(Fall 1941): 31–42; Frederick Kling, "Restrictions on the Right to Bear Arms: State and Federal Firearms Legislation," *University of Pennsylvania Law Review* 98(May 1950): 905–19.

[82] Stuart R. Hays, "The Right to Bear Arms, A Study in Judicial Misinterpretation," *William and Mary Law Review* 2(1960): 403.

[83] Compare with Bogus, "The Hidden History of the Second Amendment," 375–85; and Lois G. Schworer, "To Hold and Bear Arms: The English Perspective," *Chicago-Kent Law Review* 76(2000): 27–60.

passage of the Thirteenth and Fourteenth Amendments), and misspelled Chief Justice Roger Taney as "Tanney";[84] it incorrectly labeled the Court's opinion in *Presser v. Illinois* (1886), written by Justice Woods, as a "dissent" (there was no dissent in *Presser*);[85] it miscited and misspelled the case of *U.S. v. Cruikshank* as *Cruickshank v. U.S.*;[86] and it cited the wrong years for the cases of *Miller v. Texas* (1894, not 1893), *Presser* (1886, not 1885), and *Robertson v. Baldwin* (1897, not 1899).[87] Although some of these errors are minor, when added together, they summarize an article whose scholarship, produced by the author while he was a student[88] (and who was himself a life member of the National Rifle Association [NRA], having first joined before entering law school), was less than reliable. On this broken reed was subsequent individualist analysis built.

The next article appearing in a legal publication to advance the individualist view appeared in the *American Bar Association Journal* in 1965, authored by a Chicago lawyer, Robert A. Sprecher.[89] Sprecher argued that modern writers were "sharply divided" over the question of whether the Second Amendment endorsed a militia-based or individual right. Yet, his only evidence of a "sharp divide" consisted of two articles in support of the individualist view: the Hays article and an article published in the *University of Pennsylvania Law Review* in 1950.[90] Yet, Sprecher mischaracterized this second article (also student-authored) because it did not champion the individualist view; instead, it argued for the adoption of uniform firearms laws, including national licensing for firearms owners.[91] From 1960 through the end of the decade, another twelve articles on the Second Amendment were published in legal publications – eleven

---

[84] Hays, "The Right to Bear Arms," 397. [85] *Ibid.*, 401.

[86] *Ibid.*, 399. [87] *Ibid.*, 400, notes 82 and 84; 402, note 88.

[88] According to the Alumni Office at the College of William and Mary School of Law, Hays received his undergraduate B.A. degree from William and Mary in 1957 and a B.C.L. degree from the law school in 1960. Hays had been a hunter and gun collector since before his law school days and also had become a life member of the National Rifle Association before law school (correspondence with the author, December 15, 1999; on file with the author).

[89] Robert A. Sprecher, "The Lost Amendment," *American Bar Association Journal* 51(June/July 1965): 554–57, 665–69.

[90] Kling, "Note: Restrictions on the Right to Bear Arms: State and Federal Firearms Legislation."

[91] See Carl T. Bogus, "The History and Politics of Second Amendment Scholarship: A Primer," *Chicago-Kent Law Review* 76(2000): 6–7.

supporting the militia or collective view and one, published in 1967,[92] supporting the individualist view.

In the 1970s and 1980s, however, individualist writing in legal publications took off. From 1970 to 1989, twenty-five articles supporting the militia view were published; but, twenty-seven articles appeared that supported the individualist view. It is interesting that more than half of those (i.e., sixteen) were authored by lawyers employed at one time or another by the NRA or other gun rights groups.[93] Two individualist writers stand out as especially prolific: lawyers Stephen P. Halbrook and Don B. Kates. Up to 2000, they have together produced eight books and twenty-three law journal articles, as well as numerous other writings extolling the individualist view. Both have also been involved in gun-related litigation.[94] Halbrook is particularly notable in this regard because he has served as the NRA's lead lawyer in many suits, including the 1997 case of *Printz v. U.S.*,[95] in which the Supreme Court struck down the provision of the Brady Law that required local police to conduct background checks of prospective handgun buyers. In his writings, however, Halbrook never mentions his NRA affiliation, saying only that he "practices law in Fairfax, Virginia," which also happens to be the location of the NRA's headquarters.[96]

This assertion of little academic writing also carries within it a corollary assertion – that any relative handful of articles, by virtue of their small number, ipso facto cannot have adequately examined and discussed the issue in question. Obviously, this judgment is false, absent a content analysis of the articles, because a single, careful article might indeed examine with adequate depth and care any given subject. Beyond this, to say that few articles have been written on this subject is, in and of itself, false. In any case, the focus on simple numbers of articles says nothing about whether this or any subject has received adequate, proper, or appropriate treatment.

The second assertion, that the individualist view was the dominant one, is contradicted by the history and case law previously discussed and by the information provided in the previous discussion, encapsulated by

[92] Nicholas V. Olds, "Second Amendment and the Right to Keep and Bear Arms," *Michigan State Bar Journal* 46(October 1967): 15–25.
[93] Bogus, "The History and Politics of Second Amendment Scholarship," 8–10; Spitzer, "Lost and Found," 379–80.
[94] Bogus, "The History and Politics of Second Amendment Scholarship," 8–10.
[95] 521 U.S. 898 (1997).   [96] Spitzer, "Lost and Found," 380.

the existence of twenty-four articles taking the militia view published until 1970, compared with just three articles taking the individualist view. In the decade of the 1980s, seventeen militia/collective articles were published, compared with twenty-one taking the individualist view.[97] The numbers jumped again in the 1990s, with twenty-nine taking the militia view and fifty-eight taking the individualist view.[98]

The assertion that the individualist view has been the dominant one is also contradicted by standard reference works. For example, in his foundational reference book on the Constitution, Jack Peltason says that the Second Amendment "was designed to prevent Congress from disarming the state militias, not to prevent it from regulating private ownership of firearms."[99] In his classic book on the Bill of Rights, Irving Brant says: "The Second Amendment, popularly misread, comes to life chiefly on the parade floats of rifle associations and in the propaganda of mail-order houses selling pistols to teenage gangsters. . . ."[100] Similar if less sarcastic sentiments are found in other standard works.[101]

[97] Don B. Kates has been quick to mischaracterize the literature, saying that before the 1980s there was "scant historical support" for the court/collective view (an assertion contradicted by the bibliographic data presented herein), and as seen also in his false assertion that "thirty-six law review articles" addressed the Second Amendment from 1980 to the early 1990s, and that "only four" take the court/collectivist view. "Gun Control: Separating Reality from Symbolism," *Journal of Contemporary Law* 20(1994): 359. In fact, thirty-eight articles dealt with the subject from 1980 to 1989, with another twenty-four published from 1990 to 1993 (the year before the publication of Kates's article), totaling sixty-two articles. Of the sixty-two, twenty-six take the collectivist view, not four. See Spitzer, "Lost and Found," 384.

[98] Spitzer, "Lost and Found," 384.

[99] Jack Peltason, *Corwin and Peltason's Understanding the Constitution* (New York: Holt, Rinehart, and Winston, 1988), 168.

[100] Irving Brant, *The Bill of Rights* (Indianapolis, IN: Bobbs-Merrill Co., 1965), 486.

[101] Edward Dumbauld says: "The Second and Third Amendments stand simply as the empty symbol of what remains a living American ideal: the supremacy of the civil power over the military." He also notes that "these amendments are defunct in practice." *The Bill of Rights* (Norman, OK: University of Oklahoma Press, 1957), 62–63. See also John Sexton and Nat Brandt, *How Free Are We?* (New York: M. Evans and Co., 1986), 209–210. In the words of Robert A. Rutland, the Second Amendment (along with the Third, having to do with the quartering of troops in peoples' homes) has become "obsolete." *The Birth of the Bill of Rights* (Chapel Hill, NC: University of North Carolina Press, 1955), 229. Standard legal reference works used by lawyers and judges parallel this perspective. See *American Law Reports, Federal* (Rochester, NY: The Lawyers Co-Operative Pub. Co., 1983), 700–729. In 1975, the American Bar Association endorsed the understanding that the Second Amendment is connected with militia service, as has the American Civil Liberties Union. See Anthony J. Dennis, "Clearing the Smoke," *Akron Law Review* 29(Summer 1995): 65, note 29.

The third assertion – that the courts have committed a kind of dereliction of duty with respect to the Second Amendment – is also false, given the existence of the Supreme Court cases discussed previously, all of which explicate and support the interpretation that the Second Amendment comes into play only in connection with citizen service in a government-organized and -regulated militia, and that this amendment has not been incorporated under the Fourteenth Amendment, despite the opportunity to do so afforded by numerous lower-court appeals spanning the last sixty years. Further, these recent lower federal court opinions have been even more emphatic and detailed in asserting that, as the Ninth Circuit noted in 1996, "We follow our sister circuits in holding that the Second Amendment is a right held by the states, and does not protect the possession of a weapon by a private citizen."[102] The inescapable conclusion is that the Supreme Court simply has no inclination to revisit the issue. The high court may, of course, change its mind on the matter, and there is reason to believe that at least two justices are interested in revisiting the subject (see subsequent discussion).

The fourth assertion – that because three of the four key Supreme Court cases on the Second Amendment came in the nineteenth century they are therefore now somehow irrelevant or deficient – is transparently false because no legal doctrine imposes a statute of limitations or expiration date on binding Court precedent unless the precedent is ignored or overturned, neither of which has occurred for Second Amendment law.[103] Whereas it is true that the three earlier cases came before the Supreme Court began the piecemeal incorporation of the Bill of Rights in 1897, the process has never been extended by the Court to the entire Bill of Rights, and there is no expectation that it will.[104] Since then, the Third

---

[102] *Hickman v. Block*, 81 F.3d 98 (9th Cir., 1996), at 101. See also the other federal cases cited in footnote 39 of this chapter.

[103] Thomas M. Moncure says that the three nineteenth-century cases "are as unillustrative as they are unpleasant." Whether true or not, I know of no legal doctrine that invalidates cases because of these traits. "The Second Amendment Ain't About Hunting," 592.

[104] The late Supreme Court Justices John Marshall Harlan, William O. Douglas, and Hugo Black argued for total incorporation of the Bill of Rights, but no one else on the Court has since embraced such an argument. The first incorporation case applied the Fifth Amendment protection to the states pertaining to just compensation in cases of eminent domain in *Chicago, Burlington, and Quincy Railroad v. Chicago*, 166 U.S. 226 (1897). Other significant incorporation cases included First Amendment free speech in *Gitlow v. New York*, 268 U.S. 652 (1925); First Amendment press freedom in *Near v. Minnesota*, 283 U.S. 697 (1931); First Amendment religious freedom in *Hamilton v.*

Amendment, the grand jury clause of the Fifth Amendment, the Seventh Amendment, the fines-and-bails clause of the Eighth Amendment, as well as the Ninth and Tenth Amendments, have not been incorporated. The pre-incorporation Second Amendment cases thus continue to stand as good law.[105]

Seeking Shelter under the Fourteenth Amendment

This discussion of incorporation raises an additional, related argument offered by a few – namely, that the Fourteenth Amendment somehow created, enhanced, or validated a constitutionally based individual right to bear arms aside or apart from citizen militia service. To support this claim, advocates generally cite post–Civil War debate in Congress that referenced the Second Amendment or the bearing of arms. Typical of these claims is that of Halbrook, who quotes Senator Jacob M. Howard's (R-MI) comments during debate over the Fourteenth Amendment in 1866. "When he introduced the Fourteenth Amendment in Congress, Senator Jacob M. Howard . . . referred to 'the personal rights guaranteed and secured by the first eight amendments of the Constitution; such as freedom of speech and of the press; . . . *the right to keep and bear arms*. . . . [emphasis added by Halbrook]'."[106] Halbrook makes two claims from this and related quotes. One is that the reference to "personal rights,"

Regents of the University of California, 293 U.S. 245 (1934); First Amendment freedom of assembly and petitioning the government for redress of grievances, *De Jonge v. Oregon*, 299 U.S. 353 (1937); Fourth Amendment search and seizure, *Mapp v. Ohio*, 367 U.S. 643 (1961); Sixth Amendment right to counsel in *Gideon v. Wainwright*, 372 U.S. 335 (1963); and Fifth Amendment protection against double jeopardy in *Benton v. Maryland*, 395 U.S. 784 (1969). For an excellent summary of incorporation, see Henry J. Abraham, *Freedom and the Court* (New York: Oxford University Press, 1972), chap. 3. See also Brant, *The Bill of Rights*, chaps. 27–40. Richard C. Cortner notes that the last incorporation case was 1969 and suggests that only the fines and bail clause might one day be incorporated. *The Supreme Court and the Second Bill of Rights* (Madison, WI: University of Wisconsin Press, 1981), 279.

[105] The Courts of Appeal have repeatedly recognized the validity of the earlier Supreme Court cases dealing with the Second Amendment. Some individualist writers misconstrue incorporation entirely. Halbrook, for example, claims that the *Presser* case "plainly suggests that the second amendment applies to the States through the fourteenth amendment" when, in fact, the Court said precisely the opposite. "To Keep and Bear Their Private Arms," 85.

[106] Stephen P. Halbrook, *That Every Man Be Armed* (Oakland, CA: The Independent Institute, 1984), 112.

apparently offered in the same context as the mention of the right to bear arms, means that this "personal right" is an "individual right." The second claim is to argue for total incorporation – that is, application of all of the Bill of Rights to the states. Whereas even this abbreviated quote suggests that Senator Howard was merely listing the parts of the Bill of Rights, the full quote from Senate debate clarifies the point:

> To these privileges and immunities [referenced in Article IV of the Constitution], whatever they may be – for they are not and cannot be fully defined in their entire extent and precise nature – to these should be added the personal rights guarantied and secured by the first eight amendments of the Constitution; such as the freedom of speech and of the press [First Amendment]; the right of the people peaceably to assemble and petition the Government for redress of grievances, a right appertaining to each and all the people [First Amendment]; the right to keep and bear arms [Second Amendment]; the right to be exempted from the quartering of soldiers in a house without the consent of the owner [Third Amendment]; the right to be exempt from unreasonable searches and seizures, and from any search or seizure except by virtue of a warrant issued upon formal oath or affidavit [Fourth Amendment]; the right of an accused person to be informed of the nature of the accusation against him, and his right to be tried by an impartial jury of the vicinage [Sixth Amendment]; and also the right to be secure against excessive bail and against cruel and unusual punishments [Eighth Amendment].[107]

The senator's reference to "personal rights" in the quote was simply a synonym for all of the rights of the Bill of Rights. There is no reason to believe that this reference articulates or implies an individual right to bear arms aside or apart from the conventional understanding of citizen participation in a government-organized and -regulated militia. As for the question of full incorporation of the Bill of Rights under the Fourteenth Amendment, one may argue that this quote supports the contention. Although the argument that the Fourteenth Amendment was designed to provide for total incorporation is a minority viewpoint among constitutional scholars[108] (and it has been rejected by the courts), it is at least a bona fide argument. The claim that the Fourteenth Amendment somehow created, elevated, or ratified an individual right to bear arms, either as part of the

---

[107] Alfred Avins, *The Reconstruction Amendments' Debates* (Richmond, VA: Virginia Commission on Constitutional Government, 1967), 219.

[108] For example, Andrea L. Bonnicksen, *Civil Rights and Liberties* (Palo Alto, CA: Mayfield Publishing, 1982), 12–14.

Second or Fourteenth Amendment, is not.[109] In any case, to make such an argument about the Fourteenth Amendment is also to argue implicitly that the Second Amendment, as originally drafted, did not create such an individual right in the first place (otherwise, there would be no reason to resort to the Fourteenth to support such a line of reasoning). Amar, in fact, makes this argument explicitly when he says that "Creation-era arms bearing was collective. . . . Reconstruction gun-toting was individualistic. . . ."[110]

Quinlan offers the same kind of analysis when, for example, he quotes Representative Roswell Hart (R-NY) when he said the following during House of Representatives debate in 1866:

> "citizens shall be entitled to all privileges and immunities of other citizens;" where "no law shall be made prohibiting the free exercise of religion;" where "the right of the people to keep and bear arms shall not be infringed;" where "the right of the people to be secure in their persons, houses, papers, and effects, against unreasonable searches and seizures, shall not be violated,". . . . [quotation marks in original][111]

From this quote, Quinlan concludes that "Apparently, several commentators in the Reconstruction Congress considered the Second Amendment's right to keep and bear arms an individual right."[112] Once again, the speaker is simply reciting Bill of Rights protections, as demarcated by the use of quotation marks. The quote does nothing to support the individualist view, as even Quinlan's use of the modifier "apparently" suggests.

Halbrook expands this Fourteenth Amendment analysis when he attempts to link together the Fourteenth Amendment with the

---

[109] Michael J. Quinlan makes the same error in "Is There a Neutral Justification for Refusing to Implement the Second Amendment or Is the Supreme Court Just 'Gun Shy'?" *Capital University Law Review* 22(Summer 1993): 661.

[110] Akhil Reed Amar, *The Bill of Rights* (New Haven, CT: Yale University Press, 1998), 259. Amar concludes that the Second Amendment "was reglossed by a later constitutional text [i.e., the Fourteenth Amendment]. . . ." (297). Amar cites the same kind of sources as Halbrook to support his "floor wax" theory of this supposed relationship between the two amendments. In his analysis, Amar confuses politics and law, citing congressional debate over Southern turmoil to support his argument, yet he never cites or even mentions the *Cruikshank* or *Presser* cases (or, for that matter, *U.S. v. Miller*), which falsify his argument. Amar makes similar arguments in "The Second Amendment: A Case Study in Constitutional Interpretation," *Utah Law Review* (2001): 899–900, 907–8.

[111] Quinlan, "Is There a Neutral Justification," 662.

[112] *Ibid.*

Freedman's Bureau Act of 1866 and the Civil Rights Act of 1866, so he can draw on the debate and text of these bills to argue that, when taken together, they provide "the rights of personal security and personal liberty [and] include the 'constitutional right to bear arms.'"[113] Again, Halbrook culls congressional and state debate for any and all references to firearms, the bearing of arms, the word *individual*, and the like. Not only is Halbrook seeking to argue that "the Fourteenth Amendment was intended to incorporate the Second Amendment" but also further to argue that the "Fourteenth Amendment protects the rights to personal security and personal liberty, which its authors declared in the Freedmen's Bureau Act to include 'the constitutional right to bear arms.' To the members of the Thirty-Ninth Congress, possession of arms was a fundamental, individual right worthy of protection from both federal and state violation."[114] In other words, beyond arguing for total incorporation, Halbrook argues that the Fourteenth Amendment itself protects the bearing of arms.

This line of reasoning has several obvious problems. First and foremost, while it is true that the same congress sought to extend similar, basic rights through the trio of enactments, including the Fourteenth Amendment, the Fourteenth Amendment simply does not stipulate anything like a right to bear arms. No court has ever found or suggested that the Second Amendment was somehow repeated, amplified, or elevated by the Fourteenth. And, although similar, each of these three enactments is – as a matter of law – different, and to attempt to draw out legislative intent behind one enactment (i.e., the Fourteenth Amendment) by bringing in others (i.e., the Civil Rights Act and the Freedmen's Bureau Act) is both desperate and erroneous.[115]

Second, the discussion of arms, personal security, and militias in Congress during this time is by no means a discussion that revolves solely

---

[113] Stephen P. Halbrook, *Freedmen, the Fourteenth Amendment, and the Right to Bear Arms, 1866–1876* (Westport, CT: Praeger, 1998), viii.

[114] Halbrook, *Freedmen, the Fourteenth Amendment*, 43. See also 71.

[115] Akhil Reed Amar also wants to argue for a kind of total incorporation by saying that "the Second Amendment right to bear arms – and presumably all other rights and freedoms in the Bill of Rights – were encompassed by both the Freedman's Bureau Act and its companion Civil Rights Act. (Of course, adoption of both Acts presupposed congressional power to impose the general requirements of the Bill of Rights on states. [Rep.] Bingham . . . denied that Congress had such power, and therefore argued that a constitutional amendment was required to validate the Civil Rights Act. . . .)" Amar does note the key difference between the two bills and the Fourteenth Amendment. "The Bill of Rights and the Fourteenth Amendment," 1245, note 228.

around the Second Amendment. Remember that the American South was in a state of near-total destruction and utter chaos, a fact heightened by the race hatred found in the region in the aftermath of the freeing of millions of former slaves (some of whom formed militias for their own protection), and the presence of thousands of former Confederate soldiers who were allowed to keep their arms. Little wonder that there was so much discussion in Congress of security and safety issues.[116]

Third, as an interpretation of the Second Amendment, the congressional debates of the 1860s deserve no special, if any, consideration. These debates were not debates over the meaning of that amendment per se, occurring as they did more than seventy years after adoption of the Bill of Rights. They were political debates over how best to extend hard-won rights, restore order, and reconfigure governance in the American South.

Fourth, the yearning for total incorporation or any kind of elevation of the Second Amendment was rejected by political contemporaries. Eight years after adoption of the Fourteenth Amendment, the Supreme Court explicitly rejected the idea in *U.S. v. Cruikshank*, as quoted previously in this chapter. And, the Court did not incorporate any part of the Bill of Rights until 1897. This fact alone puts to rest Halbrook's assertions.

The research tactic applied to attempting to find a connection between the Fourteenth and Second Amendments follows that described by Garry Wills in characterizing individualist research on the Second Amendment. "The tactic . . . is to ransack any document, no matter how distant from the . . . debates, in the hope that someone, somewhere, ever used 'bear arms' in a non-military way. . . ."[117] In the case of incorporation, this search extends, fruitlessly, to eight decades after the writing of the Second Amendment.

Public Policy Consequences

As this discussion has described, efforts to win legitimacy for the individualist view of the Second Amendment in the courts have, with one exception, fallen flat to date. That exception, the Fifth Circuit Court of Appeals case of *U.S. v. Emerson* from 2001,[118] has proven to be a pyrrhic

---

[116] Nicholas Lemann, *Redemption: The Last Battle of the Civil War* (New York: Farrar, Straus and Giroux, 2006).

[117] Wills, *A Necessary Evil*, 257–58.   [118] 270 F.3d 203 (5th Cir. 2002).

victory. Yes, the two-member majority authored a lengthy opinion that embraced the individualist view. Yet, it proved no help to the man whose prosecution gave rise to the case because the appeals court also over-turned a lower court ruling that dismissed the charges against Emerson on Second Amendment grounds, upheld the federal law that barred gun possession for persons under a domestic violence restraining order, and remanded the case to trial in Texas, where Emerson was convicted on the weapons possession charges (his conviction was upheld on appeal). Further, *Emerson*'s Second Amendment theorizing has been ignored to date by every other circuit and even by the Fifth Circuit.

Still, apropos the theme of this chapter and book, individualist law journal writing was central to the majority decision's reasoning, evidence, and conclusion. In addition to citing individualist law journal writers,[119] the lengthy decision parrots the arguments and evidence found in the individualist writings cited herein and elsewhere.[120]

When *Emerson* was appealed to the Supreme Court, it refused to hear the case. But *Emerson* has arguably opened the door to future consid-eration by the high court, given that it contradicts the many Second Amendment rulings from the other circuits. And, some sympathy for the individualist view may already exist on the Supreme Court.

In the 1997 case of *Printz v. U.S.*, Justice Clarence Thomas noted in his concurring opinion:

> The Court has not had recent occasion to consider the nature of the sub-stantive right safeguarded by the Second Amendment. If, however, the Second Amendment is read to confer a *personal* right to "keep and bear arms," a colorable argument exists that the Federal Government's regula-tory scheme . . . runs afoul of that Amendment's protection. As the parties did not raise this argument, however, we need not consider it here.[121]

In a footnote to this comment, Thomas characterizes the individualist law journal writing this way: "Marshaling an impressive array of histori-cal evidence, a growing body of scholarly commentary indicates that the 'right to keep and bear arms' is, as the Amendment's text suggests, a per-sonal right."[122] He then cites a series of law journal articles authored

---

[119] 270 F.3d 203 at 220–22.
[120] See Spitzer, "The Second Amendment 'Right to Bear Arms' and *United States v. Emerson*."
[121] 521 U.S. 898 (1997), at 938–39.   [122] 521 U.S. 898 at 939, note 2.

by Halbrook, William Van Alstyne, Amar, Robert Cottrol and Raymond Diamond, Levinson, Kates, and David Williams. Justice Antonin Scalia raised similar suggestions in a talk that was published as part of a book.[123] And Chief Justice John Roberts echoed sympathies for the individualist view during his confirmation hearings in 2005.[124] Whatever else may be said of this writing, it has deeply infused the Second Amendment debate in the courts and won for itself the lofty, if undeserved, mantle of "impressive ... scholarly commentary."

Individualist writing has had a more direct effect on decisions within the executive branch's Justice Department. Shortly after taking office in 2001, Bush administration Attorney General John Ashcroft moved to codify and legitimize the individualist view of the Second Amendment. In one of his first legal pronouncements, Ashcroft outlined his views on the meaning of the Second Amendment's right to bear arms in a two-page letter sent on May 17, 2001, to NRA Executive Director James Jay Baker shortly before the NRA's annual convention, in which Ashcroft said: "Let me state unequivocally my view that the text and the original intent of the Second Amendment clearly protect the right of individuals to keep and bear firearms." As a formal issuance from the nation's chief law-enforcement officer, the letter merits particular scrutiny not only because it argued that the individualist view "is not a novel position" but also because it

---

[123] Antonin Scalia, "Common-Law Courts in a Civil-Law System," in *A Matter of Interpretation: Federal Courts and the Law*, ed. Amy Gutmann (Princeton, NJ: Princeton University Press, 1997), 3, 43.

[124] During questioning by U.S. Senate Judiciary Committee member Russell Feingold (D-WI) on September 14, 2005, Roberts was asked about his views of the Second Amendment's right to bear arms. In his question, Feingold said that the 1939 *Miller* case "saw the right to bear arms as a collective right." Roberts responded by saying that *Miller* did not, in fact, endorse the collective view: "I know that the Miller case side-stepped that issue. An argument was made back in 1939 that this provides only a collective right. And the court didn't address that. They said, instead, that the firearm at issue there – I think it was a sawed-off shotgun – is not the type of weapon protected under the militia aspect of the Second Amendment. So people try to read the tea leaves about Miller and what would come out on this issue. But that's still very much an open issue." Transcript accessed at www.washingtonpost.com on September 12, 2006. Debate about Justice Samuel Alito's views on gun control and the Second Amendment that arose during his confirmation hearings focused on his dissenting opinion in a 1996 case, *U.S. v. Rybar* (103 F.3d 273; 3d Cir.), in which Alito argued in favor of striking down the 1934 National Firearms Act's prohibition against possession of machine guns. But Alito's dissent was based on the argument that Congress had exceeded its authority under the commerce power. Alito made no mention of the Second Amendment. His extreme conservatism, however, suggests that he might be sympathetic to an individualist interpretation if others on the Court already share that view.

contradicted the existing position that the Justice Department had taken in the then-pending *Emerson* case and was sent to a group, the NRA, which had filed an opposing friend-of-the-court brief in the very same case.

Beyond these particulars, the letter was remarkable, first, because it represented an offhanded, informal, and political means to articulate and inaugurate what proved to be an abrupt and total about-face in decades of Justice Department policy on the meaning of the Second Amendment. Second, the letter's arguments contradicted the numerous federal court rulings discussed in this chapter that have rejected the view embraced by Ashcroft. Third, the evidence and sources cited in the letter to support Ashcroft's claim do no such thing. Fourth, the letter failed to cite the most important sources explaining what the right to bear arms does mean. And, fifth, law journal articles received prominent mention as authoritative sources supporting the letter's arguments. Further, Ashcroft moved ahead to make the views expressed in this letter the policy of the Justice Department when he sent a subsequent memorandum to all ninety-three U.S. Attorneys in November 2001 directing them to adopt the individualist view as law, seizing on the *Emerson* ruling (handed down the previous month) to buttress his case. Ashcroft's decision was made without the usual vetting process that it normally follows whenever the Justice Department considers a change in policy. In fact, it was produced by the "political echelon" of the Justice Department. The Solicitor General's Office was not consulted nor were career Justice Department attorneys who had specific authority over the government's position concerning the Second Amendment.[125] Even though Ashcroft's two-page letter was not in and of itself a legal issuance, it proved to be the linchpin of Justice Department policy and, therefore, warrants careful attention.

By way of background, the Justice Department has consistently embraced the collective or militia view for decades, including both Democratic and Republican presidents. Investigations by a former Justice Department employee who later worked for a pro-gun control policy group traced Justice Department Office of Legal Counsel (OLC) policy statements on the Second Amendment back to 1954.[126] From that point forward, the position of the Justice Department was uniform – that

[125] Mathew Nosanchuk, "The Embarrassing Interpretation of the Second Amendment," *Northern Kentucky Law Review* 29(2002): 766.
[126] Nosanchuk," The Embarrassing Interpretation of the Second Amendment," 751–61.

the Second Amendment, in the words of President Reagan's Solicitor General, Charles Fried, "guarantees no right to keep and bear a firearm that does not have 'some reasonable relationship to . . . a well-regulated militia.'" The first President Bush's Solicitor General, Kenneth Starr, similarly concluded that "possession of [a] firearm did not fall within the rights guaranteed by the Second Amendment."[127] This was also the position of the Clinton Justice Department, articulated as recently as 2000.

Attorney General Ashcroft's letter cited a variety of historical sources to buttress his new individualist view, from the *Federalist Papers*, to congressional hearings in the 1930s, to legislation from the 1980s. Yet, examination of these sources reveals that none of them supported the claims Ashcroft made.[128] Also prominently mentioned in his letter as

---

[127] Jeffrey Toobin, "Ashcroft's Ascent," *The New Yorker*, April 15, 2002, 60.

[128] In his May 2001 letter, Ashcroft argued that President Franklin D. Roosevelt's Attorney General, Homer Cummings, had embraced the individualist interpretation of the Second Amendment in testimony offered in 1934 before the Ways and Means Committee of the House of Representatives on a bill that was enacted later that year as the National Firearms Act. Although Cummings acknowledged at one point during the hearings that he had concerns about the constitutionality of a proposal to require all existing gun owners to register their handguns (a proposal based on the government's powers to tax), at no time did Cummings say that such a proposal might run afoul of the Second Amendment, nor did Cummings ever say anywhere in the 166-page printed hearings that he supported or believed the idea that the Second Amendment protected an individual right to own guns. In fact, Cummings was the most strongly pro-gun-control attorney general in the nation's history, who aggressively advocated a wide range of gun-control measures.

Further, during its hearings, the Ways and Means Committee took extensive testimony from two NRA officers, including NRA President Karl T. Frederick. At no point in their testimony did either object to the proposed law as a violation of the Second Amendment. Both NRA representatives did raise objections to the legislation but did so primarily because they were concerned that the law might interfere with honest citizens attempting to defend themselves from lawless individuals. Thus, Ashcroft's claim that his position on the Second Amendment "was not a novel one" was, for the purposes of the Justice Department's long-held position on the issue, false. See Hearings Before the Committee on Ways and Means, "National Firearms Act," 73rd Cong., 2nd Sess., April 16, 18, May 14–16, 1934.

Ashcroft further cited various statements from the Constitution's founders, including correspondence and debate by early American leaders and the *Federalist Papers*, all to argue that these writings supported his individualist views. As other research demonstrates, however, none of this writing supports Ashcroft's arguments; in fact, it all supports the opposite conclusion that the right to bear arms was invariably linked with issues of militia service and the government's ability to meet military emergencies. See, for example, Spitzer, *The Right to Bear Arms*, chap. 2.

Finally, Ashcroft cited a 1986 federal gun law, the Firearms Owners Protection Act (P.L. 99–308), as having "explicitly adopted" the individualist view. It does nothing of the sort. In fact, all the law does is refer to "the right of citizens to keep

authoritative sources were law review articles by four individualist writers (i.e., Van Alstyne, Amar, Levinson, and Kates). Based on these writers and their articles, Ashcroft concluded that "the individuals [*sic*] rights view is embraced by the preponderance of legal scholarship on the subject."[129] Ashcroft's close reliance on this law journal writing extends not only to the reference to it but also the ideas found within his letter that surely helped frame the case analysis in it.

Specifically, Ashcroft's letter cited five Supreme Court cases that he claimed supported his individualist interpretation. Of these, only two (i.e., *Miller v. Texas*, 1893, and *Robertson v. Baldwin*, 1897) actually address the meaning of the Second Amendment. As discussed previously, *Miller v. Texas* upheld a Texas law barring the carrying of dangerous weapons as not in violation of the Second Amendment. The Court also noted that the Second Amendment did not apply to the states. In *Robertson*, the Court ruled that the Second Amendment was not infringed by a law barring the carrying of concealed weapons. In neither case did the Court state or imply that the Second Amendment protected a private or individual right for citizens to own guns apart from their service in a government-organized and -regulated militia.

Two other cases cited in Ashcroft's letter have nothing whatsoever to do with interpreting the Second Amendment. One of the cases, *Logan v. U.S.*,[130] had to do with the propriety of a federal conspiracy prosecution arising from physical violence that occurred while a suspect was in federal custody. The only mention of the Second Amendment (which was mis-cited in Ashcroft's letter because the page of the decision he cites makes no mention of the amendment) was a passing reference to it in connection with other Bill of Rights protections to note that, in the year of the case, the Court had not applied any of the Bill of Rights to the states – that is, the Bill of Rights was interpreted as applying only to federal action. The other, *Maxwell v. Dow*,[131] had to do with procedures governing juries. *Maxwell* did, however, quote from *Presser v. Illinois*, which did rule on the

---

and bear arms under the second amendment." The Ashcroft letter is available at www.nraila.org/images/Ashcroft.pdf. Accessed on September 12, 2006.

[129] In the text of his letter, Ashcroft writes, "See, e.g. William Van Alstyne, *the Second Amendment and the Personal Right to Arms*, 43 Duke L.J. 1236 (1994); Akhil Reed Amar, *The Bill of Rights and the Fourteenth Amendment*, 101 Yale L.J. 1193 (1992); Sandford Levinson, *The Embarrassing Second Amendment*, 99 Yale L.J. 637 (1989); Don Kates, *Handgun Prohibition and the Original Meaning of the Second Amendment*, 82 Mich. L. Rev. 204 (1983)."

[130] 144 U.S. 263 (1892).   [131] 176 U.S. 581 (1899).

meaning of the Second Amendment. *Maxwell* noted that the Court had previously ruled in *Presser* that states could not keep citizens from bearing arms if it deprived the national government from "maintaining the public security, and disable the people from performing their duty to the General Government." Thus, both *Maxwell* and *Presser* as cited by the Court in *Maxwell* endorse the view that the Second Amendment applies only to citizen service in a government-organized and -regulated militia. In other words, the *Presser* case, which did deal squarely with the meaning of the Second Amendment, interpreted the amendment in diametric opposition to Ashcroft's claim. This meaning was then confirmed in *Maxwell*. To add to the confusion, Ashcroft did not cite *Presser* in his letter, even though it is central to the Court's interpretation of the amendment.

The fifth case Ashcroft cited was *U.S. v. Verdugo-Urquidez*.[132] Yet, this 1990 case has nothing to do with interpreting the Second Amendment but instead deals with the applicability of Fourth Amendment search and seizure protections to non–U.S. citizens. In a passing comment, the majority opinion mentioned several places in the Constitution where the phrase "the people" appears, including the Second Amendment. Nowhere did the Court say, as Ashcroft claimed in his letter, that the phrase "the people" "should be interpreted consistently throughout"; in fact, the Court has never adopted a single, uniform interpretation of the phrase, as its rulings on the Second Amendment alone make clear.

Aside from these errors, Ashcroft not only failed to cite *Presser* but also *U.S. v. Miller*. By omitting any reference to *Miller* in his letter, Ashcroft demonstrated either shocking incompetence in the ability to research and cite cases relevant to Bill of Rights interpretation or a tacit admission that the ruling in this case did not conform to the views he advanced in his letter. According to one critic, Ashcroft's failure to mention *Miller* was an attempt to "'overrule' *Miller* by omission."[133]

The Justice Department's directive of November 2001 was followed in May 2002 with a further, formal articulation of this new individualist view. In two cases appealed to the Supreme Court, *Haney v. U.S.*[134] and *Emerson*,[135] Solicitor General Theodore B. Olson filed briefs on behalf of the government recommending that the individuals charged in these two

---

[132] 494 U.S. 259 (1990).
[133] Nosanchuk, "The Embarrassing Interpretation of the Second Amendment," 782.
[134] 536 U.S. 907 (2002).   [135] *Ibid.*

cases be prosecuted for their respective gun-related violations. Although supporting the prosecutions in question, however, Olson also inserted in the two government briefs a footnote saying that the government's position on the Second Amendment was now that it "more broadly protects the rights of individuals, including persons who are not members of any militia or engaged in active military service or training, to possess and bear their own firearms, subject to reasonable restrictions. . . ." One news account observed that this was not only "a policy change" but noted also "the offhand manner in which the administration expressed such a major policy change, in footnotes in briefs filed without public pronouncement. . . ." In both instances, the high court ruled in June 2002 to uphold the prosecutions without comment, and declined to address the matter of interpretations of the Second Amendment.[136]

Ashcroft's departmental policy change pertaining to the Second Amendment spawned numerous challenges to gun-control laws and criminal prosecutions involving guns, including a motion on behalf of the "American Taliban," John Walker Lindh, to dismiss weapons charges against him on this basis (the motion was not sustained). In all, more than 130 court challenges were filed against federal gun laws based on the new Justice Department policy in the District of Columbia and Virginia alone. In 2004, shortly before Ashcroft left the Justice Department, the OLC issued a memorandum embracing the individualist view.[137] Former Deputy Solicitor General Andrew L. Frey, who served in the post from 1973 to 1986, said that the Justice Department's new view of the Second Amendment would both hamper prosecutors and help defendants. To add to the confusion, the Justice Department denied that this new interpretation was applicable to the numerous cases that have arisen, leading one federal prosecutor to complain that the government's position was "evasive and anemic to the point of unconsciousness."[138] This conclusion is supported by the case of Bashaun Pearson, who was charged in June 2002 by Washington, DC, authorities with unlawfully carrying a 9 mm handgun in the District of Columbia – a gun for which he had a lawful permit

---

[136] Linda Greenhouse, "Justices Reject Cases on Right to Bear Arms," *New York Times*, June 11, 2002, A24.

[137] Greenhouse, "Justices Reject Cases on Right to Bear Arms"; Nancy V. Baker, *General Ashcroft: Attorney at War* (Lawrence, KS: University Press of Kansas, 2006), 30–31.

[138] Adam Liptak, "Revised View of the 2nd Amendment Is Cited as Defense in Gun Crimes," *New York Times*, July 23, 2002, A1.

issued from Maryland. In other words, his only crime was firearms possession. Yet, the Justice Department insisted that Pearson's prosecution
and the DC law were legal, even though the department's new position
on the Second Amendment would plainly support dismissing the charges
against the man as a violation of his alleged Second Amendment rights.[139]
Conservative commentator Robert A. Levy, an avowed opponent of gun-
control laws, offered this tart assessment of Ashcroft's new policy on the
Second Amendment: "It is bizarre for Ashcroft to go out of his way to
assert a new Second Amendment theory in cases – *Emerson* and *Haney* –
where the theory almost certainly wouldn't matter, then decline to reaf-
firm the theory in cases arising under D.C. law, where it could dictate the
outcome."[140] In the second term of George W. Bush's administration, it
was not clear whether the new attorney general, Alberto Gonzales, would
continue to pursue the Ashcroft view of the Second Amendment. Yet,
it is clear that individualist writing in law journals was pivotal to legit-
imizing and elevating the policy change enacted during the second Bush
presidency.

Interest-Group Involvement

One other factor in the explosion of law journal writing on the Second
Amendment deserves mention. Unlike the other cases discussed in this
book, the effort to advance the individualist view of the Second Amendment in law journals has been propelled by the concerted efforts of gun
advocacy groups – but especially the NRA – that have a vested interest
in promoting academic writing to buttress and legitimize their political goals. The linchpin of this effort is the NRA Civil Rights Defense
Fund, established in 1978. The organization's two stated purposes are "to
become involved in court cases establishing legal precedents in favor of
gun owners," which it does by providing both financial and legal support
to individuals and organizations involved in gun-related litigation, and to
sponsor "legal research and education ... including the meaning of the
Second Amendment."[141] Since the 1970s, the NRA has also devoted personnel and other resources to encourage and support law journal writing

---

[139] "Guns and Ideology," *Washington Post*, August 5, 2002, A14.
[140] Robert A. Levy, "Bearing Arms in D.C.," *Legal Times*, July 24, 2002. Accessed at
www.law.com.
[141] www.nradefensefund.org, accessed on September 12, 2006.

to advance the individualist view.[142] It has provided funding and support to other groups composed of members with academic affiliations.[143] It has

---

[142] The most prominent example is Stephen Halbrook, who has been the NRA's lead lawyer in Court and other actions, and who has authored dozens of law journal articles on the Second Amendment and related subjects. Individualist authors including Caplan, Dowlut, Gardiner, Hardy, Kates, Kopel, Moncure, and Tahmassebi are employed by or have worked for the NRA or other gun groups. Caplan has served on the governing board of the NRA and as counsel to two New York State gun groups. See "Constitutional Rights in Jeopardy: The Push for 'Gun Control,'" a publication of the NRA, 1998. Dowlut, Gardiner, Moncure, and Tahmassebi have all worked for the Office of the General Counsel of the NRA; see Subcommittee on the Constitution, Judiciary Committee, U.S. Senate, "The Right to Keep and Bear Arms," 97th Cong., 2d sess. (Washington, DC: Government Printing Office, February 1982), iii; David Kopel has edited the Second Amendment Foundation's academic journal; Thomas M. Moncure, "Who is the Militia," *Lincoln Law Review* 19(1990): 1; Stefan B. Tahmassebi, "Gun Control and Racism," *George Mason University Civil Rights Law Journal* 2(Winter 1990): 67. Halbrook argued such cases as *Printz v. U.S.* During hearings held before the Subcommittee on the Constitution, Judiciary Committee, U.S. Senate, held in Washington, DC, on September 23, 1998, Halbrook advised NRA President Charlton Heston during Heston's testimony before the committee. Halbrook does not mention his long association with the NRA when identifying himself in print. In his book, *Freedmen, the Fourteenth Amendment, and the Right to Bear Arms*, for example, he identifies himself as having argued *Printz* before the Supreme Court but beyond that says only that he "practices law in Fairfax, Virginia." Fairfax is the home of the NRA. Kates is a long-time gun activist who is a regular contributor to anti-gun-control publications and advisor to anti-control activists. See, for example, "Readers Write," *American Rifleman*, February 1994, 10. He has authored a regular column called "Gun Rights" appearing in the magazine *Handguns*. I do not attach particular significance to these interest-group associations, however, because the key issue is the willingness of law journals to accept and print these articles rather than the occupational backgrounds or ideological predilections of the authors.

[143] A group formed in 1992 called Academics for the Second Amendment (ASA) asserted in an open letter that "The Second Amendment does not guarantee merely a 'right of the states,' but rather a 'right of the people,' a term which . . . is widely understood to encompass a personal right of citizens." The organization further stated that "Our primary goal is to give the 'right to bear arms' enshrined in the Bill of Rights its proper, prominent place in Constitutional discourse and analysis." (Of the forty-eight academics whose names appeared in the ASA advertisement, thirty-three listed law school affiliations.) See the ad reprinted in the *National Review*, March 15, 1993, 23. In the early 1990s, this group received $6,000 from the NRA, out of a total of $90,000 raised by the group. The ASA's president, Joseph Olson, a law school faculty member at Hamline Law School, has served on the NRA's governing board. In 1992, the NRA's Firearms Civil Rights Legal Defense Fund contributed $5,000 to cover the expenses for academics who attended the ASA conference that year. A 1996 article reported that the ASA's meeting that year was "funded partly by National Rifle Association" and that the ASA was "engaged in a genteel lobbying effort to popularize what many liberals consider the gun nut's view of the Second Amendment: that it confers an individual right to bear arms, not just the right to bear arms in a well-regulated militia." Wendy Kaminer,

provided financial support for research on the right to bear arms[144] and provided funding earmarked to produce "publication-quality law review pieces on gun-rights issues."[145]

In 2003, the NRA established a significant academic benchmark in the law school world when George Mason University announced that it had accepted a $1 million gift from the NRA Foundation to establish an endowed chair at its law school, titled the Patrick Henry Professorship of Constitutional Law and the Second Amendment. According to university President Alan Merten, the professorship is "dedicated to exploring the ideas and impact of the Second Amendment." Its first appointee to the chair was law professor Nelson Lund, who has long authored individualist articles on the Second Amendment.[146] NRA Vice President Wayne LaPierre was named a founding trustee and was quoted at the time of the announcement as saying, "We are proud to launch this pioneering effort as part of NRA's long-standing commitment to educating the public about the Second Amendment."[147] Although the principles of academic freedom are undoubtedly still in play, it is difficult to imagine that those

"Second Thoughts on the Second Amendment," *The Atlantic Monthly*, March 1996. Accessed at http://www.theatlantic.com/issues/96mar/guns/guns/htm.

[144] For example, in 1993, the NRA's Legal Defense Fund contributed $99,000 "for undisclosed 'right to bear arms research and education.'" Scott Heller, "The Right to Bear Arms," *The Chronicle of Higher Education*, 21 July 1995, A8, A12; Jan Hoffman, "Fund Linked to N.R.A. Gave $20,000 for Goetz's Defense," *The New York Times*, 16 April 1996.

[145] Andrew D. Herz, "Gun Crazy: Constitutional False Consciousness and Dereliction of Dialogic Responsibility," *Boston University Law Review* 75(January 1995): 138, note 358. The NRA offered a first prize of $25,000 for its 1994–95 essay contest titled "Stand Up for the Second Amendment." It continues to sponsor annual essay contests for law school students. In 2006–2007, it offered cash prizes for the top four submitted papers in its Law Student Essay Contest (top cash prize was $5,000), and a separate Scholarship Writing Contest, with the top three submissions receiving scholarships to defray tuition costs (the top prize was $12,500). According to contest guidelines, submissions "must be of quality suitable for publication in law review or journal" and subsequent publication "is encouraged" www.nradefensefund.org. For example, an article published by Scott Bursor in the *Texas Law Review* notes that an earlier version of the article "won first prize in the 1995 Firearms Civil Rights Legal Defense Fund Scholarship Contest." The author specifically thanked the 1995 conference of Academics for the Second Amendment. "Toward a Functional Framework for Interpreting the Second Amendment," *Texas Law Review* (April 1996): 1125.

[146] For example, Lund, "The Second Amendment, Political Liberty, and the Right to Self-Preservation"; "The Past and Future of the Individual's Right to Arms," *Georgia Law Review* 31(Fall 1996): 1–76.

[147] "$1 Million Endows Professorship at George Mason University," George Mason University Press Release, Media Contact Daniel Walsch, January 28, 2003.

selected for this university chair would ever express any formal views related to the Second Amendment that would contradict those favored by the NRA.

According to one critic, these activities have a very specific public policy purpose – namely, they are "part of a concerted campaign to persuade the courts to reconsider the Second Amendment, to reject what has long been a judicial consensus, and to adopt a different interpretation – one that would give the Amendment judicial as well as political vitality and would erect constitutional barriers to gun control legislation."[148] Another critic has charged that, at least with respect to the debate over the Second Amendment, "constitutional scholarship has been hijacked for ideological purposes. . . ."[149]

The NRA's involvement in promoting individualist law journal writing is part of this story but is not central to the arguments made here. Regardless of the résumés of law journal article authors, or their motivations – after all, academics in other disciplines have partisan motivations as well – law journals again prove themselves a uniquely fertile breeding ground for wayward constitutional theorizing. One can hardly fault a political group like the NRA for exploiting a publication system so unencumbered by scholarly and academic standards or practices.

Conclusion

As I noted at the beginning of this chapter, this analysis of law journal writing is not concerned with whether gun control is good or bad public policy. That debate is, in and of itself, as legitimate as any debate about a controversial issue of public concern. Rather, this chapter examines, yet again, the genesis of a constitutional theory that purports to offer an understanding of original constitutional intent and of judicial interpretation. Here as well, the question is not whether one ought to rely a little, a lot, or not at all on intent and interpretation in divining modern constitutional meaning. It is merely a question of getting the facts right, the story straight.

[148] Bogus, "The Hidden History of the Second Amendment," 316.
[149] Saul Cornell, "St. George Tucker and the Second Amendment: Original Understandings and Modern Misunderstandings," *William and Mary Law Review* 47(February 2006): 1124.

Advocates of the individualist view could offer a bona fide constitutional argument about the Second Amendment that might go something like this: the original, collective/militia-based meaning of the Second Amendment is now obsolete, given the decline of the old-style general militias, the transformation of the volunteer militias into the National Guard, the rise of the modern standing army and a government more than able and willing to arm its soldiers and employ the option of the military draft to swell the military's ranks, and a concomitant contemporary desire or need to facilitate the arming of civilians to improve domestic criminal suppression or as a kind of domestic defense against the prospect of political violence of the sort epitomized by the war on terrorism. Therefore, the Second Amendment should be vested with a twenty-first-century meaning to confront contemporary needs.

Instead, individualist advocates have proceeded to invent an imaginary past for the Second Amendment in order to serve contemporary political goals. This invention fairly brims with irony because its advocates, in the words of historian Jack Rakove, rely on the idea of constitutional originalism to a degree rarely found in other constitutional debates.[150] Yet, individualists have ignored, distorted, and disfigured constitutional meaning, history, and past court rulings. After several decades of concerted effort, the individualist view has won a not-inconsiderable degree of constitutional legitimacy in public policy circles, thanks largely to the law journal breeding ground. Yes, there are numerous legitimate disputes about constitutional meaning, including in the realm of the Second Amendment. But most of the individualist writing falls outside of any "reasonable minds may differ" standard. It is a grand constitutional house of cards, the fragility of which is ever more concealed as numerous new layers are pasted onto it. On this matter as in any other, if the Constitution can be said to mean the opposite of what it does mean, then it has no meaning at all.

---

[150] Jack N. Rakove, "The Second Amendment: The Highest Stage of Originalism," *Chicago-Kent Law Review* 76(2000): 107.

6 . . . . . Conclusion

An immediate and inevitable question arises at the end of this book. If it is true, as I argue, that legal training and law reviews cultivate a breeding ground for wayward constitutional theorizing, what then is to be done about it?

To this, I offer two responses. The first is that strategies aimed at reform are beyond the scope of this book because its foremost purpose has been to establish the validity of my claim that legal training and law reviews are unique in their intellectual and publishing traits, as compared with every other academic discipline, and that these unique traits have the pernicious consequences I have outlined in the examination of three areas of constitutional law. If this project succeeds in simply identifying the problems arising from legal writing, then that purpose alone is more than enough to justify this work. The second response, however, is to acknowledge that the consideration of possible reforms herein is appropriate because the subject of this inquiry is not one about which one may be sanguine. Beyond that, some consideration of reform is valuable for two reasons: it rounds out the logic of the analysis and may encourage some small steps in this direction.

As discussed particularly in Chapter 2, the legal community has long engaged in critical analysis and discussion about its professional training, norms, and values, ranging from law school education to the problems associated with student-run law reviews. For that reason, my treatment of reform herein is brief. Yet, this project's interest in reform extends beyond otherwise laudable efforts to improve legal education and writing. As federal judge, law professor, and law review critic Richard Posner observed in an article taking law reviews to task for many of the problems described herein, "The situation is basically hopeless, though fortunately not serious."[1] It may or may not be hopeless but, as I have argued, it is far from "not serious."

The three cases examined herein – the inherent item veto debate, the interpretation of the president's CIC power, and the debate over the meaning of the Second Amendment's right to bear arms – all depict pathological constitutional interpretation that has shaped – or, more accurately, misshaped – intellectual discourse, political debate, and even public policy outcomes. The Constitution is a vague and elastic document, and there is plenty to argue over regarding its meaning, interpretation, and application in contemporary America. But, the three examples of constitutional theorizing born, cultivated, and grown in the pages of law reviews take us far beyond the realm of reasonable, evidence-based analysis of constitutional meaning. In each instance, the goals of advocates for a presidential item veto, expanded CIC powers, and an individualist interpretation of the Second Amendment could be pursued through perfectly legitimate political or even constitutional means. The Constitution could be amended to grant the president item veto powers; the president's CIC powers could be expanded further – although here the unitary executive theorists simply have it wrong to say that these powers have not increased over two centuries – through constitutional amendment or additional statutory enhancement; and an individualist view of the Second Amendment could be advanced through a combination of an elastic Constitution argument and statutory enhancement. Instead, in each of these three instances, advocates have attempted to invent and legitimize as "scholarly" arguments that are literally contrary to any sane reading of what the Constitution actually says. If the Constitution can be said to mean the opposite of what it does mean, then it has no meaning at all.

Let me again emphasize that the purpose of this book is not to debate the merits of whether the president should or should not have an item veto, or whether the president's CIC powers should be defined in a way that allows the chief executive to nullify law and circumvent judicial review, or whether gun control is good or bad as a matter of public policy. All are

---

[1] Richard A. Posner, "The Future of the Student-Edited Law Review," *Stanford Law Review* 47(Summer, 1995): 1135.

perfectly legitimate public and academic debates. What is not legitimate, however, is to offer up a partisan lawyer's brief as scholarship; to make arguments and assertions based on obvious distortions and misrepresentations of evidence; to advance conclusions purportedly constructed on evidence that, when examined, leads to a contrary conclusion. There is a place for advocacy, and even partisanship, in any academic discipline, and only a fool would pretend that these preferences do not exist or are irrelevant to academic inquiry. But partisan advocacy cannot be allowed to twist evidence, distort or ignore the rules of inquiry, or offer up certainty for that which is anything but certain. Advocacy scholarship as it appears in the law journals is an oxymoron. Scholars may also be advocates and advocates scholars, but the merging of the two as "advocacy scholarship" is not scholarship as that term is defined and applied in every other discipline.

Reform

As I discussed in the first two chapters, much thoughtful consideration of the reform of legal writing and analysis is already to be found in the legal literature. Whereas that discussion does not specifically address the arguments raised in this book, the effects of such changes would indeed address at least some of the critical problems described herein.

Two sets of problems are identifiable: (1) the inappropriateness of legal training for scholarly analysis, and (2) the structure and operation of the publishing forum for legal writers. In conceptual terms, changes in legal training could be complicated yet in practice be relatively easy. As discussed in Chapter 1, the main purpose of law school is to train students for the legal profession, so it is essential that they learn the values and principles that underlie the profession. The principles and rules of academic inquiry, on the other hand, represent a conceptually different (and even contradictory) intellectual approach to a subject matter, so any effort to reconcile the two would require a careful rethinking of how the training of lawyers would be reconciled with the research methodologies one might apply to, for example, the academic study of constitutional law. In practical terms, legal training could readily include basic courses on philosophy of science, research methods, and similar subjects, akin to the standard coursework offered in virtually any graduate program in every other discipline.

Reforming the law reviews would pose an opposing set of problems: in conceptual terms, principles behind law-review reform are simple but, in practice, any widespread change would be difficult. Indeed, the conceptual answer is simple: turn editorial and review control over to competent faculty and impose peer review. Yet, the practical problem is daunting, indeed: How does one implement such a vast change when applied to more than six hundred law reviews, with many thousands of manuscripts to be evaluated every year? Yes, every other academic field of inquiry relies on faculty control and peer review, but these systems have existed for many decades; faculty participation is ingrained as a part of their professional obligations; and reviewers and often editors are accustomed to performing these services without direct financial remuneration (although indirect financial support may be provided to underwrite the costs of running an academic journal). The problem, in other words, is not what to do but how to do it.

Legal Training and Research

Much reformist literature in legal writing addresses legal training and curriculum and has done so for more than a century. But, its concerns have centered almost exclusively on the consequences of such training on the practice of law in America and the professionalization of the discipline, not on its effects on legal academic writing or the effects of that writing outside of the legal community. Yet, some calls for curricular reform would have direct consequences for the problems identified in this book. For example, some have proposed that academic legal writing return to its traditional (and narrower) subjects: case and doctrinal writing.[2] Although one can scarcely imagine legal writers voluntarily abandoning the multifarious fields and subjects that now consume legal publications, the call for a return to these subjects recognizes the belief of some in the legal community that, in straying from its traditional subjects, it abandons that which is most useful for and germane to lawyers' core professional training and activities. Aggressive solicitation and cultivation of

---

[2] Two chief proponents of the return to doctrinal and case writing are both federal judges: Harry T. Edwards, "The Growing Disjunction Between Legal Education and the Legal Profession," *Michigan Law Review* (October 1992): 34–78; Posner, "The Future of the Student-Edited Law Review," 1131–38; Posner, "Against the Law Reviews," *Legal Affairs*, November/December 2004. Accessed at http://www.legalaffairs.org/issues/November-December-2004 on November 5, 2004.

case and doctrinal writing by law reviews would promote such writing by the discipline, and it would address a critical and growing problem in the discipline and in the judiciary – that courts rely less and less on law journal writing. And, as noted in Chapter 2, law journal writing today suffers from an overweening emphasis on the relative handful (i.e., seventy to eighty) of Supreme Court cases handed down annually, with a comparable neglect in the law reviews of the many lower federal court rulings.

A conference held at the Benjamin N. Cardozo School of Law in 2007 that brought together federal judges and legal academics addressed this very concern. As *New York Times* law specialist Adam Liptak reported, both judges and law professors agreed that law scholarship "no longer had any impact on the courts." Whereas some law faculty argued that this trend represented "an anti-intellectual know-nothingism" on the part of judges, most seemed to agree that legal writing had rendered itself irrelevant because of the writing's increasing obscurity, poor quality, and irrelevance to actual cases confronting the courts. The plea from the assembled judges was clear in asking the academics "to write about actual cases and doctrines."[3] Underscoring the conference theme was the report of a study examining the frequency with which law review articles from top law journals were cited in court decisions. It chronicled a precipitous decline in such citations. In the case of the *Harvard Law Review*, for example, more than 4,400 citations in cases to articles in this one law review (the publication most often cited) were found in the decade of the 1970s; in the 1990s, the number had dropped to 1,956; and from 2000 to the beginning of 2007, there were only 937 citations. Comparable if less dramatic drops were found in the other law reviews examined.[4] The idea that theory-based or abstract writing be somehow abandoned is neither feasible nor desirable, but the principle that more law journal writing hew to traditional case and doctrinal writings is both feasible and desirable. It would not only help the courts but also play to the traditional intellectual strengths of legal scholars.

---

[3] Adam Liptak, "When Rendering Decisions, Judges Are Finding Law Reviews Irrelevant," *New York Times*, March 19, 2007, A8.

[4] Carissa Alden et al., "Trends in Federal Judicial Citations and Law Review Articles," presented at the Benjamin N. Cardozo School of Law Conference, March 8, 2007. Accessed June 1, 2007, at http://graphics8.nytimes.com/packages/pdf/national/20070319_federal_citations.pdf.

A parallel if different call for pedagogical reform comes from two political scientists, Lee Epstein and Gary King, whose landmark critique of empirical law review writing takes much of that literature to task for its failure to follow the rules of inference that guide every other academic discipline. Recognizing that legal writers will not abandon their new modes of inquiry, they are nevertheless optimistic that meaningful reforms can be instituted because law schools "appear highly organized, efficient, well funded, and most seem collegial and congenial." These traits, they argue, mean that "opportunities for quickly and significantly improving the research infrastructure in law schools are substantial."[5] They urge that law schools offer courses on empirical research (or coursework aimed more broadly at research strategies, the study of causal inference, and other elements of academic inquiry not limited to strictly empirical research), so that future lawyers and law faculty can acquire the necessary training on proper research methodology. Although such coursework would seem of greatest benefit to legal scholars as distinct from practicing attorneys, they argue persuasively that the acquisition of such skills by lawyers would enhance their marketability. They also propose that quantitative and qualitative data gathered by legal researchers be archived to preserve it and make it accessible to others,[6] an obvious benefit of which would be the reduction of duplication in legal publications and a more clearly additive disciplinary trajectory. Although the large majority of legal writing is not "empirical" in the way that term is normally understood, the broad principles of academic inquiry applied in every other academic discipline could be rolled into the law school curriculum in the manner proposed by Epstein and King. And, such proposed curricular changes could be implemented on a more limited basis for that subset of law school graduates who do eventually find themselves teaching at law schools.

Law Reviews

Any system that leaves law students in charge of the meaningful decisions concerning publication, including the initial culling of manuscripts, evaluation of their content, the decision whether to publish, and even editing, leaves the fundamental problem unaddressed. Only the replacement

---

[5] Lee Epstein and Gary King, "The Rules of Inference," *The University of Chicago Law Review* 69(Winter 2002): 115.
[6] Epstein and King, "The Rules of Inference," 115–124.

of student editors with content-based evaluation conducted by subject-matter experts operating under some system of peer review can address the otherwise insurmountable problem of leaving students in charge, especially because law review articles are not treated as the product of a student-run system. Only the substitution of expertise for student control can mend this problem.[7]

Many have suggested that law reviews transition to a system in which faculty play a greater or even controlling role (noting that faculty do play an important role at a few law schools), both in terms of managing the flow of submissions and in the actual manuscript review process.[8] Such a change is as laudable as it is unlikely, at least in the near term: given the hundreds of university-attached law reviews and the preexisting obligations of law school faculty, the sheer mechanics of such a change – not to mention the additional faculty workload that would suddenly exist to accommodate this massive review task (a task that, although performed in every other discipline, is normally one that is both voluntary and unpaid) – make the widespread implementation of such a change a long-term goal at best. The task would be eased if fewer law reviews existed to begin with;[9] yet, which law schools would voluntarily abolish their publications and what incentive could possibly precipitate such a decision?

Change of this magnitude is possible, but just as an aircraft carrier cannot turn on a dime, law school publication practices cannot be remade overnight. Short of change on this scale, others have suggested more limited changes that would continue to maintain some degree of student control but that would provide greater and more systematic training for student law review editors rolled into the curriculum, where law faculty could also provide at least some of the expertise-based evaluation

---

[7] Bernard J. Hibbitts argues for reforming the problems of student-run law journals by having faculty self-publish directly on the Web. Although bypassing student control, this proposal also sidesteps any kind of quality control based on peer or even prior review. "Last Writes? Reassessing the Law Review in the Age of Cyberspace," *New York University Law Review* 71(June 1996): 615–88.

[8] For example, Afton Dekanal, "Faculty-Edited Law Reviews: Should the Law Schools Join the Rest of Academe?," *University of Missouri Kansas City Law Review* 57(1989): 233–40; James Lindgren, "An Author's Manifesto," *University of Chicago Law Review* 61(Spring 1994): 535–38; Richard A. Epstein, "Faculty-Edited Law Journals," *Chicago-Kent Law Review* 70(1994): 87–94.

[9] Kenneth Lasson, "Scholarship Amok: Excesses in the Pursuit of Truth and Tenure," *Harvard Law Review* 103(February 1990): 935.

that occurs in other disciplines through peer review.[10] Recognizing the immense practical problems, Epstein and King propose leaving students in charge but also propose that editorial boards be expanded to include faculty, that student editors obtain at least one blind peer review from a subject-matter expert, that final approval from the full board would be required for publication, and that both student editors and editorial boards retain the option of rejecting manuscripts for review for any reasons they determine.[11] Such a hybrid system might most realistically reconcile the need for expertise-based peer review with the preexisting structures and norms of American law schools – although this plan, too, would make greater demands on faculty and students.[12]

The imposition of strict length restrictions (perhaps including limits on footnote length[13]) on manuscript submissions is an easily implemented reform that would reduce workload (and improve readability), based on the simple proposition that a shorter article takes less time to read and assess than a longer one and would thereby economize on the time commitments involved in manuscript review and editing. In 2005, the *Harvard Law Review* imposed a 25,000-word limit on submissions,[14] a move that prompted ten other law schools to adopt a policy of giving preference to shorter submissions, although the new policy did not necessarily exclude longer articles from review consideration. If adopted by other law reviews, these steps could, in time, make shorter submissions the norm across the discipline. As Columbia Law professor and former school dean Michael Dorf argues, these changes, "if complemented by greater reliance on outside experts in the selection of articles for publication and by the law schools' own rethinking of tenure standards and procedures," could move the discipline toward an expertise-based system.[15]

---

[10] James Lindgren, "Reforming the American Law Review," *Stanford Law Review* (Summer 1995): 1123–30; Carol Sanger, "Editing," *Georgetown Law Review* 82(December 1993): 513–27; Nathan H. Saunders, "Reflections and Responses of an Inmate," *Duke Law Journal* 49(April 2000): 1682–83.

[11] Epstein and King, "The Rules of Inference," 127–29.

[12] Even critics of Epstein and King concede that their plan for mixed student-faculty control would be a positive step. See Frank Cross, Michael Heise, and Gregory C. Sisk, "Above the Rules: A Response to Epstein and King," *University of Chicago Law Review* 69(Winter 2002): 149.

[13] Lasson, "Scholarship Amok," 939.

[14] Robert C. Berring, "Less Is More. Really," *Green Bag* 8(Spring 2005): 231–34.

[15] Michael C. Dorf, "Thanks to a Joint Statement by Top Law Journals, Law Review Articles Will Get Shorter, But Will They Get Better?," *Findlaw*, February 28, 2005, http://writ.news.findlaw.com/Dorf/20050228.html, accessed on March 1, 2005.

Although an arbitrary limit on article length might seem like an artificial or purely mechanical change disconnected from the substance of an article implemented purely for the sake of convenience, such length limitations are the norm for academic journals in other disciplines.[16] More important, they are based not only on practical concerns but also on an important intellectual caveat: the value and importance of an idea or argument is not correlated with sheer length. In fact, it is an article of faith in the journal-publishing world that authors unable to express themselves concisely have probably not mastered the ideas and arguments they are advancing. And, as discussed in Chapter 2, most law journal articles are long for indefensible reasons – that is, because of a kind of law journal vanity that accepts, even extols, the needless repetition of information, digressions into subjects not relevant to the core subject, and the filling of articles with numerous citations that are utterly unnecessary. A certain kind of intellectual "brag" often seems to accompany the authoring of a law review article that is exceptionally long, yet it is a hollow and empty brag, and it should be exposed as such by the legal community.

One other growing trend would facilitate reformation: an increase in cross-disciplinary publication and review. Just as more law faculty now publish outside of the law review realm, historians, political scientists, and others have also increasingly published in law reviews. Both trends should be encouraged because it is one way in which interdisciplinary ideas, methods, values, and norms can be exchanged. Such exchange already occurs to a limited degree in the study of constitutional law, for example. Although one might quibble with the suggestion that more historians, political scientists, and other nonlawyers should seek to publish in law reviews given my criticisms of the law review system, I believe it to be beneficial because it is the most direct way in which nonlawyers can speak to the academic legal community.[17]

---

[16] For example, the flagship journal of the American Political Science Association, the *American Political Science Review*, stipulates this regarding length: "Manuscripts should not be longer than 45 pages including text, all tables and figures, notes, references, and appendices. This page size guideline is based on the U.S. standard 8.5 × 11 inch paper; if you are submitting a manuscript printed on longer paper, you must adjust accordingly. Font size must be at least 11 point for all parts of the paper, including notes and references. The entire paper, including references, must be double-spaced, with the sole exception of tables for which double-spacing would require a second page otherwise not needed." See http://www.apsanet.org/imgtest/apsrinst.pdf.

[17] The law review article I have cited and discussed repeatedly in this book by the political scientists Epstein and King, "The Rules of Inference," is an exemplar of the virtues and value of such cross-disciplinary writing.

Law Reviews Will Still Matter

Lawyers will continue to expound, through professional writings and by other means, on the important (and not so important) constitutional matters of the day. Their contributions have been enormous, important, and thought-provoking. But, this does not excuse or mitigate the fact that legal training, by its very nature, extols values that are as indispensable in the courtroom as they are inimical to the principles of academic inquiry when applied to constitutional interpretation. And, the huge primary publishing venue in which legal academics expound on constitutional meaning is run by people who do not and cannot make publishing judgments based on subject-specific, merit-based expertise. These are institutional traits that are the result of decades of evolution. The participation of lawyers and law students in this system of academic expression as it has evolved over many decades is both logical and understandable, yet neither trait justifies the current system. Yes, many good and smart people participate in the law review system, but that does not and cannot excuse a system that, as it has evolved and operated in the last few decades, is uniquely flawed as a mode of academic inquiry. In a nation where the Constitution is the first and most important political talisman,[18] the stakes for wayward constitutional theorizing are simply too high.

---

[18] See Mary Ann Glendon, *Rights Talk* (New York: Free Press, 1991); Robert J. Spitzer, *The Right to Bear Arms* (Santa Barbara, CA: ABC-CLIO, 2001), 82–83.

About the Author

ROBERT J. SPITZER (Ph.D. Cornell, 1980) is Distinguished Service Professor of Political Science at the State University of New York, College at Cortland. His books include *The Presidency and Public Policy* (1983), *The Right to Life Movement and Third Party Politics* (1987), *The Presidential Veto* (1988), *The Bicentennial of the U.S. Constitution* (1990), *President and Congress* (1993), *Media and Public Policy* (1993), *The Politics of Gun Control* (1995; 2nd ed. 1998; 3rd ed. 2004; 4th ed. 2007), *Politics and Constitutionalism* (2000), *The Right to Bear Arms* (2001), *Essentials of American Politics* (co-authored, 2002; 2nd ed. 2006), and *The Presidency and the Constitution* (co-authored, 2005). He is also Series Editor for the book series "American Constitutionalism" for SUNY Press. In 2003, he received the SUNY Chancellor's Award for Excellence in Scholarship. Spitzer is the author of more than three hundred articles and papers appearing in many journals and books on a variety of American politics subjects. He served as President of the Presidency Research Group of the American Political Science Association from 2001 to 2003. He also served as a member of the New York State Commission on the Bicentennial of the U.S. Constitution and has testified before Congress on several occasions. Spitzer has appeared on NBC's *Today Show*, ABC's *Good Morning America* and *Network Nightly News*, PBS's *News Hour With Jim Lehrer*, CNN, CNBC, NHK Television (Japan), CBC (Canada), BBC (Britain), and the PBS documentary film *Guns and Mothers*, and he has been quoted in or by the *New York Times*, *Washington Post*, *Time Magazine*, *Los Angeles Times*, *USA Today*, *Wall Street Journal*, *Christian Science Monitor*, *Boston Globe*, *Chicago Tribune*, *Philadelphia Enquirer*, *Miami Herald*,

Dallas Morning News, Detroit Free Press, Kansas City Star, Seattle Post-Intelligencer, Newsday, Denver Post, Toronto Globe, Congress Daily, The Hill, Rolling Stone, The Nation, National Journal, The Spectator, Reuters, AP, Gannett, Knight Ridder, BBC (Britain), CBC (Canada), ABC News Online, Fox News Online, National Public Radio, and CBS Radio, among others. His op-ed articles have appeared in many newspapers around the country. He is also a regular panelist on the weekly public affairs program, *The Ivory Tower Half Hour*, broadcast on WCNY-TV in Syracuse, New York.

Index

For EU product safety concerns, contact us at Calle de José Abascal, 56–1°,
28003 Madrid, Spain or eugpsr@cambridge.org.

www.ingramcontent.com/pod-product-compliance
Ingram Content Group UK Ltd.
Pitfield, Milton Keynes, MK11 3LW, UK
UKHW020326140625
459647UK00018B/2034